Kaplan Publishing are constantly fi[nding new] ways to make a difference to your s[tudies and our] exciting online resources really do [make something] different to students looking for ex[am success.]

This book comes with free MyKaplan online resources so that you can study anytime, anywhere. This free online resource is not sold separately and is included in the price of the book.

Having purchased this book, you have access to the following online study materials:

CONTENT	ACCA (including FFA,FAB,FMA)		FIA (excluding FFA,FAB,FMA)	
	Text	Kit	Text	Kit
iPaper version of the book	✓	✓	✓	✓
Interactive electronic version of the book	✓			
Check Your Understanding Test with instant answers	✓			
Material updates	✓	✓	✓	✓
Latest official ACCA exam questions*		✓		
Extra question assistance using the signpost icon*		✓		
Timed questions with an online tutor debrief using the clock icon*		✓		
Interim assessment including questions and answers	✓		✓	
Technical articles	✓	✓	✓	✓

* Excludes F1, F2, F3, FFA, FAB, FMA

How to access your online resources

Kaplan Financial students will already have a MyKaplan account and these extra resources will be available to you online. You do not need to register again, as this process was completed when you enrolled. If you are having problems accessing online materials, please ask your course administrator.

If you are already a registered MyKaplan user go to www.MyKaplan.co.uk and log in. Select the 'add a book' feature and enter the ISBN number of this book and the unique pass key at the bottom of this card. Then click 'finished' or 'add another book'. You may add as many books as you have purchased from this screen.

If you purchased through Kaplan Flexible Learning or via the Kaplan Publishing website you will automatically receive an e-mail invitation to MyKaplan. Please register your details using this email to gain access to your content. If you do not receive the e-mail or book content, please contact Kaplan Flexible Learning.

If you are a new MyKaplan user register at www.MyKaplan.co.uk and click on the link contained in the email we sent you to activate your account. Then select the 'add a book' feature, enter the ISBN number of this book and the unique pass key at the bottom of this card. Then click 'finished' or 'add another book'.

Your Code and Information

This code can only be used once for the registration of one book online. This registration and your online content will expire when the final sittings for the examinations covered by this book have taken place. Please allow one hour from the time you submit your book details for us to process your request.

Please scratch the film to access your MyKaplan code.

Please be aware that this code is case-sensitive and you will need to include the dashes within the passcode, but not when entering the ISBN. For further technical support, please visit www.MyKaplan.co.uk

KAPLAN PUBLISHING

ACCA
Paper F2

FIA
Diploma in Accounting and Business

Management Accounting (MA/FMA)

EXAM KIT

KAPLAN
PUBLISHING

British Library Cataloguing-in-Publication Data

A catalogue record for this book is available from the British Library.

Published by:

Kaplan Publishing UK

Unit 2 The Business Centre

Molly Millar's Lane

Wokingham

Berkshire

RG41 2QZ

ISBN: 978-1-78415-447-9

© Kaplan Financial Limited, 2015

Printed and bound in Great Britain

The text in this material and any others made available by any Kaplan Group company does not amount to advice on a particular matter and should not be taken as such. No reliance should be placed on the content as the basis for any investment or other decision or in connection with any advice given to third parties. Please consult your appropriate professional adviser as necessary. Kaplan Publishing Limited and all other Kaplan group companies expressly disclaim all liability to any person in respect of any losses or other claims, whether direct, indirect, incidental, consequential or otherwise arising in relation to the use of such materials.

All rights reserved. No part of this examination may be reproduced or transmitted in any form or by any means, electronic or mechanical, including photocopying, recording, or by any information storage and retrieval system, without prior permission from Kaplan Publishing.

Acknowledgements

The past ACCA examination questions are the copyright of the Association of Chartered Certified Accountants. The original answers to the questions from June 1994 onwards were produced by the examiners themselves and have been adapted by Kaplan Publishing.

We are grateful to the Chartered Institute of Management Accountants and the Institute of Chartered Accountants in England and Wales for permission to reproduce past examination questions. The answers have been prepared by Kaplan Publishing.

CONTENTS

		Page
Index to questions and answers		v
Exam Technique		vii
Paper specific information		ix
Kaplan's recommended revision approach		xi
Formulae and Tables		xv

Section

1	Section A-type questions	1
2	Section B-type questions	121
3	Free text questions (paper based exam only)	135
4	Answers to Section A-type questions	139
5	Answers to Section B-type questions	211
6	Answers to free text questions	217
7	Practice exam questions	225
8	Answers to practice exam questions	239
9	Specimen exam	247

New features in this edition

In addition to providing a wide ranging bank of practice questions, we have also included in this edition:

- Paper specific information and advice on exam technique.
- Our recommended approach to make your revision for this particular subject as effective as possible.

    This includes step by step guidance on how best to use our Kaplan material (Complete text, pocket notes and exam kit) at this stage in your studies.

You will find a wealth of other resources to help you with your studies on the following sites:

www.mykaplan.co.uk and www.accaglobal.com/students/

KAPLAN PUBLISHING

Quality and accuracy are of the utmost importance to us so if you spot an error in any of our products, please send an email to mykaplanreporting@kaplan.com with full details.

Our Quality Co-ordinator will work with our technical team to verify the error and take action to ensure it is corrected in future editions.

INDEX TO QUESTIONS AND ANSWERS

	Page number	
	Question	*Answer*

SECTION A-TYPE QUESTIONS

Accounting for management	1	139
Sources of data	4	140
Presenting information	8	142
Cost classification	12	143
Accounting for materials	22	149
Accounting for labour	33	157
Accounting for overheads	38	160
Absorption and Marginal costing	44	164
Cost accounting methods	48	168
Alternative costing principles	59	176
Nature and purpose of budgeting	61	177
Statistical techniques	62	177
Budget preparation	72	183
Flexible budgets	79	188
Capital budgeting	83	190
Budgetary control and reporting	87	193
Behavioural aspects of budgeting	89	194
Standard costing systems	91	196
Variance calculations and analysis	92	196
Reconciliation of budgeted and actual profit	101	202
Performance measurement overview	103	204
Performance measurement – application	104	204
Cost reduction and value enhancement	115	209
Monitoring performance and reporting	116	209

SECTION B-TYPE QUESTIONS

Budgeting	121	211
Standard costing	125	213
Performance measurement	131	214

KAPLAN PUBLISHING

FREE TEXT QUESTIONS (PAPER BASED EXAM ONLY)

The nature, source and purpose of management information	135	217
Cost accounting methods and systems	135	218
Budgeting	136	219
Standard costing	136	219
Performance measurement	137	221

EXAM TECHNIQUE

- **Do not skip any of the material** in the syllabus.
- **Read each question** *very* carefully.
- **Double-check your answer** before committing yourself to it.
- Answer **every** question – if you do not know an answer, you don't lose anything by guessing. Think carefully before you **guess**. The examiner has indicated that many candidates are still leaving blank answers in the real exam.
- If you are answering a multiple-choice question, **eliminate first those answers that you know are wrong**. Then choose the most appropriate answer from those that are left.
- Remember that **only one answer to a multiple-choice question can be right**. After you have eliminated the ones that you know to be wrong, if you are still unsure, guess. Only guess after you have double-checked that you have only eliminated answers that are *definitely* wrong.
- **Don't panic** if you realise you've answered a question incorrectly. Getting one question wrong will not mean the difference between passing and failing

Computer-based exams – tips

- Do not attempt a CBE until you have **completed all study material** relating to it.
- On the ACCA website there is a CBE demonstration. It is **ESSENTIAL** that you attempt this before your real CBE. You will become familiar with how to move around the CBE screens and the way that questions are formatted, increasing your confidence and speed in the actual exam.
- Be sure you understand how to use the **software** before you start the exam. If in doubt, ask the assessment centre staff to explain it to you.
- Questions are **displayed on the screen** and answers are entered using keyboard and mouse. At the end of the exam, you are given a certificate showing the result you have achieved.
- In addition to the traditional multiple-choice question type, CBEs might also contain **other types of questions**, such as number entry questions, formula entry questions, and stem questions with multiple parts. There are also questions that carry several marks.
- You need to be sure you **know how to answer questions** of this type before you sit the exam, through practice.

KAPLAN PUBLISHING

PAPER SPECIFIC INFORMATION

THE EXAM

FORMAT OF THE PAPER-BASED AND COMPUTER BASED EXAM

	Number of marks
35 compulsory multiple choice questions (2 marks each)	70
3 compulsory long form questions (10 marks each)	30
	100

Total time allowed: 2 hours

Section A will assess the whole syllabus. Section B will assess Budgeting, Standard costing and Performance management. Question styles in section B will include Number entry, Drop down lists, MCQ and Multiple response.

Note: The paper based exam will contain 'free text' response questions.

AIM

To develop knowledge and understanding of providing basic management information in an organisation to support management in planning and decision-making

OBJECTIVES

On successful completion of this paper, candidates should be able to:

- explain the nature, source and purpose of management information
- explain and apply cost accounting techniques
- prepare budgets for planning and control
- compare actual costs with standard costs and analyse any variances
- analyse, interpret and monitor business performance
- ACCA official statistics have shown that most students do not find the exam time pressured

PASS MARK

The pass mark for all ACCA Qualification examination papers is 50%.

DETAILED SYLLABUS

The detailed syllabus and study guide written by the ACCA can be found at:

www.accaglobal.com/students/

KAPLAN'S RECOMMENDED REVISION APPROACH

QUESTION PRACTICE IS THE KEY TO SUCCESS

Success in professional examinations relies upon you acquiring a firm grasp of the required knowledge at the tuition phase. In order to be able to do the questions, knowledge is essential.

However, the difference between success and failure often hinges on your exam technique on the day and making the most of the revision phase of your studies.

The **Kaplan complete text** is the starting point, designed to provide the underpinning knowledge to tackle all questions. However, in the revision phase, pouring over text books is not the answer.

Kaplan Online fixed tests help you consolidate your knowledge and understanding and are a useful tool to check whether you can remember key topic areas.

Kaplan pocket notes are designed to help you quickly revise a topic area, however you then need to practice questions. There is a need to progress to full exam standard questions as soon as possible, and to tie your exam technique and technical knowledge together.

The importance of question practice cannot be over-emphasised.

The recommended approach below is designed by expert tutors in the field, in conjunction with their knowledge of the examiner.

The approach taken for the fundamental papers is to revise by topic area.

You need to practice as many questions as possible in the time you have left.

OUR AIM

Our aim is to get you to the stage where you can attempt exam standard questions confidently, to time, in a closed book environment, with no supplementary help (i.e. to simulate the real examination experience).

Practising your exam technique on real past examination questions, in timed conditions, is also vitally important for you to assess your progress and identify areas of weakness that may need more attention in the final run up to the examination.

The approach below shows you which questions you should use to build up to coping with exam standard question practice, and references to the sources of information available should you need to revisit a topic area in more detail.

Remember that in the real examination, all you have to do is:

- attempt all questions required by the exam
- only spend the allotted time on each question, and
- get them at least 50% right!

Try and practice this approach on every question you attempt from now to the real exam.

THE KAPLAN PAPER F2/FMA REVISION PLAN

Stage 1: Assess areas of strengths and weaknesses

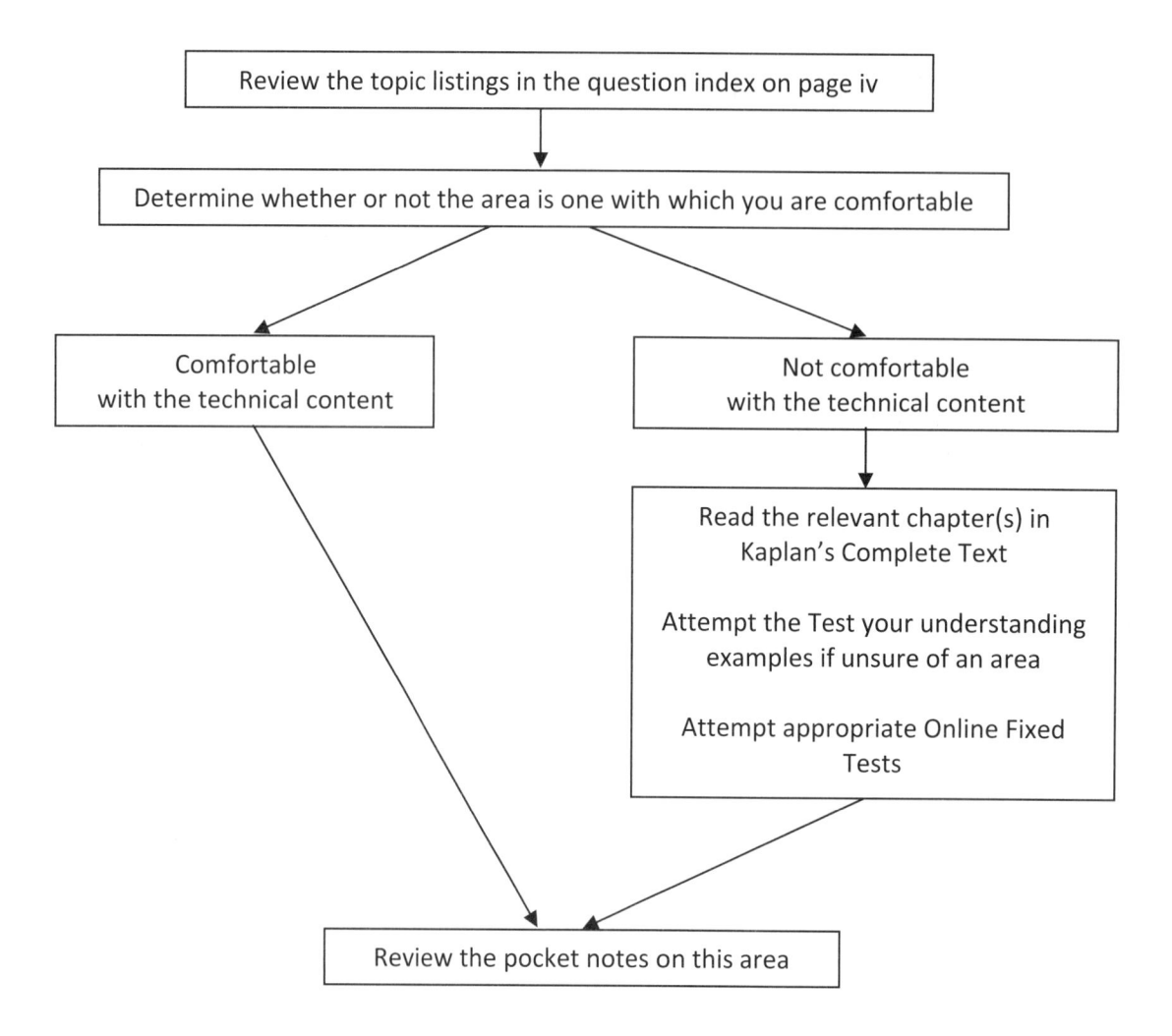

```
Review the topic listings in the question index on page iv
                        │
                        ▼
Determine whether or not the area is one with which you are comfortable
            │                                    │
            ▼                                    ▼
     Comfortable                           Not comfortable
 with the technical content            with the technical content
            │                                    │
            │                                    ▼
            │                       Read the relevant chapter(s) in
            │                            Kaplan's Complete Text
            │
            │                       Attempt the Test your understanding
            │                         examples if unsure of an area
            │
            │                       Attempt appropriate Online Fixed
            │                                    Tests
            │                                    │
            ▼                                    ▼
              Review the pocket notes on this area
```

Stage 2: Practice questions

Ensure that you revise all syllabus areas as questions could be asked on anything.

Try to avoid referring to text books and notes and the model answer until you have completed your attempt.

Try to answer the question in the allotted time.

Review your attempt with the model answer. If you got the answer wrong, can you see why? Was the problem a lack of knowledge or a failure to understand the question fully?

Fill in the self-assessment box below and decide on your best course of action.

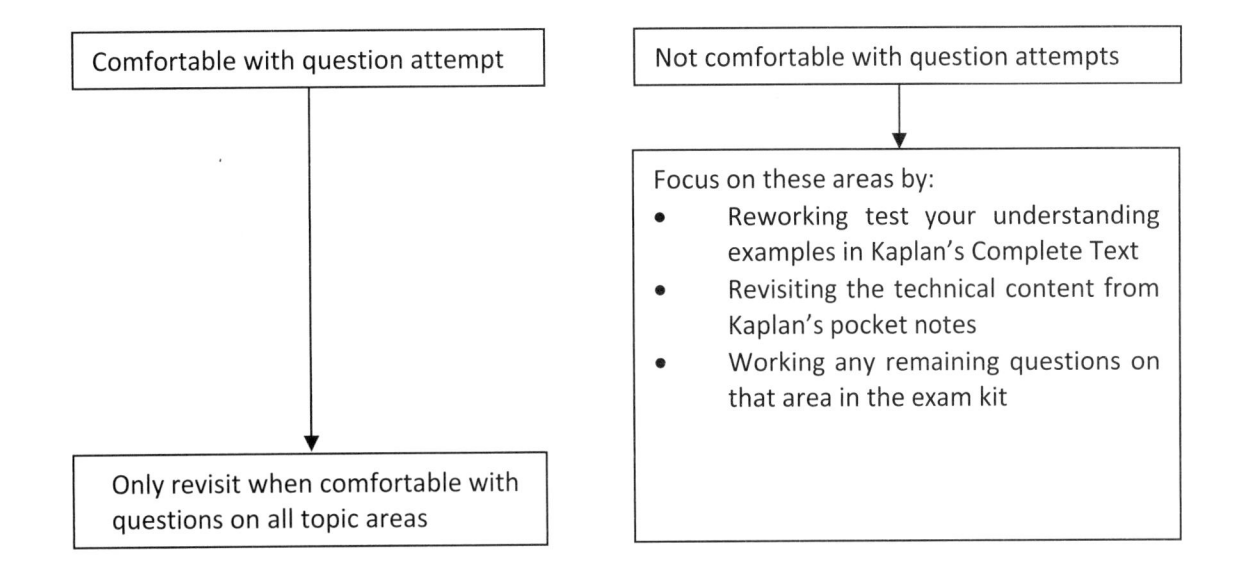

```
┌─────────────────────────────────────┐        ┌─────────────────────────────────────┐
│ Comfortable with question attempt   │        │ Not comfortable with question attempts │
└──────────────┬──────────────────────┘        └──────────────┬──────────────────────┘
               │                                               │
               │                                               ▼
               │                               ┌──────────────────────────────────────┐
               │                               │ Focus on these areas by:             │
               │                               │  • Reworking test your understanding │
               │                               │    examples in Kaplan's Complete Text│
               │                               │  • Revisiting the technical content  │
               │                               │    from Kaplan's pocket notes        │
               │                               │  • Working any remaining questions   │
               │                               │    on that area in the exam kit      │
               │                               └──────────────────────────────────────┘
               ▼
┌─────────────────────────────────────┐
│ Only revisit when comfortable with  │
│ questions on all topic areas        │
└─────────────────────────────────────┘
```

Stage 3: Final pre-exam revision

We recommend that you **attempt at least one two hour mock examination** containing a set of previously unseen exam standard questions.

It is important that you get a feel for the breadth of coverage of a real exam without advanced knowledge of the topic areas covered – just as you will expect to see on the real exam day.

Ideally this mock should be sat in timed, closed book, real exam conditions and could be:

- a mock examination offered by your tuition provider, and/or
- the pilot paper in this exam kit, and/or
- the practice exam paper in this kit

FORMULAE AND TABLES

Regression analysis

$$y = a + bx$$

$$a = \frac{\Sigma y}{n} - \frac{b \Sigma x}{n}$$

$$b = \frac{n \Sigma xy - \Sigma x \Sigma y}{n \Sigma x^2 - (\Sigma x)^2}$$

$$r = \frac{n \Sigma xy - \Sigma x \Sigma y}{\sqrt{(n \Sigma x^2 - (\Sigma x)^2)(n \Sigma y^2 - (\Sigma y)^2)}}$$

Economic order quantity

$$= \sqrt{\frac{2C_0 D}{C_h}}$$

Economic batch quantity

$$= \sqrt{\frac{2C_0 D}{C_h \left(1 - \frac{D}{R}\right)}}$$

PRESENT VALUE TABLE

Present value of 1, i.e. $(1 + r)^{-n}$

Where r = interest rate

n = number of periods until payment.

Periods (n)	1%	2%	3%	4%	5%	6%	7%	8%	9%	10%
1	0.990	0.980	0.971	0.962	0.952	0.943	0.935	0.926	0.917	0.909
2	0.980	0.961	0.943	0.925	0.907	0.890	0.873	0.857	0.842	0.826
3	0.971	0.942	0.915	0.889	0.864	0.840	0.816	0.794	0.772	0.751
4	0.961	0.924	0.888	0.855	0.823	0.792	0.763	0.735	0.708	0.683
5	0.951	0.906	0.863	0.822	0.784	0.747	0.713	0.681	0.650	0.621
6	0.942	0.888	0.837	0.790	0.746	0.705	0.666	0.630	0.596	0.564
7	0.933	0.871	0.813	0.760	0.711	0.665	0.623	0.583	0.547	0.513
8	0.923	0.853	0.789	0.731	0.677	0.627	0.582	0.540	0.502	0.467
9	0.914	0.837	0.766	0.703	0.645	0.592	0.544	0.500	0.460	0.424
10	0.905	0.820	0.744	0.676	0.614	0.558	0.508	0.463	0.422	0.386
11	0.896	0.804	0.722	0.650	0.585	0.527	0.475	0.429	0.388	0.350
12	0.887	0.788	0.701	0.625	0.557	0.497	0.444	0.397	0.356	0.319
13	0.879	0.773	0.681	0.601	0.530	0.469	0.415	0.368	0.326	0.290
14	0.870	0.758	0.661	0.577	0.505	0.442	0.388	0.340	0.299	0.263
15	0.861	0.743	0.642	0.555	0.481	0.417	0.362	0.315	0.275	0.239

(n)	11%	12%	13%	14%	15%	16%	17%	18%	19%	20%
1	0.901	0.893	0.885	0.877	0.870	0.862	0.855	0.847	0.840	0.833
2	0.812	0.797	0.783	0.769	0.756	0.743	0.731	0.718	0.706	0.694
3	0.731	0.712	0.693	0.675	0.658	0.641	0.624	0.609	0.593	0.579
4	0.659	0.636	0.613	0.592	0.572	0.552	0.534	0.516	0.499	0.482
5	0.593	0.567	0.543	0.519	0.497	0.476	0.456	0.437	0.419	0.402
6	0.535	0.507	0.480	0.456	0.432	0.410	0.390	0.370	0.352	0.335
7	0.482	0.452	0.425	0.400	0.376	0.354	0.333	0.314	0.296	0.279
8	0.434	0.404	0.376	0.351	0.327	0.305	0.285	0.266	0.249	0.233
9	0.391	0.361	0.333	0.308	0.284	0.263	0.243	0.225	0.209	0.194
10	0.352	0.322	0.295	0.270	0.247	0.227	0.208	0.191	0.176	0.162
11	0.317	0.287	0.261	0.237	0.215	0.195	0.178	0.162	0.148	0.135
12	0.286	0.257	0.231	0.208	0.187	0.168	0.152	0.137	0.124	0.112
13	0.258	0.229	0.204	0.182	0.163	0.145	0.130	0.116	0.104	0.093
14	0.232	0.205	0.181	0.160	0.141	0.125	0.111	0.099	0.088	0.078
15	0.209	0.183	0.160	0.140	0.123	0.108	0.095	0.084	0.079	0.065

FORMULAE AND TABLES

ANNUITY TABLE

Present value of an annuity of 1 i.e. $\dfrac{1-(1+r)^{-n}}{r}$

Where r = interest rate

n = number of periods.

Periods (n)	1%	2%	3%	4%	5%	6%	7%	8%	9%	10%
1	0.990	0.980	0.971	0.962	0.952	0.943	0.935	0.926	0.917	0.909
2	1.970	1.942	1.913	1.886	1.859	1.833	1.808	1.783	1.759	1.736
3	2.941	2.884	2.829	2.775	2.723	2.673	2.624	2.577	2.531	2.487
4	3.902	3.808	3.717	3.630	3.546	3.465	3.387	3.312	3.240	3.170
5	4.853	4.713	4.580	4.452	4.329	4.212	4.100	3.993	3.890	3.791
6	5.795	5.601	5.417	5.242	5.076	4.917	4.767	4.623	4.486	4.355
7	6.728	6.472	6.230	6.002	5.786	5.582	5.389	5.206	5.033	4.868
8	7.652	7.325	7.020	6.733	6.463	6.210	5.971	5.747	5.535	5.335
9	8.566	8.162	7.786	7.435	7.108	6.802	6.515	6.247	5.995	5.759
10	9.471	8.983	8.530	8.111	7.722	7.360	7.024	6.710	6.418	6.145
11	10.368	9.787	9.253	8.760	8.306	7.887	7.499	7.139	6.805	6.495
12	11.255	10.575	9.954	9.385	8.863	8.384	7.943	7.536	7.161	6.814
13	12.134	11.348	10.635	9.986	9.394	8.853	8.358	7.904	7.487	7.103
14	13.004	12.106	11.296	10.563	9.899	9.295	8.745	8.244	7.786	7.367
15	13.865	12.849	11.938	11.118	10.380	9.712	9.108	8.559	8.061	7.606

(n)	11%	12%	13%	14%	15%	16%	17%	18%	19%	20%
1	0.901	0.893	0.885	0.877	0.870	0.862	0.855	0.847	0.840	0.833
2	1.713	1.690	1.668	1.647	1.626	1.605	1.585	1.566	1.547	1.528
3	2.444	2.402	2.361	2.322	2.283	2.246	2.210	2.174	2.140	2.106
4	3.102	3.037	2.974	2.914	2.855	2.798	2.743	2.690	2.639	2.589
5	3.696	3.605	3.517	3.433	3.352	3.274	3.199	3.127	3.058	2.991
6	4.231	4.111	3.998	3.889	3.784	3.685	3.589	3.498	3.410	3.326
7	4.712	4.564	4.423	4.288	4.160	4.039	3.922	3.812	3.706	3.605
8	5.146	4.968	4.799	4.639	4.487	4.344	4.207	4.078	3.954	3.837
9	5.537	5.328	5.132	4.946	4.772	4.607	4.451	4.303	4.163	4.031
10	5.889	5.650	5.426	5.216	5.019	4.833	4.659	4.494	4.339	4.192
11	6.207	5.938	5.687	5.453	5.234	5.029	4.836	4.656	4.486	4.327
12	6.492	6.194	5.918	5.660	5.421	5.197	4.988	7.793	4.611	4.439
13	6.750	6.424	6.122	5.842	5.583	5.342	5.118	4.910	4.715	4.533
14	6.982	6.628	6.302	6.002	5.724	5.468	5.229	5.008	4.802	4.611
15	7.191	6.811	6.462	6.142	5.847	5.575	5.324	5.092	4.876	4.675

Section 1

SECTION A-TYPE QUESTIONS

Note: All questions carry two marks

SYLLABUS AREA A – THE NATURE, SOURCE AND PURPOSE OF MANAGEMENT INFORMATION

ACCOUNTING FOR MANAGEMENT

1   Which of the following statements are correct?

   (i)   Strategic information is mainly used by senior management in an organisation.

   (ii) Productivity measurements are examples of tactical information.

   (iii) Operational information is required frequently by its main users.

   A   (i) and (ii) only

   B   (i) and (iii) only

   C   (ii) and (iii) only

   D   (i), (ii) and (iii)

2   Reginald is the manager of production department M in a factory which has ten other production departments.

   He receives monthly information that compares planned and actual expenditure for department M. After department M, all production goes into other factory departments to be completed prior to being despatched to customers. Decisions involving capital expenditure in department M are not taken by Reginald.

   Which of the following describes Reginald's role in department M?

   A   A cost centre manager

   B   An investment centre manager

   C   A revenue centre manager

   D   A profit centre manager

PAPER F2/FMA : MANAGEMENT ACCOUNTING

3   Which of the following is NOT CORRECT?

   A   Cost accounting can be used for inventory valuation to meet the requirements of internal reporting only.

   B   Management accounting provides appropriate information for decision making, planning, control and performance evaluation.

   C   Routine information can be used for both short-term and long-run decisions.

   D   Financial accounting information can be used for internal reporting purposes.

4   The following statements relate to financial accounting or to cost and management accounting:

   (i)   Financial accounts are historical records.

   (ii)   Cost accounting is part of financial accounting and establishes costs incurred by an organisation.

   (iii) Management accounting is used to aid planning, control and decision making.

   Which of the statements are correct?

   A   (i) and (ii) only

   B   (i) and (iii) only

   C   (ii) and (iii) only

   D   (i), (ii) and (iii)

5   Which of the following is correct?

   A   Qualitative data is generally non-numerical information

   B   Information can only be extracted from external sources

   C   Operational information gives details of long-term plans only

   D   Quantitative data is always accurate

6   The manager of a profit centre is responsible for which of the following?

   (i)   Revenues of the centre

   (ii)   Costs of the centre

   (iii) Assets employed in the centre

   A   (i) only

   B   (ii) only

   C   (i) and (ii) only

   D   (i), (ii) and (iii)

SECTION A-TYPE QUESTIONS : SECTION 1

7 Which of the following would be best described as a short-term tactical plan?

- A Reviewing cost variances and investigate as appropriate
- B Comparing actual market share to budget
- C Lowering the selling price by 15%
- D Monitoring actual sales to budget

8 Which of the following relates to management accounts and which to financial accounts?

	Management accounts	Financial accounts
Prepared yearly		✓
For internal use	✓	
Contains future information	✓	

9 The following statements refer to strategic planning:

- (i) It is concerned with quantifiable and qualitative matters.
- (ii) It is mainly undertaken by middle management in an organisation.
- (iii) It is concerned predominantly with the long term.

Which of the statements are correct?

- A (i) and (ii) only
- B (i) and (iii) only
- C (ii) and (iii) only
- D (i), (ii) and (iii)

10 The following statements relate to responsibility centres:

- (i) Return on capital employed is a suitable measure of performance in both profit and investment centres.
- (ii) Cost centres are found in manufacturing organisations but not in service organisations.
- (iii) The manager of a revenue centre is responsible for both sales and costs in a part of an organisation.

Which of the statements are incorrect?

- A (i) and (ii)
- B (ii) and (iii)
- C (i) and (iii)
- D All of them

KAPLAN PUBLISHING

11 In which ways do management accountants helps manager of a business?

	YES	NO
Control	✓	
Plan	✓	
Co-ordinate	✓	
Make decisions	✓	
Motivate	✓	

12 A paint manufacturer has a number of departments. Each department is located in a separate building on the same factory site. In the mixing department the basic raw materials are mixed together in very large vessels. These are then moved on to the colour adding department where paints of different colours are created in these vessels. In the next department – the pouring department – the paint is poured from these vessels into litre sized tins. The tins then go on to the labelling department prior to going on to the finished goods department.

The following statements relate to the paint manufacturer:

(i) The mixing department is a cost centre.

(ii) A suitable cost unit for the colour adding department is a litre tin of paint.

(iii) The pouring department is a profit centre.

Which statement or statements is/are correct?

A (i) only

B (i) and (ii) only

C (i) and (iii) only

D (ii) and (iii) only

SOURCES OF DATA

13 The following statements refer to qualities of good information:

(i) It should be communicated to the right person.

(ii) It should always be completely accurate before it is used.

(iii) It should be understandable by the recipient.

Which of the above statements are correct?

A (i) and (ii) only

B (i) and (iii) only

C (ii) and (iii) only

D (i), (ii) and (iii)

SECTION A-TYPE QUESTIONS : SECTION 1

14 Which of the following statements describes the essence of systematic sampling?

- A each element of the population has an equal chance of being chosen
- B members of various strata are selected by the interviewers up to predetermined limits
- C every nth member of the population is selected
- D every element of one definable sub-section of the population is selected

15 A firm which bottles shampoo selects some filled bottles for examination. The procedure used is to select a random starting point x (xth bottle filled) and every bottle at an interval of y is then chosen for examination.

What is this type of sampling known as?

- A Multi-stage
- B Random
- C Systematic
- D Stratified

16 The following statements are often made about 'simple random sampling'.

(i) It ensures a representative sample.

(ii) It eliminates selection bias.

Which of the following is always true?

- A (i) only
- B (ii) only
- C Both (i) and (ii)
- D Neither (i) nor (ii)

17 An accountant has to check a sample of invoices. The invoices are divided into three groups, by value as follows: 'under £100', '£100 – £500' and 'over £500'. Samples are then selected randomly from each group.

Which ONE of the following sampling methods is involved?

- A Cluster
- B Multi-stage
- C Quota
- D Stratified

KAPLAN PUBLISHING

PAPER F2/FMA : MANAGEMENT ACCOUNTING

18 A sample of 10% of ACCA students is required. Which ONE of the following methods will provide the best simple random sample?

- A Select every tenth ACCA student to arrive at their college/institute on one specific day.
- B Select randomly, using random number tables, one in ten of every ACCA class.
- C Select 10% of colleges/institutions providing ACCA courses, then from these choose all students who are registered with ACCA.
- D Select 10% of all students registered with ACCA, giving each a chance of 0.1 of being picked.

19 Which of the following describes Secondary data?

- A data that does not provide any information
- B data collected for another purpose
- C data collected specifically for the purpose of the survey being undertaken
- D data collected by post or telephone, not by personal interview

20 Which of the following are primary sources of data and which are secondary sources of data?

	Primary	Secondary
Data collected outside a polling station regarding voters choices	✓	
An internet search for the cheapest fuel available in the area		✓
Government statistics on the levels of unemployment		✓
Data collected by observation on the number of cars flowing through a junction during peak travel hours	✓	

21 When gathering information you would use both internal sources of information and external sources of information.

Which of the following are examples of external information?

- (i) Trade references.
- (ii) Sales representatives' knowledge.
- (iii) A credit agency report
- (iv) Bank references.

Options:

- A (ii) only
- B (ii), (iii) and (iv) only
- C All of the above
- D (i), (iii) and (iv) only

SECTION A-TYPE QUESTIONS : SECTION 1

22 When gathering information on a potential client you can use both internal sources of information and external sources of information.

Which TWO of the following would be classified as internally generated information?

- A   Supplier references
- B   Credit reference agency reports
- C   Sales information
- D   Ratio calculations

23 Which of the following only contains essential features of useful management information?

- A   Accurate, understandable, presented in report format
- B   Timely, reliable, supported by calculations
- C   Regular, complete, communicated in writing
- D   Understandable, accurate, relevant for its purpose

24 Which of the following describes 'Information'?

- A   data that consists of facts and statistics before they have been processed
- B   data that consists of numbers, letters, symbols, events and transactions which have been recorded but not yet processed into a form that is suitable for making decisions
- C   facts that have been summarised but not yet processed into a form that is suitable for making decisions
- D   data that has been processed in such a way that it has a meaning to the person who receives it, who may then use it to improve the quality of decision making

25 Which one of the following statements is correct?

- A   Data is held on computer in digital form whereas information is in a form that is readable to human beings
- B   Information is obtained by processing data
- C   Data and information mean the same thing
- D   Data consists of numerical or statistical items of information

26 Which of the following is an example of external information that could be used in a management accounting system?

- A   Consumer price index statistics
- B   Price list for the products sold by the business
- C   Production volume achieved by the production department
- D   Discounts given to customers

PAPER F2/FMA : MANAGEMENT ACCOUNTING

27 Which of the following would be classified as data?

   A   Number of purchase requisitions

   B   Analysis of wages into direct and indirect costs

   C   Table showing variances from budget

   D   Graph showing the number of labour hours worked

28 Which of the following are primary data?

   (i)   Information on timesheets used for making up wages

   (ii)   Information from a government publication concerning forecast inflation rates used for budgeting

   (iii) Information from a trade publication used to choose a supplier of raw materials

   A   (i) and (ii)

   B   (i) and (iii)

   C   (i) only

   D   (i), (ii) and (iii)

29 Which one of the following is an example of internal information for the wages department of a large company?

   A   A Code of Practice issued by the Institute of Directors

   B   A new national minimum wage

   C   Changes to tax coding arrangements issued by the tax authorities

   D   The company's employees' schedule of hours worked

PRESENTING INFORMATION

30 The following table shows that the typical salary of part qualified accountants in five different regions of England.

Area	Typical salary $
South-east	21,500
Midlands	20,800
North-east	18,200
North-west	17,500
South-west	16,700

   Which diagram would be the best one to draw to highlight the differences between areas?

   A   a pie diagram

   B   a multiple bar chart

   C   a percentage component bar chart

   D   a simple bar chart

SECTION A-TYPE QUESTIONS : SECTION 1

31 A line graph is being produced to show the cost of advertising and sales revenue for a business. Which values would be shown on which axis?

  A Both on the y-axis

  B Both on the x-axis

  C Cost of advertising on the x-axis and sales revenue on the y-axis

  D Sales revenue on the x-axis and cost of advertising on the y-axis

32 A pie chart is being produced to represent the sales from different regional offices of a business:

	$000
North	125
North West	180
East	241
South	691
South East	147
Total	1,384

What would be the angle of the East divisions section on the pie chart (to the nearest whole degree)? 63 °

241/1384 × 360 = 62.69

33 The overhead cost of a business has been allocated and apportioned into the different cost centres. A pie chart has been used to present this information. The assembly department is represented by a section that has an angle of 45°. The total overhead cost is $800,000.

What is the value of the overhead that has been allocated and apportioned to assembly?

  A $360,000

  B $100,000

  C $120,000

  D $640,000

45/360 × 800,000 = 100,000

34 XYZ produces three main products. Which would be the most appropriate chart or diagram for showing total revenue analysed into product revenue month by month?

  A Scatter graph

  B Line graph

  C Pie chart

  D Component bar chart

PAPER F2/FMA : MANAGEMENT ACCOUNTING

35 The pie chart shows the sales volumes of 4 different products.

Product sales 20X4

If the products are ranked from largest sales volume to smallest sales volume what would be the correct order for the products?

A   K, Q, A, W

B   Q, K, A, W

C   K, A, Q, W

D   K, Q, W, A

36 Which member of the sales team had the highest sales in February?

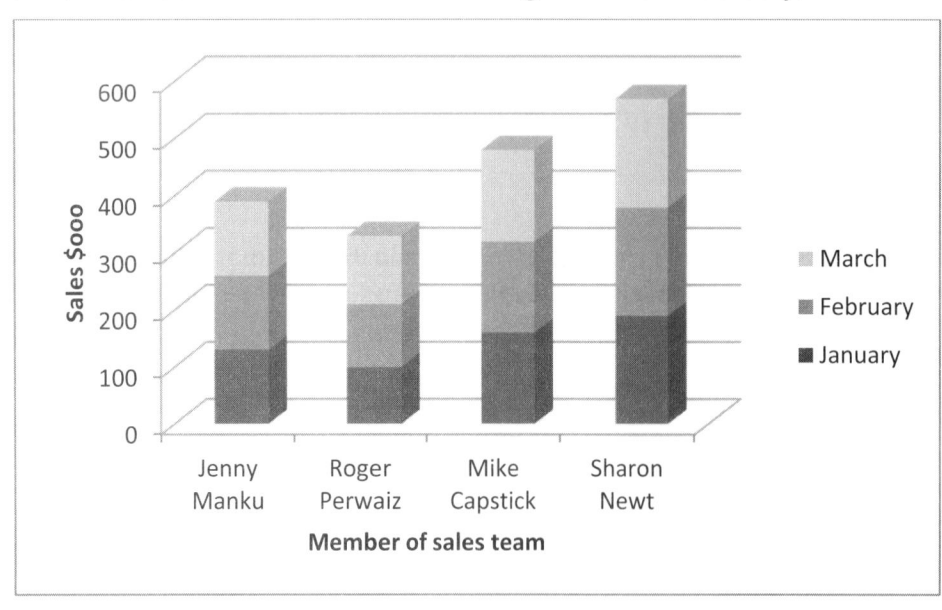

A   Jenny Manku

B   Roger Perwaiz

C   Mike Capstick

D   Sharon Newt

10   KAPLAN PUBLISHING

37 Referring to the graph which statements are true and which are false?

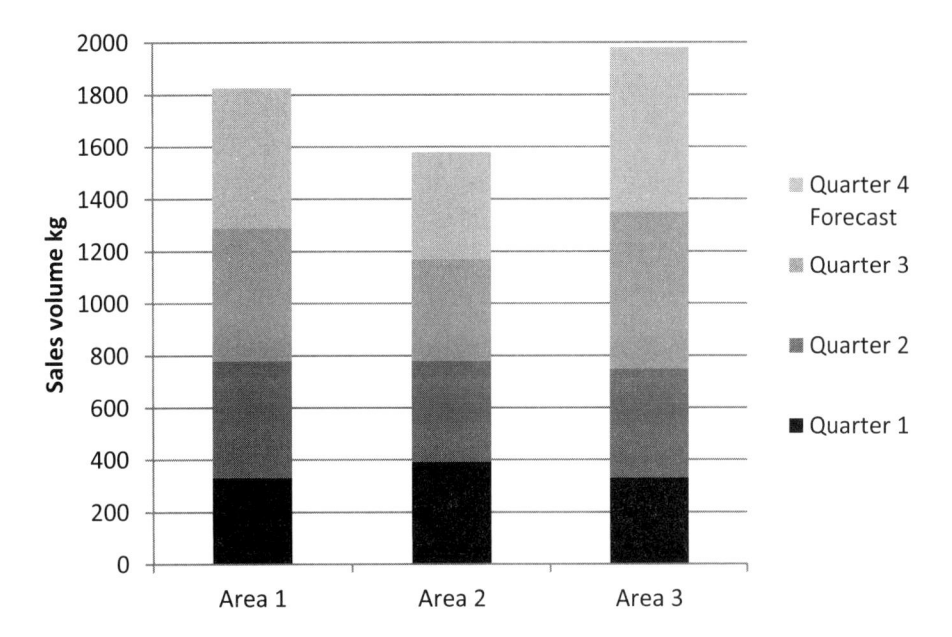

	True	False
Area 3 shows the best performance in Q3	✓	
Area 2 sales are consistent quarter on quarter		✓
Q4 has the largest volume of sales across all areas	✓	
Area 1 shows the best performance in Q2	✓	

PAPER F2/FMA : MANAGEMENT ACCOUNTING

COST CLASSIFICATION

38 The following diagram represents the behaviour of one element of cost:

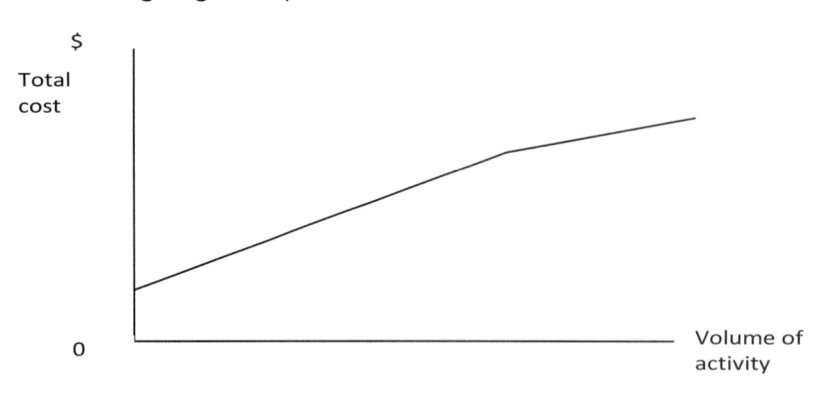

Which one of the following descriptions is consistent with the above diagram?

A Annual total cost of factory power where the supplier sets a tariff based on a fixed charge plus a constant unit cost for consumption which is subject to a maximum annual charge.

B Total annual direct material cost where the supplier charges a constant amount per unit which then reduces to a lower amount per unit after a certain level of purchases.

C Total annual direct material cost where the supplier charges a constant amount per unit but when purchases exceed a certain level a lower amount per unit applies to all purchases in the year.

D Annual total cost of telephone services where the supplier makes a fixed charge and then a constant unit rate for calls up to a certain level. This rate then reduces for all calls above this level.

39 An organisation has the following total costs at three activity levels:

Activity level (units)	8,000	12,000	15,000
Total cost	$204,000	$250,000	$274,000

Variable cost per unit is constant within this activity range and there is a step up of 10% in the total fixed costs when the activity level exceeds 11,000 units.

What is the total cost at an activity level of 10,000 units?

A $220,000
B $224,000
C $227,000
D $234,000

40 A firm has to pay a $0.50 per unit royalty to the inventor of a device which it manufactures and sells.

How would the royalty charge be classified in the firm's accounts?

A   selling expense

B   direct expense

C   production overhead

D   administrative overhead

41 Pliant plc produces cars and motorbikes. The company is split into four different divisions:

Car sales division – this department's manager has been given responsibility for selling the cars, as well as keeping control of the division's costs.

Motorbike sales division – this department's manager has been given responsibility for selling the motorbikes as well as controlling divisional costs. In addition, he has been told to plan what assets he should purchase for the coming year.

Manufacturing division – this division makes the cars and bikes and passes them to the finishing division. The divisional manager is only responsible for controlling the division's costs.

Finishing division – this division tests the cars and cleans them ready to be sold. They transfer the goods to the sales divisions and charge the sales divisions a set price, which is set by the finishing division's manager. The manager is also responsible for managing the division's costs as well as the investment in divisional assets.

Are these centres being operated as a cost, profit or investment centre?

Division	Cost centre	Profit centre	Investment centre
Car sales		✓	
Motorbike sales			✓
Manufacturing	✓		
Finishing			✓

42 Which of the following can be included when valuing inventory?

(i)   Direct material

(ii) Direct labour

(iii) Administration costs

(iv) Production overheads

A   (i) and (ii) only

B   (i), (ii) and (iv)

C   (I), (ii) and (iii)

D   all of them

PAPER F2/FMA : MANAGEMENT ACCOUNTING

43 Which of the following is usually classed as a step cost?

A Supervisor's wages

B Raw materials

C Rates

D Telephone

44 Which of the following is not a cost objects?

A a cost centre

B a customer

C a manager

D a product

45 Which of the following describes depreciation of fixtures?

A not a cash cost so is ignored in the cost accounts

B part of overheads

C part of prime cost

D is a cash outflow

46 Which of the following costs would NOT be classified as a production overhead cost in a food processing company?

A The cost of renting the factory building

B The salary of the factory manager

C The depreciation of equipment located in the materials store

D The cost of ingredients

47 Which TWO of the following are included in the prime cost of a product?

A Direct material

B Direct labour

C Administration costs

D Production overheads

SECTION A-TYPE QUESTIONS : SECTION 1

48 There is to be an increase next year in the rent from $12,000 to $14,000 for a warehouse used to store finished goods ready for sale.

What will be the impact of this increase on the value of inventory manufactured and held in the warehouse?

A   an increase of $14,000

B   a decrease of $14,000

C   no change

D   an increase of $2,000

49 Gilbert plc is a furniture manufacturer. How would he classify the following costs?

Cost	Fixed	Variable	Semi-variable
Director's salary	✓		
Wood		✓	
Rent of factory	✓		
Phone bill – includes a line rental			✓
Factory workers wage		✓	

50 The diagram represents the behaviour of a cost item as the level of output changes:

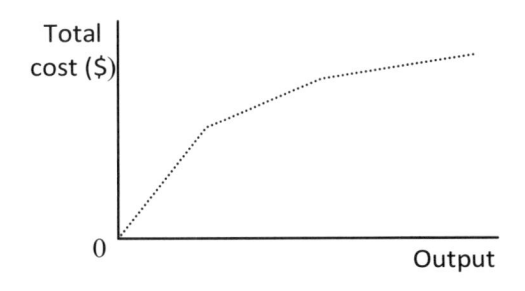

Which ONE of the following situations is described by the graph?

A   Discounts are received on additional purchases of material when certain quantities are purchased

B   Employees are paid a guaranteed weekly wage, together with bonuses for higher levels of production

C   A licence is purchased from the government that allows unlimited production

D   Additional space is rented to cope with the need to increase production

PAPER F2/FMA : MANAGEMENT ACCOUNTING

51 Bytes Limited operates an IT consultancy business and uses a coding system for its elements of cost (materials, labour or overheads) and then further classifies each element by nature (direct or indirect cost):

Element of cost	Code	Nature of cost	Code
Materials	A	Direct	100
		Indirect	200
Labour	B	Direct	100
		Indirect	200
Overheads	C	Direct	100
		Indirect	200

What would the codes be for the following costs?

Cost	Code
Salary of trainee IT consultant	B100
Planning costs to renew lease of the office	C200
Wages of the office manager	B200
Cleaning materials used by cleaner	A200

52 **How would a clothes retailer classify the following costs?**

Cost	Materials	Labour	Expenses
Designer skirts	✓		
Heating costs			✓
Depreciation of fixtures and fittings			✓
Cashier staff salaries		✓	

53 **Which of the following would be classified as direct labour?**

A   Personnel manager in a company servicing cars

B   Bricklayer in a construction company

C   General manager in a DIY shop

D   Maintenance manager in a company producing cameras

54 **Which of the following describes Cost centres?**

A   units of product or service for which costs are ascertained

B   amounts of expenditure attributable to various activities

C   functions or locations for which costs are ascertained

D   a section of an organisation for which budgets are prepared and control exercised

55 The following data relate to two output levels of a department:

Machine hours	17,000	18,500
Overheads	$246,500	$251,750

What is the amount of fixed overheads?

$187,000

56 A kitchen fitting company receives an invoice for sub-contractors who were used to connect the gas supply to a cooker installed in a new kitchen.

How would this invoice be classified?

A   Direct expenses

B   Indirect expenses

C   Direct labour

D   Indirect labour

57 A manufacturing company has four types of cost (identified as T1, T2, T3 and T4).

The total cost for each type at two different production levels is:

Cost type	Total cost for 125 units	Total cost for 180 units
	$	$
T1	1,000	1,260
T2	1,750	2,520
T3	2,475	2,826
T4	3,225	4,644

Which two cost types would be classified as being semi-variable?

A   T1 and T3

B   T1 and T4

C   T2 and T3

D   T2 and T4

58 P Harrington is a golf ball manufacturer. Classify the following costs by nature (direct or indirect) in the table below.

Cost	Direct	Indirect
Machine operators wages	✓	
Supervisors wages		✓
Resin for golf balls	✓	
Salesmen's salaries		✓

PAPER F2/FMA : MANAGEMENT ACCOUNTING

59 The following data relate to the overhead expenditure of contract cleaners at two activity levels:

Square metres cleaned	12,750	15,100
Overheads	$73,950	$83,585

Using the high-low method, what is the estimate of the overhead cost if 16,200 square metres are to be cleaned?

A $88,095
B $89,674
C $93,960
D $98,095

60 A company manufactures and sells toys and incurs the following three costs:

(i) Rental of the finished goods warehouse
(ii) Depreciation of its own fleet of delivery vehicles
(iii) Commission paid to sales staff.

Which of these are classified as distribution costs?

A (i) and (ii) only
B (ii) and (iii) only
C (ii) and (iii) only
D (i), (ii) and (iii)

61 A company incurs the following costs at various activity levels:

Total cost	Activity level
$	Units
250,000	5,000
312,500	7,500
400,000	10,000

Using the high-low method what is the variable cost per unit?

A $25
B $30
C $35
D $40

62 An organisation manufactures a single product. The total cost of making 4,000 units is $20,000 and the total cost of making 20,000 units is $40,000. Within this range of activity the total fixed costs remain unchanged.

What is the variable cost per unit of the product?

A $0.80
B $1.20
C $1.25
D $2.00

63 The total materials cost of a company is such that when total purchases exceed 15,000 units in any period, then all units purchased, including the first 15,000, are invoiced at a lower cost per unit.

Which of the following graphs is consistent with the behaviour of the total materials cost in a period?

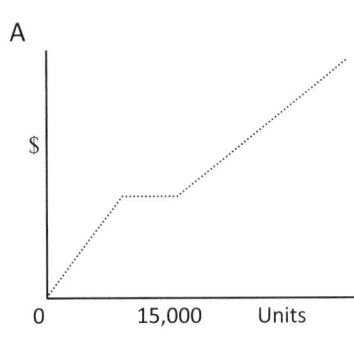

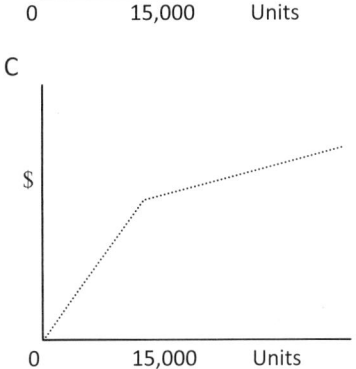

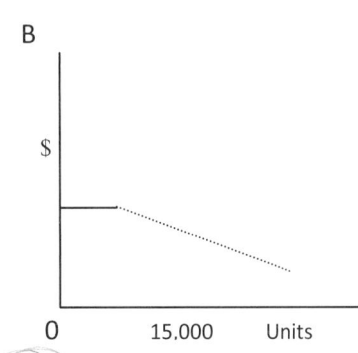

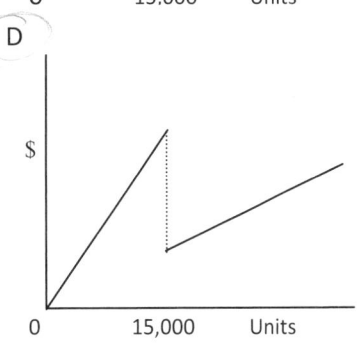

64 George plc makes stationery. How would he classify the following costs?

Cost	Production	Administration	Distribution
Purchases of plastic to make pens	✓		
Managing director's bonus		✓	
Depreciation of factory machinery	✓		
Salaries of factory workers	✓		
Insurance of sales team cars			✓

PAPER F2/FMA : MANAGEMENT ACCOUNTING

65 A supplier of telephone services charges a fixed line rental per period. The first 10 hours of telephone calls by the customer are free, after that all calls are charged at a constant rate per minute up to a maximum, thereafter all calls in the period are again free.

Which of the following graphs depicts the total cost to the customer of the telephone services in a period?

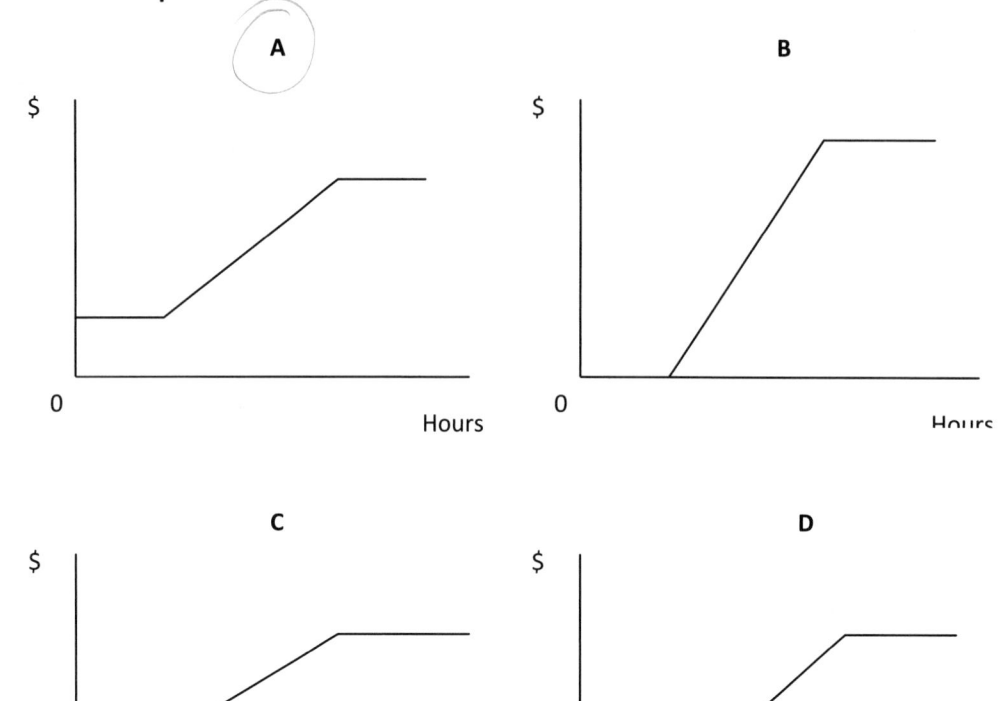

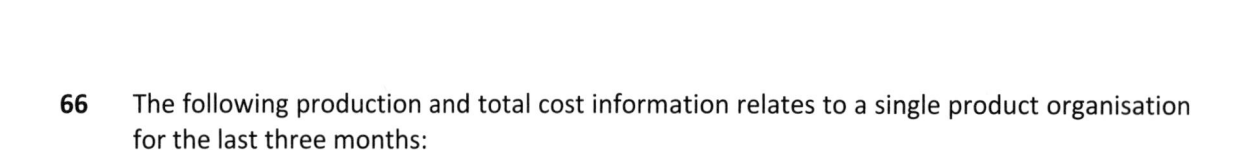

A

B

C

D

66 The following production and total cost information relates to a single product organisation for the last three months:

Month	Production units	Total cost $
1	1,200	66,600
2	900	58,200
3	1,400	68,200

The variable cost per unit is constant up to a production level of 2,000 units per month but a step up of $6,000 in the monthly total fixed cost occurs when production reaches 1,100 units per month.

What is the total cost for a month when 1,000 units are produced?

A $54,200
B $55,000
C $59,000
D $60,200

67 Camberwell runs a construction company. Classify the following costs by nature (direct or indirect) in the table below.

Cost	Direct	Indirect
Bricks	✓	
Plant hire for long term contract	✓	
Builders' wages	✓	
Accountants' wages		✓

PAPER F2/FMA : MANAGEMENT ACCOUNTING

SYLLABUS AREA B – COST ACCOUNTING TECHNIQUES

ACCOUNTING FOR MATERIALS

68 A manufacturing company uses 28,000 components at an even rate during the year. Each order placed with the supplier of the components is for 1,500 components, which is the economic order quantity. The company holds a buffer inventory of 700 components. The annual cost of holding one component in inventory is $3.

What is the total annual cost of holding inventory of the component?

$4,350

69 The following represent the materials transactions for a company for the month of December 20X6:

	$000s
Materials purchases	176
Issued to production	165
Materials written off	4
Returned to stores	9
Returned to suppliers	8

The material inventory at 1 December 20X6 was $15,000.

What is the closing balance on the materials inventory account at 31 December 20X6?

A $5,000
B $16,000
C $23,000
D $31,000

70 **Which of the following statements is correct?**

A A stores ledger account will be updated from a goods received note only

B A stores requisition will only detail the type of product required by a customer

C The term 'lead time' is best used to describe the time between receiving an order and paying for it

D To make an issue from stores authorisation should be required

71 **What is the correct description of perpetual inventory?**

A The counting and valuing of selected items on a rotating basis

B The recording, as they occur, of receipts, issues and the resulting balances of individual items of inventory

C The recording of inventory that is constantly changing

D The counting and valuing inventory on a regular (e.g. weekly) basis

SECTION A-TYPE QUESTIONS : SECTION 1

72 What would be the double entry for an issue of indirect production materials?

   A   Dr Materials control account   Cr Finished goods control account
   B   Dr Production overhead control a/c   Cr Materials control account
   C   Dr Work-in-progress control account   Cr Production overhead control a/c
   D   Dr Work-in-progress control account   Cr Materials control account

73 Which of the following documents would be completed in each situation?

	Material Requisition	Purchase Requisition	Goods received note	Goods returned note
Material returned to stores from production				✓
Form completed by the stores department detailing inventory requirements		✓		
Materials returned to supplier				✓
Form completed by stores on receipt of goods			✓	
Form completed by production detailing inventory requirements.	✓			

74 Which of the following will be completed by a production department requiring new materials to be obtained from suppliers?

   A   A purchase order
   B   A delivery note
   C   A goods requisition note
   D   A goods received note

75 The following represent transactions on the material account for a company for the month of March 20X8:

                              $000s
   Issued to production   144
   Returned to stores   5

   The material inventory at 1 March 20X8 was $23,000 and at 31 March 20X8 was $15,000.

   How much material was purchased in March 20X8?

   $131,000

KAPLAN PUBLISHING   23

76 Which of the following procedures are carried out to minimise losses from inventory?

(i) use of standard costs for purchases

(ii) restricted access to stores

(iii) regular stocktaking

A (i) and (ii)

B (ii) and (iii)

C (ii) only

D All of them

77 Appleby buys and sells inventory during the month of August as follows:

Opening inventory		100 units	$2.52/unit
4 August	Sales	20 units	
8 August	Purchases	140 units	$2.56/unit
10 August	Sales	90 units	
18 August	Purchases	200 units	$2.78/unit
20 August	Sales	180 units	

The periodic weighted average for the month is calculated as follows:

Total value of inventory (opening inventory plus purchase costs during the month) divided by total units (opening inventory plus purchase costs during the month).

Which of the following statements is true?

A Closing inventory is $19.50 higher when using the FIFO method instead of the periodic weighted average.

B Closing inventory is $19.50 lower when using the FIFO method instead of the periodic weighted average.

C Closing inventory is $17.50 higher when using the FIFO method instead of the periodic weighted average.

D Closing inventory is $17.50 lower when using the FIFO method instead of the periodic weighted average.

78 In the year ended 31 August 20X4, Aplus' records show closing inventory of 1,000 units compared to 950 units of opening inventory. Which of the following statements is true assuming that prices have fallen throughout the year?

A Closing inventory and profit are higher using FIFO rather than AVCO

B Closing inventory and profit are lower using FIFO rather than AVCO

C Closing inventory is higher and profit lower using FIFO rather than AVCO

D Closing inventory is lower and profit higher using FIFO rather than AVCO

SECTION A-TYPE QUESTIONS : SECTION 1

79 Inventory movements for product X during the last quarter were as follows:

January	Purchases	10 items at $19.80 each
February	Sales	10 items at $30 each
March	Purchases	20 items at $24.50
	Sales	5 items at $30 each

Opening inventory at 1 January was 6 items valued at $15 each.

What would the Gross profit be for the quarter using the weighted average cost method?

A $135.75

B $155.00

C $174.00

D $483.00

80 Your firm values inventory using the weighted average cost method. At 1 October 20X8, there were 60 units in inventory valued at $12 each. On 8 October, 40 units were purchased for $15 each, and a further 50 units were purchased for $18 each on 14 October. On 21 October, 75 units were sold for $1,200.

What was the value of closing inventory at 31 October 20X8?

$ [   ]

81 An organisation's inventory at 1 July is 15 units at $3.00 each. The following movements occur:

3 July 20X4	5 units sold at $3.30 each
8 July 20X4	10 units bought at $3.50 each
12 July 20X4	8 units sold at $4.00 each

What would be the closing inventory valuation at 31 July using the FIFO method of inventory valuation?

A $31.50

B $36.00

C $39.00

D $41.00

82 In times of rising prices, the valuation of inventory using the First In First Out method, as opposed to the Weighted Average Cost method, will result in which ONE of the following combinations?

	Cost of sales	Profit	Closing inventory
A	Lower	Higher	Higher
B	Lower	Higher	Lower
C	Higher	Lower	Higher
D	Higher	Higher	Lower

PAPER F2/FMA : MANAGEMENT ACCOUNTING

83 A company determines its order quantity for a component using the Economic Order Quantity (EOQ) model.

What would be the effects on the EOQ and the total annual ordering cost of an increase in the annual cost of holding one unit of the component in inventory?

	EOQ	Total annual ordering cost
A ⊙	Lower	Higher
B	Higher	Lower
C	Lower	No effect
D	Higher	No effect

84 A company uses the Economic Order Quantity (EOQ) model to establish reorder quantities. The following information relates to the forthcoming period:

Order costs = $25 per order

Holding costs = 10% of purchase price

Annual demand = 20,000 units

Purchase price = $40 per unit

EOQ = 500 units

No safety inventory is held.

What are the total annual costs of inventory (i.e. the total purchase cost plus total order cost plus total holding cost)?

- A $22,000   Purchase costs (20,000 units × 40)   800,000
- B $33,500   order costs (20,000/500 order × 25/order)   1000
- C ⊙ $802,000   Holding costs 500/2 average unit × $4/unit   1000
- D $803,000   802,000

85 Data relating to a particular stores item are as follows:

Average daily usage	400 units
Maximum daily usage	520 units
Minimum daily usage	180 units
Lead time for replenishment of inventory	10 to 15 days
Reorder quantity	8,000 units

What is the reorder level (in units) that avoids inventory stockouts?

| 7800 | units |

max usage × max lead time
520 × 15 = 7800

SECTION A-TYPE QUESTIONS : SECTION 1

86 A large store selling office furniture stocks a popular chair for which the following information is available:

Annual demand:	4,000 chairs
Maximum inventory:	75 chairs
Minimum inventory:	20 chairs
Lead time:	5 days
Re-order quantity:	100 chairs

What is the average inventory level?

A 75 chairs

B 70 chairs

C 55 chairs

D 47 chairs

ROQ/2 + min inventory
= 100/2 + 20 = 70

87 What is the economic batch quantity used to establish?

A Optimal reorder quantity

B Optimal reorder level

C Maximum inventory levels

D Optimal quantity to be manufactured

88 Which method of inventory valuation is being described?

Characteristic	FIFO	LIFO	AVCO
Potentially out of date valuation on issues.	✓		
The valuation of inventory rarely reflects the actual purchase price of the material.			✓
Potentially out of date closing inventory valuation.		✓	
This inventory valuation method is particularly suited to inventory that consist of liquid materials e.g. oil.			✓
This inventory valuation method is particularly suited to inventory that has a short shelf life e.g. dairy products.	✓		
This inventory valuation method is suited to a wheat farmer who has large silos of grain. Grain is added to and taken from the top of these silos.		✓	
In times of rising prices this method will give higher profits.	✓		
In times of rising prices this method will give lower profits.		✓	
In times of rising prices this method gives a middle level of profits compared to the other two.			✓
Issues are valued at the most recent purchase cost.		✓	
Inventory is valued at the average of the cost of purchases.			✓
Inventory is valued at the most recent purchase cost.	✓		

PAPER F2/FMA : MANAGEMENT ACCOUNTING

89 A company manufactures a product in batches and then holds the items produced in finished goods inventory until they are sold. It is capable of replenishing the product at the rate of 100,000 units/year, but annual sales demand is just 40,000 units. The cost of setting up a batch production run is $1,500 and the cost of holding a unit of the product in inventory is $25/year.

What is the economic batch quantity for manufacturing this product?

A 2,191 units

B 2,828 units

C 4,472 units

D 10,954 units

90 Which TWO of the following are included in the cost of holding inventory?

A The cost of insurance

B The delivery costs

C Rental payments on storage space

D The cost of placing an order

91 A manufacturing company uses 25,000 components at an even rate during a year. Each order placed with the supplier of the components is for 2,000 components, which is the economic order quantity. The company holds a buffer inventory of 500 components. The annual cost of holding one component in inventory is $2.

What is the total annual cost of holding inventory of the component?

A $2,000

B $2,500

C $3,000

D $4,000

92 The purchase price of an inventory item is $42 per unit. In each three-month period the usage of the item is 2,000 units. The annual holding costs associated with one unit is 5% of its purchase price. The EOQ is 185 units.

What is the cost of placing an order (to 2 decimal places)?

$4.49

SECTION A-TYPE QUESTIONS : SECTION 1

93 Are the following statements true or false?

Statement	True	False
In periods of rising prices, FIFO gives a higher valuation of closing inventory than LIFO or AVCO.	✓	
In periods of falling prices, LIFO gives a higher valuation of issues of inventory than FIFO or AVCO.		✓
AVCO would normally be expected to produce a valuation of closing inventory somewhere between valuations FIFO and LIFO.	✓	
FIFO costs issues of inventory at the most recent purchase price.		✓
AVCO costs issues of inventory at the oldest purchase price.		✓
LIFO costs issues of inventory at the oldest purchase price.		✓
FIFO values closing inventory at the most recent purchase price.	✓	
LIFO values closing inventory at the most recent purchase price.		✓
AVCO values closing inventory at the latest purchase price.		✓

The following information applies to questions 94, 95 and 96

Point uses the economic order quantity (EOQ) model to establish the reorder quantity for raw material Y. The company holds no buffer inventory. Information relating to raw material Y is as follows:

Annual usage	48,000 units
Purchase price	$80 per unit
Ordering costs	$120 per order
Annual holding costs	10% of the purchase price

94 What is the EOQ for raw material Y?

    A   438

    B   800

    C   1,200

    D   3,795

95 What is the total annual cost of purchasing, ordering and holding inventory of raw material Y?

    A $3,849,600

    B $3,850,400

    C $3,853,600

    D $3,854,400

KAPLAN PUBLISHING

96 The supplier has offered Point a discount of 1% on the purchase price if each order placed is for 2,000 units.

What is the total annual saving to Point of accepting this offer?

A $29,280

B $30,080

C $37,200

D $38,000

97 A company uses components at the rate of 600 units per month, which are bought in at a cost of $2.24 each from the supplier. It costs $8.75 each time to place an order, regardless of the quantity ordered. The supplier offers a 5% discount on the purchase price for order quantities of 2,000 items or more. The current EOQ is 750 units. The total holding cost is 10% per annum of the value of inventory held.

What is the change in total cost to the company of moving to an order quantity of 2,000 units?

A $601 additional cost

B $730 additional cost

C $730 saving

D $601 saving

98 A company makes a component for one of its products in-house. It uses an average of 5,000 of these throughout the year. The production rate for these components is 500 per week and the cost of holding one item for the year is $1.50. The factory is open for 50 weeks per year. The company has calculated that the economic batch quantity is 2,000. What is the production setup cost per batch?

A $213

B $240

C $480

D $960

99 Which of the following is in the correct chronological sequence for sales documents?

A   Enquiry – Order – Invoice – Payment

B   Order – Enquiry – Invoice – Payment

C   Enquiry – Order – Payment – Invoice

D   Enquiry – Invoice – Order – Payment

SECTION A-TYPE QUESTIONS : SECTION 1

100 Which of the following is in the correct chronological sequence for purchase documents?

- A   Purchase order – Invoice – Goods received note – Delivery note
- B   Delivery note – Goods received note – Purchase order – Invoice
- C   Purchase order – Delivery note – Goods received note – Invoice
- D   Goods received note – Delivery note – Purchase order – Invoice

101 Which of the following describes a purchase order?

- A   Issued by the purchasing department, sent to the supplier requesting materials
- B   Issued by the stores department, sent to the purchasing department requesting materials
- C   Received together with the materials and compared to the materials received
- D   Issued by the production department, sent to the stores department requesting materials

102 Which TWO of the following statements describe the information a Goods Received Note (GRN) provides?

- A   Information used to update inventory records
- B   Information to check that the correct price has been recorded on the supplier's invoice
- C   Information to check that the correct quantity of goods has been recorded on the supplier's invoice
- D   Information to record any unused materials which are returned to stores

103 When charging direct material cost to a job or process, the details would be taken from which document?

- A   Purchase requisition
- B   Material requisition
- C   Goods received note
- D   Purchase order

104 Which TWO of these documents are matched with the goods received note in the buying process?

- A   Invoice from supplier
- B   Purchase order
- C   purchase requisition
- D   Stores requisition

KAPLAN PUBLISHING

31

105 The following relate to the management of raw materials:

(i) Holding costs per unit of inventory would increase

(ii) The economic order quantity would decrease

(iii) Average inventory levels would increase

(iv) Total ordering costs would decrease

Which of the above would result from the introduction of buffer (safety) inventory?

A (iii) only

B (ii) and (iii) only

C (ii), (iii) and (iv) only

D (i), (ii), (iii) and (iv)

106 Which of the following is least relevant to the simple economic order quantity model for inventory?

A Safety inventory

B Annual demand

C Holding costs

D Ordering costs

107 The following documents are used in accounting for raw materials:

(i) goods received note

(ii) materials returned note

(iii) materials requisition note

(iv) delivery note

Which of the documents may be used to record raw materials sent back to stores from production?

A (i) and (ii)

B (i) and (iv)

C (ii) only

D (ii) and (iii)

108 Which of the following documents should be checked before a purchase invoice is paid, to confirm that the price and quantities are correct?

	Price check	Quantity check
A	Purchase order	Purchase order
B	Goods received note	Delivery note
C	Purchase invoice	Goods received note
D	Purchase order	Goods received note

ACCOUNTING FOR LABOUR

109 The following statements relate to labour costs:

There would be an increase in the total cost for labour as a result of:

(i) additional labour being employed on a temporary basis

(ii) a department with spare capacity being made to work more hours

(iii) a department which is at full capacity switching from the production of one product to another.

Which of the above is/are correct?

A (i) only

B (ii) only

C (iii) only

D (i) and (iii) only

110 A manufacturing firm is very busy and overtime is being worked.

What would the amount of overtime premium contained in direct wages normally be classed as?

A part of prime cost

B factory overheads

C direct labour costs

D administrative overheads

111 KL currently pays its direct production workers on a time basis at a rate of $6.50 per hour. In an effort to improve productivity, the company is introducing a bonus based on (time taken/time allowed) × time saved × rate per hour. The standard time allowed for a worker in the Assembly Department to perform this particular operation once has been agreed at 37.5 minutes.

In the first week of the scheme's operation, one employee worked for a total of 44 hours and performed 94 operations.

What are the gross wages for this employee based on a time rate of $6.50 per hour plus the productivity bonus based on (time taken/time allowed) × time saved × rate per hour, to 2 decimal places?

A $214.20

B $357.80

C $381.88

D $977.60

PAPER F2/FMA : MANAGEMENT ACCOUNTING

112 How would the cost be recorded in the cost ledger if the direct labour costs in a manufacturing company are $95,000?

    A ⊙ Debit Work-in-progress $95,000, Credit Wages and salaries $95,000

    B   Debit Wages and salaries $95,000, Credit Bank $95,000

    C   Debit Wages and salaries $95,000, Credit Work-in-progress $95,000

    D   Debit Bank $95,000, Credit Wages and salaries $95,000

113 How would the following labour costs be classified?

Cost	Direct	Indirect
Basic pay for production workers	✓	
Supervisors wages		✓
Bonus for salesman		✓
Production workers overtime premium due to general pressures.		✓
Holiday pay for production workers		✓
Sick pay for supervisors		✓
Time spent by production workers cleaning the machinery		✓

114 Budgeted production in a factory for next period is 4,800 units. Each unit requires five labour hours to make. Labour is paid $10 per hour. Idle time represents 20% of the total labour time.

What is the budgeted total labour cost for the next period?

$300,000   4800 units × 5hrs × 10 p/h ÷ 0.80 = 300,000

115 The following statements refer to situations occurring in Process Q of an organisation which operates a series of consecutive processes:

    (i)   Direct labour is working at below the agreed productivity level.

    (ii)   A machine breakdown has occurred.

    (iii)   Direct labour is waiting for work to be completed in a previous process.

Which of these situations could give rise to idle time?

    A   (i) and (ii) only

    B   (i) and (iii) only

    C ⊙ (ii) and (iii) only

    D   (i), (ii) and (iii)

116 A direct labour employee works a standard 37 hour week and is paid a basic rate of $15 per hour. Overtime is paid at time and a half. In a week when 40 hours were worked and a bonus of $20 was paid, what was the direct labour cost?

   A $555
   B $600
   C $622.50
   D $642.50

117 At 1 January a company employed 5,250 employees. Due to expansion the number of employees increased to 5,680 by 31 December. During the year 360 staff left the company and were replaced. What was the labour turnover rate?

   A   6.3%
   B   6.6%
   C   6.9%
   D   360 staff

The following information applies to questions 118, 119 and 120

A company records the following information concerning a product:

Standard time allowed per unit	16 minutes
Actual output in period	720 units
Actual hours worked	180
Budgeted hours	185

118 What is the labour efficiency ratio?

   A   93.75%
   B   97.3%
   C   102.5%
   D   106.7%

119 What is the labour capacity ratio?

   A   102.8%
   B   99.4%
   C   98.6%
   D   97.3%

120 What is the production volume ratio?

   A   97.3%
   B   102.5%
   C   103.8%
   D   106.7%

PAPER F2/FMA : MANAGEMENT ACCOUNTING

121 What is the hourly payment method being described?

Payment method	Basic rate	Overtime premium	Overtime payment
This is the amount paid above the basic rate for hours worked in excess of the normal hours.		✓	
This is the total amount paid per hour for hours worked in excess of the normal hours.			✓
This is the amount paid per hour for normal hours worked.	✓		

122 H&H operates an incentive scheme based on differential piecework. Employees are paid on the following basis:

Weekly output up to:
- 600 units — $0.40 per unit
- 601–650 units — $0.50 per unit
- 650 units + — $0.75 per unit

Only the additional units qualify for the higher rates.

In Week 17, an employee produced 660 units. What would be the gross pay for the week?

- A $260.40
- B $272.50
- C $325.75
- D $488.25

600 units at 0.40 — 240.00
50 units at 0.50 — 25.00
10 units at 0.75 — 7.50
for 660 units — (272.50)

123 Which of the following methods of remuneration is not an incentive-based scheme?

- A Straight piecework
- B Day rate
- C Group bonus
- D Differential piecework

124 A differential piecework scheme has a basic rate of $0.50 per unit. Output in addition to 500 units is paid at higher rates. The premiums over and above the basic rate, which apply only to additional units over the previous threshold, are:

Output (units)	Premium (per unit)
501–600	$0.05
above 600	$0.10

What is the total amount paid if output is 620 units?

- A $317
- B $318
- C $322
- D $372

(500 × 0.50) + (100 × 0.55) + (20 × 0.60) = 317

SECTION A-TYPE QUESTIONS : SECTION 1

125 Which remuneration method is being described?

Payment method	Time-rate	Piecework	Piece-rate plus bonus
Labour is paid based solely on the production achieved.		✓	
Labour is paid extra if an agreed level of output is exceeded.			✓
Labour is paid according to hours worked.	✓		

126 Which TWO of the following labour records may be used to allocate costs to the various cost units in a factory?

    A   Employee record card

    B   Attendance record card

    C   Timesheet

    D   Job card

127 A business employs two grades of labour in its production department. Grade A workers are considered direct labour employees, and are paid $10 per hour. Grade B workers are considered indirect labour employees, and are paid $6 per hour.

In the week just ended, Grade A labour worked 30 hours of overtime, 10 hours on a specific customer order at the customer's request, and the other 20 hours as general overtime. Grade B labour worked 45 hours of overtime, as general overtime. Overtime is paid at time-and-one-half.

What would be the total amount of pay for overtime worked in the week that is considered to be a direct labour cost?

    A $50

    B $150

    C $285

    D $350

128 An employee is paid on a piecework basis. The scheme is as follows:

1 – 200 units per day	$0.15 per unit
201 – 500 units per day	$0.20 per unit
> 500 units per day	$0.25 per unit

Only the additional units qualify for the higher rates. Rejected units do not qualify for payment. An employee produced 512 units in a day of which 17 were rejected as faulty.

What wage is paid to the employee?

    A $128

    B $103

    C $99

    D $89

129 H&H employed on average 55 employees during the year. There had been 8 leavers all of whom were replaced. What was the company's labour turnover ratio?

    A   7.30%

    B   8.50%

    C   14.55%

    D   17.00%

ACCOUNTING FOR OVERHEADS

130 A factory consists of two production cost centres (G and H) and two service cost centres (J and K). The total overheads allocated and apportioned to each centre are as follows:

G	H	J	K
$40,000	$50,000	$30,000	$18,000

The work done by the service cost centres can be represented as follows:

	G	H	J	K
Percentage of service cost centre J to	30%	70%	–	–
Percentage of service cost centre K to	50%	40%	10%	–

The company apportions service cost centre costs to production cost centres using a method that fully recognises any work done by one service cost centre for another.

What are the total overheads for production cost centre G after the reapportionment of all service cost centre costs?

$ ☐

131 What is an overhead absorption rate used for?

    A   share out common costs over benefiting cost centres

    B   find the total overheads for a cost centre

    C   charge overheads to products

    D   control overheads

132 A factory consists of two production cost centres (P and Q) and two service cost centres (X and Y). The total allocated and apportioned overhead for each is as follows:

P	Q	X	Y
$95,000	$82,000	$46,000	$30,000

It has been estimated that each service cost centre does work for the other cost centres in the following proportions:

	P	Q	X	Y
Percentage of service cost centre X to	40	40	–	20
Percentage of service cost centre Y to	30	60	10	–

After the reapportionment of service cost centre costs has been carried out using a method that fully recognises the reciprocal service arrangements in the factory, what is the total overhead for production cost centre P?

A $122,400

B $124,716

C $126,000

D $127,000

133 A cost centre has an overhead absorption rate of $4.25 per machine hour, based on a budgeted activity level of 12,400 machine hours.

In the period covered by the budget, actual machine hours worked were 2% more than the budgeted hours and the actual overhead expenditure incurred in the cost centre was $56,389.

What was the total over or under absorption of overheads in the cost centre for the period?

A $1,054 over absorbed

B $2,635 under absorbed

C $3,689 over absorbed

D $3,689 under absorbed

134 When do over-absorbed overheads occur?

A absorbed overheads exceed actual overheads

B absorbed overheads exceed budgeted overheads

C actual overheads exceed budgeted overheads

D budgeted overheads exceed absorbed overheads

PAPER F2/FMA : MANAGEMENT ACCOUNTING

135 The management accountant's report shows that fixed production overheads were over-absorbed in the last accounting period. What is the combination that is certain to lead to this situation?

A production volume is lower than budget and actual expenditure is higher than budget

B production volume is higher than budget and actual expenditure is higher than budget

C production volume and actual cost are as budgeted

D production volume is higher than budget and actual expenditure is lower than budget

136 What would the accounting entries be for $10,000 of over-absorbed overheads?

A	Dr	Work-in-progress control account	Cr	Overhead control account
B	Dr	Statement of profit or loss	Cr	Work-in-progress control account
C	Dr	Statement of profit or loss	Cr	Overhead control account
D	Dr	Overhead control account	Cr	Statement of profit or loss

137 During a period $50,000 were incurred for indirect labour. What would the double entry be in a typical cost ledger?

A	Dr	Wages control	Cr	Overhead control
B	Dr	WIP control	Cr	Wages control
C	Dr	Overhead control	Cr	Wages control
D	Dr	Wages control	Cr	WIP control

138 Iddon makes two products, Pye and Tan, in a factory divided into two production departments, machining and assembly. In order to find a fixed overhead cost per unit, the following budgeted data are relevant.

	Machining	Assembly
Direct and allocated fixed costs	$120,000	$72,000
Labour hours per unit		
Pye	0.50 hour	0.20 hour
Tan	1.00 hour	0.25 hour

Budgeted production is 4,000 units of each product (8,000 units in all) and fixed overheads are to be absorbed by reference to labour hours.

What is the budgeted fixed overhead cost of a unit of Pye (to 2 decimal places)?

$ 18

139 What is cost apportionment?

- A The charging of discrete identifiable items of cost to cost centres or cost units
- B The collection of costs attributable to cost centres and cost units using the costing methods, principles and techniques prescribed for a particular business entity
- C The process of establishing the costs of cost centres or cost units
- D The division of costs amongst two or more cost centres in proportion to the estimated benefit received, using a proxy, e.g. square metres

140 A law firm recovers overheads on chargeable consulting hours. Budgeted overheads were $615,000 and actual consulting hours were 32,150. Overheads were under-recovered by $35,000. Actual overheads were $694,075.

What is the budgeted overhead absorption rate per hour (to 2 decimal places)?

- A $20.21
- B $20.50
- C $21.59
- D $22.68

141 A finishing department absorbs production overheads using a direct labour hour basis. Budgeted production overheads for the year just ended were $268,800 for the department, and actual production overhead costs were $245,600.

If actual labour hours worked were 45,000 and production overheads were over-absorbed by $6,400, what was the overhead absorption rate per labour hour?

- A $5.32
- B $5.60
- C $5.83
- D $6.12

142 A firm absorbs overheads on labour hours. In one period 11,500 hours were worked, actual overheads were $138,000 and there was $23,000 over-absorption.

What was the overhead absorption rate per hour (to 2 decimal places)?

$ _____

PAPER F2/FMA : MANAGEMENT ACCOUNTING

143 A factory has two production departments, X and Y, and two service departments C and D.

The following information costs relates to the overhead costs in each department.

	Manufacturing departments		Service departments	
	X	Y	C	D
Overhead costs	$5,000	$7,500	$3,200	$4,600
Proportion of usage of services of C	50%	40%	–	10%
Proportion of usage of services of D	20%	60%	20%	–

Using the reciprocal method of apportioning service department costs what is the total overhead cost allocated to department X?

- A $5,000
- B $7,520
- C $8,106
- D $12,195

144 The following budgeted and actual results relate to production activity and overhead costs in WX.

	Budget	Actual
Production overhead costs		
Fixed	$36,000	$39,000
Variable	$9,000	$12,000
Direct labour hours worked	18,000 hours	20,000 hours

An absorption costing system is used and production overhead costs are absorbed into output costs on a direct labour hour basis.

What is the total production overhead (both fixed and variable) during the period?

- A   over-absorbed by $1,000
- B   under-absorbed by $1,000
- C   under-absorbed by $5,000
- D   under-absorbed by $6,000

145 Lerna produces hydras in three production departments and needs to apportion budgeted monthly fixed costs between those departments. Budgeted costs are as follows:

	$
Rent	2,000
Rates	1,000
Plant insurance	1,000
Plant depreciation	10,000
Supervisor's salary	7,000
	21,000

The following additional information is available.

	Department A	Department B	Department C
Area (square feet)	3,800	3,500	700
Value of machinery ($000)	210	110	80
Number of employees	34	16	20

What is the total budgeted monthly fixed overhead cost for Department C?

A $1,837.50

B $4,462.50

C $7,000.00

D $10,600.00

146 The following information is available regarding the fixed overhead costs and output of the two production departments of a firm.

Department	S	T
Allocated or apportioned fixed overhead	$60,000	$100,000
Total cost of direct materials used	$120,000	$100,000
Total productive labour hours	5,000	10,000

A particular product has the following variable cost.

				$
Materials				
Department S	3 kg	@	$4 per kg	12
Department T	2 kg	@	$4 per kg	8
Labour				
Department S	½ hour	@	$10 per hour	5
Department T	1½ hours	@	$10 per hour	15
Variable overheads	1 hour	@	$5 per hour	5
				45

What is the fixed overhead cost per unit if fixed overheads are absorbed on the basis of departmental material cost?

A $5.50

B $12.00

C $14.00

D $21.00

PAPER F2/FMA : MANAGEMENT ACCOUNTING

ABSORPTION AND MARGINAL COSTING

147 PQR sells one product. The cost card for that product is given below:

	$
Direct materials	4
Direct labour	5
Variable production overhead	3
Fixed production overhead	2
Variable selling cost	3

The selling price per unit is $20. Budgeted fixed overheads are based on budgeted production of 1,000 units. Opening inventory was 200 units and closing inventory was 150 units. Sales during the period were 800 units and actual fixed overheads incurred were $1,500.

What was the total contribution earned during the period?

- A $2,000
- B $2,500
- **C $4,000**
- D $2,500

Total variable cost = (4 + 5 + 3 + 3) = 15
Contribution per unit = 20 − 15 = 5
Total Contribution earned = 5 × 800 = 4,000

148 E operates a marginal costing system. For the forthcoming year, variable costs are budgeted to be 60% of sales value and fixed costs are budgeted to be 10% of sales value.

If E were to increase the selling price by 10% and all other costs and production and sales volumes were to remain the same what would be the effect on E's contribution?

- A a decrease of 2%
- B an increase of 5%
- C an increase of 10%
- **D an increase of 25%**

$100 per unit

	100	110
Selling price	100	110
Variable cost	60	60
Contribution	40	50

(50−40)/40 × 100 = 25%

149 Last month a manufacturing company's profit was $2,000, calculated using absorption costing principles. If marginal costing principles had been used, a loss of $3,000 would have occurred. The company's fixed production cost is $2 per unit. Sales last month were 10,000 units.

What was last month's production (in units)?

> 12,500 units

2000 → marginal costing of 3000 = Sales by 5000
5000 = OAR × number of units
5000 = 2 × number of units
number of units = 5000/2 = 2500

Sales of 10,000 + 2500 = 12,500

SECTION A-TYPE QUESTIONS : SECTION 1

150 A company produces and sells a single product whose variable cost is $6 per unit.

Fixed costs have been absorbed over the normal level of activity of 200,000 units and have been calculated as $2 per unit.

The current selling price is $10 per unit.

How much profit is made under marginal costing if the company sells 250,000 units?

- A $500,000
- (B) $600,000
- C $900,000
- D $1,000,000

Handwritten working:
Contribution per unit = (10 − 6) = 4
Total contribution = 250,000 × 4 = 1,000,000
Fixed overhead = 200,000 × 2 = 400,000
Profit = 600,000

151 A company manufactures and sells a single product. For this month the budgeted fixed production overheads are $48,000, budgeted production is 12,000 units and budgeted sales are 11,720 units.

The company currently uses absorption costing.

If the company used marginal costing principles instead of absorption costing for this month, what would be the effect on the budgeted profit?

- A $1,120 higher
- (B) $1,120 lower
- C $3,920 higher
- D $3,920 lower

Handwritten working:
Production overhead / budgeted production
48,000 / 12,000 = 4
280 units × 4 = 1,120

152 When opening inventory was 8,500 litres and closing inventory was 6,750 litres, a firm had a profit of $62,100 using marginal costing.

Assuming that the fixed overhead absorption rate was $3 per litre, what would be the profit using absorption costing?

$ **56,850**

Handwritten working:
(8,500 − 6,750) × 3 = 5,250
62,100 − 5,250 = 56,850

153 A company has established a marginal costing profit of $72,300. Opening inventory was 300 units and closing inventory is 750 units. The fixed production overhead absorption rate has been calculated as $5/unit.

What was the profit under absorption costing?

- A $67,050
- B $70,050
- C $74,550
- D $77,550

KAPLAN PUBLISHING

PAPER F2/FMA : MANAGEMENT ACCOUNTING

154 Which of the following relate to marginal costing and which to absorption costing?

	Marginal costing	Absorption costing
The cost of a product includes an allowance for fixed production costs.		✓
The cost of a product represents the additional cost of producing an extra unit.	✓	

The following data are for questions 155 and 156

The budget for Bright's first month of trading, producing and selling boats was as follows:

	$000
Variable production cost of boats	45
Fixed production costs	30
Production costs of 750 boats	75
Closing inventory of 250 boats	(25)
Production cost of 500 sold	50
Variable selling costs	5
Fixed selling costs	25
	80
Profit	10
Sales revenue	90

The budget has been produced using an absorption costing system.

155 What would the budgeted profit be if a marginal costing system were used?

- A $22,500 lower
- B $10,000 lower
- C $10,000 higher
- D $22,500 higher

30,000/750 = 40 per unit
250 units × 40 = 10,000

156 Assume that at the end of the first month unit variable costs and fixed costs and selling price for the month were in line with the budget and any inventory was valued at the same unit cost as in the above budget.

However, if production was actually 700 and sales 600, what would be the reported profit using absorption costing?

- A $9,000
- B $12,000
- C $14,000
- D $15,000

46 KAPLAN PUBLISHING

157 A new company has set up a marginal costing system and has a budgeted contribution for the period of $26,000 based on sales of 13,000 units and production of 15,000 units. This level of production represents the firm's expected long-term level of production. The company's budgeted fixed production costs are $3,000 for the period.

What would the budgeted profit be if the company were to change to an absorption costing system?

  A $22,600

  B $23,400

  C $25,600

  D $26,400

158 Which of these statements are true of marginal costing?

  (i) The contribution per unit will be constant if the sales volume increases.

  (ii) There is no under- or over-absorption of overheads.

  (iii) Marginal costing does not provide useful information for decision making.

  A (i) and (ii) only

  B (ii) and (iii) only

  C (ii) only

  D (i), (ii) and (iii)

159 In a period, a company had opening inventory of 31,000 units of Product G and closing inventory of 34,000 units. Profits based on marginal costing were $850,500 and profits based on absorption costing were $955,500.

If the budgeted fixed costs for the company for the period were $1,837,500, what was the budgeted level of activity?

  A 24,300 units

  B 27,300 units

  C 52,500 units

  D 65,000 units

160 In a given period, the production level of an item exactly matches the level of sales.

How would the profit differ if marginal or absorption costing was used?

  A There would not be a difference

  B It would be higher under absorption costing

  C It would be lower under absorption costing

  D It would be higher under marginal costing

PAPER F2/FMA : MANAGEMENT ACCOUNTING

161 For a product that has a positive unit contribution, which of the following events would tend to increase total contribution by the greatest amount?

    A   10% decrease in variable cost

    B   10% increase in selling price

    C   10% increase in volume sold

    D   15% decrease in total fixed costs

162 Exp has compiled the following standard cost card for its main product.

	$
Production costs	
Fixed	33.00
Variable	45.10
Selling costs	
Fixed	64.00
Variable	7.20
Profit	14.70
Selling price	164.00

What would the closing inventory be valued at under an absorption costing system (to 2 decimal places)?

$ [   ]

COST ACCOUNTING METHODS

163 A company operates a job costing system. Job 812 requires $60 of direct materials, $40 of direct labour and $20 of direct expenses. Direct labour is paid $8 per hour. Production overheads are absorbed at a rate of $16 per direct labour hour and non-production overheads are absorbed at a rate of 60% of prime cost.

What is the total cost of Job 812?

    A $240

    B $260

    C $272

    D $320

164 **Which one of the following statements is incorrect?**

    A   Job costs are collected separately, whereas process costs are averages

    B   In job costing the progress of a job can be ascertained from the materials requisition notes and job tickets or time sheet

    C   In process costing information is needed about work passing through a process and work remaining in each process

    D   In process costing, but not job costing, the cost of normal loss will be incorporated into normal product costs

SECTION A-TYPE QUESTIONS : SECTION 1

The following data are to be used for questions 165 and 166

A firm uses job costing and recovers overheads on a direct labour cost basis.

Three jobs were worked on during a period, the details of which were:

	Job 1 $	Job 2 $	Job 3 $
Opening work-in-progress	8,500	0	46,000
Material in period	17,150	29,025	0
Labour for period	12,500	23,000	4,500

The overheads for the period were exactly as budgeted, $140,000. Actual labour costs were also the same as budgeted.

Jobs 1 and 2 were the only incomplete jobs at the end of the period.

165 What was the value of closing work-in-progress?

- A $81,900
- B $90,175
- C $140,675
- D $214,425

166 Job 3 was completed during the period and consisted of 2,400 identical circuit boards. The firm adds 50% to total production costs to arrive at a selling price.

What is the selling price of a circuit board?

- A It cannot be calculated without more information
- B $31.56
- C $41.41
- D $58.33

167 A company uses process costing to value output. During the last month the following information was recorded:

Output:	2,800 kg valued at $7.50/kg
Normal loss:	300 kg which has a scrap value of $3/kg
Abnormal gain:	100 kg

What was the value of the input?

$ 21,150

KAPLAN PUBLISHING

168 ABC manufactures product X in a single process. Normal loss (scrap) in the process is 10% of output and scrapped units can be sold off for $4/unit.

In period 8 there was no opening inventory and no closing inventory. Process costs of direct materials, direct labour and production overheads totalled $184,800. Input to the process in the month was 13,200 units.

What was the cost/unit produced?

A $12.50

B $15.00

C $15.15

D $15.40

169 A company uses process costing to value its output. The following was recorded for the period:

Input materials   2,000 units at $4.50 per unit
Conversion costs $13,340
Normal loss   5% of input valued at $3 per unit
Abnormal loss   150 units

There were no opening or closing inventories.

What was the valuation of one unit of output (to 2 decimal places)?

$ [   ]

170 A company that operates a process costing system had work-in-progress at the start of last month of 300 units (valued at $1,710) that were 60% complete in respect of all costs.

Last month a total of 2,000 units were completed and transferred to the finished goods warehouse. The cost per equivalent unit for costs arising last month was $10. The company uses the FIFO method of cost allocation.

What was the total value of the 2,000 units transferred to the finished goods warehouse last month?

A $19,910

B $20,000

C $20,510

D $21,710

SECTION A-TYPE QUESTIONS : SECTION 1

171 Vare produces various inks at its Normanton factory. Production details for Process 1 are as follows:

Opening work-in-progress, 1 April	400 units	60% complete
Closing work-in-progress, 30 April	600 units	20% complete
Units started	1,000	
Units finished	800	

The degree of completion quoted relates to labour and overhead costs. Three-quarters of the materials are added at the start of the process and the remaining quarter added when the process is 50% complete. The company uses the FIFO method of cost allocation.

What are the equivalent units of production for materials in the period?

- A 1,250
- B 1,000
- C 850
- D 680

172 Two products W and X are created from a joint process. Both products can be sold immediately after split-off. There are no opening inventories or work-in-progress. The following information is available for the last period:

Total joint production costs $776,160

Product	Production units	Sales units	Selling price per unit
W	12,000	10,000	$10
X	10,000	8,000	$12

Using the sales value method of apportioning joint production costs, what was the value of the closing inventory of product X for the last period?

$ [ ]

173 In a process where there are no work-in-progress inventories, two joint products (J and K) are created. Information (in units) relating to last month is as follows:

Product	Sales	Opening inventory of finished goods	Closing inventory of finished goods
J	6,000	100	300
K	4,000	400	200

Joint production costs last month were $110,000 and these were apportioned to joint products based on the number of units produced.

What were the joint production costs apportioned to product J for last month?

- A $63,800
- B $64,000
- C $66,000
- D $68,200

KAPLAN PUBLISHING

174 Charleville operates a continuous process producing three products and one by-product. Output from the process for a month was as follows:

Product	Selling price per unit	Units of output from process
1	$18	10,000
2	$25	20,000
3	$20	20,000
4 (by-product)	$2	3,500

Total joint costs were $277,000.

What was the unit cost valuation for product 3 using the sales revenue basis for allocating joint costs assuming that the revenue receivable from the by-product is deducted from the joint costs?

A $4.70
B $4.80
C $5.00
D $5.10

175 A business operates a job costing system and prices its jobs by adding 20% to the total cost of the job. The prime cost of a job was $6,840 and it had used 156 direct labour hours. The fixed production overheads are absorbed on the basis of direct labour hours. The budgeted overhead absorption rate was based upon a budgeted fixed overhead of $300,000 and total budgeted direct labour hours of 60,000.

What should the job be sold for?

A $7,620
B $8,208
C $9,144
D $9,525

176 If there are abnormal losses in a process how is this recorded in a process account?

A   debit with the scrap value of the abnormal loss units
B   debit with the full production cost of the abnormal loss units
C   credit with the scrap value of the abnormal loss units
D   credit with the full production cost of the abnormal loss units

SECTION A-TYPE QUESTIONS : SECTION 1

177 X uses process costing. In Process 3 the normal loss is 4% of total input.

Last period the input from Process 2 was 8,500 kg and additional material of 4,250 kg was added to process 3.

Actual output to finished goods was 12,700 kg.

There was no opening or closing work-in-progress in the period.

What was the abnormal gain or loss in kg for period 3?

A 460 kg gain
B 460 kg loss
C 290 kg gain
D 290 kg loss

178 A chemical process has a normal wastage of 10% of input. In a period, 2,500 kg of material were input and there was an abnormal loss of 75 kg.

What was the quantity of good production?

A 2,175 kg
B 2,250 kg
C 2,325 kg
D 2,675 kg

179 A company operates a job costing system.

Job number 605 requires $300 of direct materials and $400 of direct labour. Direct labour is paid at the rate of $8 per hour. Production overheads are absorbed at a rate of $26 per direct labour hour and non-production overheads are absorbed at a rate of 120% of prime cost.

What is the total cost of job number 605?

A $2,000
B $2,400
C $2,840
D $4,400

180 A factory manufactures model cars. During October work commenced on 110,000 new cars. This was in addition to 20,000 that were 50% complete at the start of the month. At the end of October there were 40,000 cars that were 50% complete.

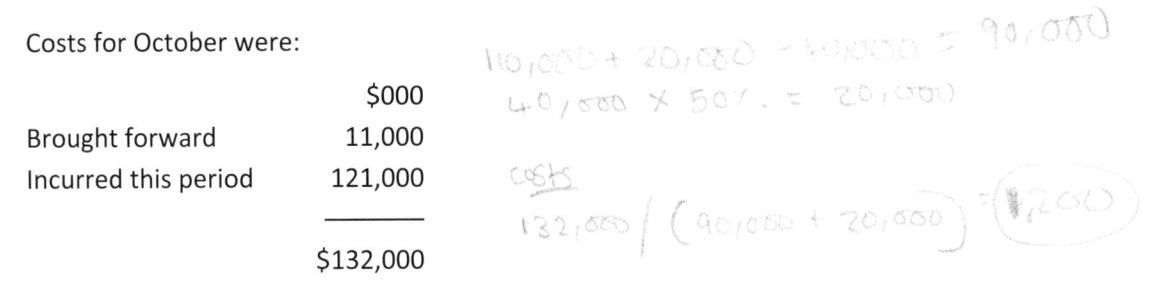

Costs for October were:

	$000
Brought forward	11,000
Incurred this period	121,000
	$132,000

KAPLAN PUBLISHING 53

PAPER F2/FMA : MANAGEMENT ACCOUNTING

If this factory chooses the weighted average method of spreading costs, what is the cost per car for October production?

A $1,100

B $1,200

C $1,210

D $1,320

181 In a production process the percentage completion of the work-in-progress (WIP) at the end of a period is found to have been understated.

When this is corrected what will be the effect on the cost per unit and the total value of the WIP?

	Cost per unit	Total value of WIP
A	Decrease	Decrease
B	Decrease	Increase
C	Increase	Decrease
D	Increase	Increase

182 The following information is available for a production process for the last period:

Material input	200 kg at $4 per kg
Labour input	100 hours at $15 per hour
Department overhead	$1,000
Transfer to finished goods	150 kg

Normal loss is 10% of input. Losses are identified when the process is 50% complete.

There is no opening or closing work-in-progress.

What is the total cost of a completed unit?

A $22.00

B $20.48

C $19.59

D $18.33

183 At the start of the month, there were 2,000 units of work-in-progress in a factory. During the month, 12,000 units were started. At the end of the month, 3,000 units were in closing work in progress. The degree of completion of opening work-in-progress was 70% and closing work in progress was 20%.

How many equivalent units of production were achieved during the month if FIFO were used?

[EU]

SECTION A-TYPE QUESTIONS : SECTION 1

184 The following information is available for a production process for the last period:

Material input   200 kg at $6 per kg
Labour and overhead input $3,500
Transfer to finished goods   190 kg

Normal loss is 15% of input and has a scrap value of $1 per kg.

There is no opening or closing work-in-progress.

What is the value of the finished output for the period (to the nearest $)?

A $4,465
B $4,670
C $5,219
D $5,253

$$\frac{1200 + 3500 - 30}{200 - 30} = 27.47$$

$$27.47 \times 190 = 5219$$

185 **Which of the following are features of process costing?**

(i)   Homogeneous products
(ii) Customer-driven production
(iii) Finished goods are valued at an average cost per unit

A   (i) and (iii)
B   (ii) and (iii)
C   (iii) only
D   (i) only

186 A builder has produced a quote for some alterations. The price is made up as follows:

		$
Direct materials	100 kg @ $4 per kg	400
Direct labour	5 hours @ $10 per hour	50
	15 hours @ $5 per hour	75
Hire of machine	1 day @ $100 per day	100
Overheads	20 hours @ $8 per hour	160
Total cost		785
Profit @ 20% of cost 0.2 × $785		157
Price quoted		$942

Actual costs for the job were as follows:

Direct materials   120 kg @ $4 per kg   480
Direct labour   3 hours @ $10 per hour   30
                   20 hours @ $5 per hour 100
Hire of machine   2 days @ $100 per day 200
                   23 hrs @ 8 per day 184

$$994 - 942 = 52 \text{ Loss}$$

KAPLAN PUBLISHING   55

PAPER F2/FMA : MANAGEMENT ACCOUNTING

What was the actual profit/(loss) made on the job?

A $52 loss

B $28 loss

C $28 profit

D $52 profit

187 A business operates a job costing system and prices its jobs by adding 20% to the total cost of the job. The prime cost of a job was $6,840 and it had used 156 direct labour hours. The fixed production overheads are absorbed on the basis of direct labour hours. The budgeted overhead absorption rate was based upon a budgeted fixed overhead of $300,000 and total budgeted direct labour hours of 60,000.

What should the job be sold for?

A $7,620

B $8,208

C $9,144

D $9,525

Handwritten: 6840 + (300,000/60,000 × 156) = 7620
7620 × 20% + 20% = 9144

188 A company operates a job costing system. Job 874 requires 110 hours of labour at $8 per hour. Materials and other expenses amount to $1,700. There are 3 employees whose basic hours are 30 hours a week. All work is to be completed in one week at the specific request of the customer. Overtime is paid at time and a quarter.

What is the total direct labour cost of Job 874?

A $880

B $920

C $2,580

D $2,620

189 Which of the following would be considered a service industry?

(i) An airline company

(ii) A railway company

(iii) A firm of accountants

A (i) and (ii) only

B (ii) and (iii) only

C (i) and (iii) only

D All of them

SECTION A-TYPE QUESTIONS : **SECTION 1**

190 Which TWO of the following are characteristics of service costing?

- A High levels of indirect costs as a proportion of total cost
- B Use of equivalent units
- C Use of composite cost units
- D Long timescale from commencement to completion of the cost unit

191 Which of the following is NOT likely to be used in a hospital run by a charitable foundation?

- A Cost per patient
- B Cost per bed-day
- C Bed throughput
- D Profit per patient

192 A hotel calculates a number of statistics including average cost per occupied bed per day.

The following information is provided for a 30-day period.

	Rooms with twin beds	Single rooms
Number of rooms in hotel	260	70
Number of rooms available to let	240	40
Average number of rooms occupied daily	200	30
Number of guests in period	6,450	
Average length of stay	2 days	
Payroll costs for period	$100,000	
Cost of cleaning supplies in period	$5,000	
Total cost of laundering in period	$22,500	

What is the average cost per occupied bed per day for the period?

- A $9.90
- B $9.88
- C $7.20
- D $8.17

193 The following figures relate to two electricity supply companies.

Meter reading, billing and collection costs

	Company A	Company B
Total cost ($000)	600	1,000
Units sold (millions)	2,880	9,600
Number of consumers (thousands)	800	1,600
Sales of electricity (millions)	$18	$50

What do the figures given indicate?

A   Company A is more efficient than Company B

B   Company A is less efficient than Company B

C   Company A and Company B are as efficient as each other

D   That neither company is efficient

194 A hotel calculates a number of statistics including average room occupancy.

Average room occupancy is calculated as the total number of rooms occupied as a percentage of rooms available to let.

The following information is provided for a 30-day period.

	Rooms with twin beds	Single rooms
Number of rooms in hotel	260	70
Number of rooms available to let	240	40
Average number of rooms occupied daily	200	30

What is the average room occupancy?

A   69.7%

B   82.1%

C   82.7%

D   84.8%

195 Which of the following are features of service organisations?

(i)   High levels of inventory

(ii) High proportion of fixed costs

(iii) Difficulty in identifying suitable cost units

A   (i) and (ii) only

B   (i) and (iii) only

C   (ii) and (iii) only

D   All of these

ALTERNATIVE COSTING PRINCIPLES

196 Which ONE of the following is an advantage of Activity Based Costing?

- A It provides more accurate product costs *(circled)*
- B It is simple to apply
- C It is a form of marginal costing and so is relevant to decision making
- D It is particularly useful when fixed overheads are very low

197 Quality control costs can be categorised into internal and external failure costs, inspection costs and prevention costs. In which of these four classifications would the following costs be included?

- The costs of a customer service team
- The cost of equipment maintenance
- The cost of operating test equipment

	Internal failure costs	External failure costs	Inspection costs	Prevention costs
Cost of the a customer service team		✓		
Cost of equipment maintenance				✓
Cost of operating test equipment			✓	

198 In the context of quality costs, what would customer compensation costs and test equipment running costs be classified as?

	Customer compensation costs	Test equipment running costs
A	Internal failure costs	Prevention costs
B	Internal failure costs	Appraisal costs
C	External failure costs	Appraisal costs *(circled)*
D	External failure costs	Prevention costs

199 The selling price of product K is set at $450 for each unit and the company requires a return of 20% from the product.

What is the target cost for each unit for the coming year?

- A $300
- B $360 *(circled)*
- C $400
- D $450

450 × 20% = 90
450 − 90 = 360

200 In calculating the life cycle costs of a product, which of the following items would be excluded?

- (i) Planning and concept design costs
- (ii) Preliminary and detailed design costs
- (iii) Testing costs
- (iv) Production costs
- (v) Distribution and customer service costs

A (iii)
B (iv)
C (v)
D None of them

201 As part of a process to achieve a target cost, GYE Inc are interviewing prospective customers to determine why they would buy the product and how they would use it.

What term best describes this process?

A Value analysis
B Operational research
C TQM
D Lifecycle costing

202 A customer returns a faulty product to a firm for repair under a warranty scheme. The firm operates a total quality management system.

Which of the following best describes the cost of the repair?

A An internal failure cost
B An external failure cost
C An appraisal cost
D A prevention cost

SYLLABUS AREA C – BUDGETING

NATURE AND PURPOSE OF BUDGETING

203 What are the main purposes of budgeting?

  (i)   to give authority to spend
  (ii) to control expenditure
  (iii) to aid decision making.

  A   (i) only
  B   (i) and (ii) only
  C   (ii) only
  D   (i), (ii) and (iii)

204 Who does the budget committee contain?

  (i)   Purchasing manager
  (ii) The chief executive
  (iii) Sales manager
  (iv) Production manager

  A   (i) and (ii) only
  B   (iii) and (iv) only
  C   (i), (ii) and (iii) only
  D   All of them

205 A budget manual will include which of the following?

  (i)   An organisation chart
  (ii) A budget timetable
  (iii) Copies of budget forms
  (iv) Key assumptions to be used in the budget

  A   (ii), (iii) and (iv)
  B   (ii) and (iv)
  C   (iii) and (iv)
  D   all of these

206 Which of the following is not a purpose of budgeting?

　A　Planning

　B　Co-ordination

　C　Consultation

　D　Communication

STATISTICAL TECHNIQUES

207 The following information for advertising and sales revenue has been established over the past six months:

Month	Sales revenue	Advertising expenditure
1	155,000	3,000
2	125,000	2,500
3	200,000	6,000
4	175,000	5,500
5	150,000	4,500
6	225,000	6,500

Using the high-low method, which of the following is the correct equation for linking advertising and sales revenue from the above data?

　A　Sales revenue = 62,500 + (25 × advertising expenditure)

　B　Advertising expenditure = –2,500 + (0.04 × sales revenue)

　C　Sales revenue = 95,000 + (20 × advertising expenditure)

　D　Advertising expenditure = –4,750 + (0.05 × sales revenue)

208 A company's weekly costs ($C) were plotted against production level (P) for the last 50 weeks and a regression line calculated to be C = 1,000 +250P. Which statement about the breakdown of weekly costs is true?

　A　Weekly fixed costs are $1,000, variable costs per unit are $5

　B　Weekly fixed costs are $250, variable costs per unit are $1000

　C　Weekly fixed costs are $1,000, variable costs per unit are $250

　D　Weekly fixed costs are $20, variable costs per unit are $5

209 If a forecasting model based on total cost = fixed cost + variable costs is graphed, the equation is C = F+Vx and the intercept is $7,788. Total costs are $14,520 and x is 3,300.

What is the value of the slope, to two decimal places?

　　☐

SECTION A-TYPE QUESTIONS : SECTION 1

210 The correlation coefficient (r) for measuring the connection between two variables (x and y) has been calculated as 0.6.

How much of the variation in the dependent variable (y) is explained by the variation in the independent variable (x)?

- A 36%
- B 40%
- C 60%
- D 64%

211 A company uses regression analysis to establish its selling overhead costs for budgeting purposes. The data used for the analysis is as follows:

Month	Number of salesmen	Sales overhead costs
1	3	35,100
2	6	46,400
3	4	27,000
4	3	33,500
5	5	41,000
	21	183,000

The gradient of the regression line is 4.20. Using regression analysis, what would be the budgeted sales overhead costs for the month, in $000, if there are 2 salesmen employed?

- A 27,360
- B 39,960
- C 41,000
- D 56,760

212 Which of the following are correct with regard to regression analysis?

(i) In regression analysis the n stands for the number of pairs of data.

(ii) Σx^2 is not the same calculation as $(\Sigma x)^2$

(iii) Σxy is calculated by multiplying the total value of x and the total value of y

- A (i) and (ii) only
- B (i) and (iii) only
- C (ii) and (iii) only
- D (i), (ii) and (iii)

KAPLAN PUBLISHING

213 Regression analysis is being used to find the line of best fit (y = a + bx) from eleven pairs of data. The calculations have produced the following information:

$\Sigma x = 440$, $\Sigma y = 330$, $\Sigma x^2 = 17,986$, $\Sigma y^2 = 10,366$ and $\Sigma xy = 13,467$

What is the value of 'b' in the equation for the line of best fit (to 2 decimal places)?

[   ]

214 An organisation is using linear regression analysis to establish an equation that shows a relationship between advertising expenditure and sales revenue. It will then use the equation to predict sales revenue for given levels of advertising expenditure. Data for the last five periods are as follows:

Period number	Advertising Expenditure $	Sales revenue $
1	17,000	108,000
2	19,000	116,000
3	24,000	141,000
4	22,000	123,000
5	18,000	112,000

What are the values of 'Σx', 'Σy' and 'n' that need to be inserted into the appropriate formula?

	Σx	Σy	n
A	$600,000	$100,000	5
B	$100,000	$600,000	5
C	$600,000	$100,000	10
D	$100,000	$600,000	10

215 The coefficient of determination (r^2) has been calculated as 60%.

What does this mean?

A 60% of the variation in the dependent variable (y) is explained by the variation in the independent variable (x)

B 40% of the variation in the dependent variable (y) is explained by the variation in the independent variable (x)

C 60% of the variation in the dependent variable (x) is explained by the variation in the independent variable (y)

D 40% of the variation in the dependent variable (x) is explained by the variation in the independent variable (y)

SECTION A-TYPE QUESTIONS : SECTION 1

216 A company has recorded its total cost for different levels of activity over the last five months as follows:

Month	Activity level (units)	Total cost ($)
7	300	17,500
8	360	19,500
9	400	20,500
10	320	18,500
11	280	17,000

The equation for total cost is being calculated using regression analysis on the above data. The equation for total cost is of the general form 'y = a + bx' and the value of 'b' has been calculated correctly as 29.53.

What is the value of 'a' (to the nearest $) in the total cost equation?

A 7,338

B 8,796

C 10,430

D 10,995

217 **Which of the following correlation coefficients indicates the weakest relationship between two variables?**

A + 1.0

B + 0.4

C − 0.6

D − 1.0

218 Regression analysis is being used to find the line of best fit (y = a + bx) from five pairs of data. The calculations have produced the following information:

$\Sigma x = 129$ $\Sigma y = 890$ $\Sigma xy = 23,091$ $\Sigma x^2 = 3,433$ $\Sigma y^2 = 29,929$

What is the value of 'a' in the equation for the line of best fit (to the nearest whole number)?

A 146

B 152

C 210

D 245

219 **Which of the following is a feasible value for a correlation coefficient?**

A +1.2

B 0

C −1.2

D −2.0

KAPLAN PUBLISHING

65

PAPER F2/FMA : MANAGEMENT ACCOUNTING

220 What is the correct order for the stages of the product life cycle?

(i) Growth
(ii) Decline
(iii) Maturity
(iv) Development
(v) Introduction

A (i), (v), (iii), (iv), (ii)
B (v), (iv), (i), (iii), (ii)
C (iv), (v), (i), (iii), (ii)
D (iv), (i), (iv), (iii), (ii)

221 An inflation index and index numbers of a company's sales ($) for the last year are given below.

Quarter:	1	2	3	4
Sales ($) index:	109	120	132	145
Inflation index:	100	110	121	133

How are the 'Real' sales performing, i.e. adjusted for inflation?

A approximately constant and keeping up with inflation
B growing steadily and not keeping up with inflation
C growing steadily and keeping ahead of inflation
D falling steadily and not keeping up with inflation

222 Four years ago material X cost $5 per kg and the price index most appropriate to the cost of material X stood at 150. The same index now stands at 430.

What is the best estimate of the current cost of material X per kg?

A $1.74
B $9.33
C $14.33
D $21.50

The following data are to be used for questions 223 and 224

The managers of the catering division of a hospital wish to develop an index number series for measuring changes in food prices. As an experiment, they have chosen four items in general use which are summarised below:

	Prices per unit		Quantities	
	20X1	20X2	20X1	20X2
Flour (kgs)	0.25	0.30	8,000	10,000
Eggs (boxes)	1.00	1.25	4,000	5,000
Milk (litres)	0.30	0.35	10,000	10,000
Potatoes (kgs)	0.05	0.06	6,000	10,000

SECTION A-TYPE QUESTIONS : SECTION 1

223 Based on 20X1 as 100, what is the Paasche price index for 20X2?

A 82.4

B 121.36

C 121.08

D 82.6

224 Based on 20X1 as 100, what is the Laspeyres price index for 20X2?

A 82.4

B 121.36

C 121.08

D 82.6

The following data are to be used for questions 225 and 226

A company is preparing its forecast sales information for the end of the current year. The actual sales information for the first nine months of the current year (20X1) is below:

	Sales volume (units)
January	172,100
February	149,600
March	165,800
April	182,600
May	160,100
June	197,100
July	174,600
August	190,800
September	207,600

225 The sales volume trend is to be identified using a 5-point moving average.

What is the monthly trend?

A 50 units

B 500 units

C 5,000 units

D 50,000 units

226 What is the expected sales volume including seasonal variation for December 20X1?

A 206,040 units

B 211,040 units

C 222,480 units

D 199,600 units

KAPLAN PUBLISHING 67

PAPER F2/FMA : MANAGEMENT ACCOUNTING

227 Which of the following are components of a time series analysis?

(i) Trend

(ii) Seasonal variation

(iii) Cyclical variation

A (i) and (ii) only

B (i) and (iii) only

C (ii) and (iii) only

D (i), (ii) and (iii) ✓

228 Two years ago the price index appropriate to the cost of material X had a value of 120. It now has a value of 160.

If material X costs $2,000 per kg today, what would its cost per kg have been two years ago?

A $1,500 ✓

B $1,667

C $2,667

D $3,200

2000 × 120/160

229 A time series model of sales volume has the following trend and additive seasonal variation.

Trend

Y = 5,000 + 4,000 X.

Where Y = quarterly sales volume in units.

X = the quarter number (Where the first quarter of 2009 = quarter 17, the second quarter of 2009 = quarter 18 etc).

Seasonal variation

Quarter	Seasonal variation (units)
First	+3,000
Second	+1,000
Third	−1,500
Fourth	−2,500

What would be the time series forecast of sales units for the third quarter of 2010?

A 79,500

B 95,500

C 97,000

D 98,500

68 KAPLAN PUBLISHING

SECTION A-TYPE QUESTIONS : SECTION 1

The following data are to be used for questions 230 and 231

A company is preparing its annual budget and is estimating the cost of production. The company has the identified the following trend for the production of its product:

y = a + bx where

y = number of units produced in a month

a = 3,000 units

b = 150 units

x = the month number (January 20X1 is month 1, February 20X1 is month 2, etc).

For the first 6 months of 20X1 the actual production, which was affected by seasonal variations, was as follows:

	Units produced
January	3,000
February	3,250
March	3,500
April	3,750
May	3,825
June	3,825

230 What is the seasonal variation for March 20X1?

- A +50
- B −50
- C +75
- D −75

231 What is the expected production for March 20X2 after adjusting for the seasonal variation using the additive model?

- A 5,250 units
- B 5,200 units
- C 5,300 units
- D 5,150 units

232 The product life cycle model has 5 stages – for how many of the stages is it thought that a loss could be made?

- A 1
- B 2
- C 3
- D 4

The following data are to be used for questions 233 and 234

A company buys and uses five different materials. Details of the actual prices and quantities used for 20X1 and the budgeted figures for 20X2 are as follows:

	Actual 20X1		Budgeted 20X2	
Material	Quantity (000)	Unit price $	Quantity (000)	Unit price $
F	21	11	25	12
G	56	22	52	26
H	62	18	79	18
I	29	20	35	22
J	31	22	36	23

233 What is the Laspeyre price index for material prices based on 20X1 = 100?

  A   108.7

  B   92.0

  C   107.8

  D   92.7

234 What is the Paasche price index for material prices based on 20X1 = 100?

  A   108.7

  B   92.0

  C   107.8

  D   92.7

235 Which TWO of the following statements are true in relation to spreadsheets?

  A   A spreadsheet consists of records and files.

  B   Most spreadsheets have a facility to allow data within them to be displayed graphically.

  C   A spreadsheet could be used to prepare a budgeted statement of profit or loss.

  D   A spreadsheet is the most suitable software for storing large volumes of data.

236 John has produced the following spreadsheet to calculate the correlation coefficient between average daily fruit and vegetable intake (measured in normal portions) and success in exams (number of passes above C grade).

	A	B	C	D	E	F
1	Correlation					
2		Vitamins	Exam			
3		x	y	xy	x^2	y^2
4		0	6			
5		1	5			
6		2	4			
7		3	4			
8		4	6			
9		5	7			
10		6	7			
11	Totals					
12						
13	Correlation coefficient		=			
14						
15						

What should the formula in cell D13 be?

A (6*D11-B11*C11)/((6*E11-B11^2)*(6*F11-C11^2))^0.5

B (7*D11-B11*C11)/((7*E11-B11^2)*(7*F11-C11^2))

C (7*D11-B11*C11)/((7*E11-B11^2)*(7*F11-C11^2))^0.5

D (6*D11-B11*C11)/((6*E11-B11^2)*(6*F11-C11^2))

237 Which of the following are advantages of spreadsheet software over manual approaches?

(i) Security

(ii) Speed

(iii) Accuracy

(iv) Legibility

A All of them

B (ii), (iii) and (iv)

C (ii) and (iv)

D (i) and (iv)

238 A company manufactures a single product. In a computer spreadsheet the cells F1 to F12 contain the budgeted monthly sales units for the 12 months of next year in sequence with January sales in cell F1 and finishing with December sales in F12. The company policy is for the closing inventory of finished goods each month to be 10% of the budgeted sales units for the following month.

Which of the following formulae will generate the budgeted production (in units) for March next year?

A = [F3 +(0.1*F4)]

B = [F3 – (0.1*F4)]

C = [(1.1*F3) – (0.1*F4)]

D = [(0.9*F3) + (0.1*F4)]

239 Which of the following is not one of the main aspects of formatting cells?

A Wrapping text

B Using graphics

C Setting number specification, e.g. working to 2 decimal places

D Changing the font, size or colour of text

BUDGET PREPARATION

240 A business is preparing its production budget for the year ahead for product A998. It is estimated that 100,000 units of A998 can be sold in the year and the opening inventory is currently 14,000 units. The inventory level is to be reduced by 40% by the end of the year.

How many units of A998 need to be produced? ☐

241 What is the formula to calculate the production budget?

A Sales budget + opening inventory – closing inventory

B Sales budget – opening inventory + closing inventory

C Sales budget – opening inventory – closing inventory

D Sales budget + opening inventory + closing inventory

242 A process has a normal loss of 10% and budgeted output is 4,500 litres for the period. Opening inventory of raw material is 600 litres and is expected to increase by 20% by the end of the period.

The material usage budget is:

A 4,500 litres

B 5,000 litres

C 5,133 litres

D 5,120 litres

243 What is the formula to calculate the material usage budget?

    A   Production budget multiplied by the standard material quantity per unit

    B   Sales budget multiplied by the standard material quantity per unit

    C   Production budget less opening inventory plus closing inventory

    D   Production budget plus opening inventory less closing inventory

244 A company has a budget for two products A and B as follows:

	Product A	Product B
Sales (units)	2,000	4,500
Production (units)	1,750	5,000
Labour:		
Skilled at $10/hour	2 hours/unit	2 hours/unit
Unskilled at $7/hour	3 hours/unit	4 hours/unit

What is the budgeted cost for unskilled labour for the period?

    A $105,000

    B $135,000

    C $176,750

    D $252,500

245 What would be the principal budget factor for a footwear retailer?

    A   The cost item taking the largest share of total expenditure

    B   The product line contributing the largest amount to sales revenue

    C   The product line contributing the largest amount to business profits

    D   The constraint that is expected to limit the retailer's activities during the budget period

246 A company makes 2 products, X and Y, which are sold in the ratio 1:2. The selling prices are $50 and $100 respectively. The company wants to earn $100,000 over the next period. What should the sales budget be?

	X (units)	Y (units)
A	1,334	667
B	800	400
C	667	1,334
D	400	800

247 A business is preparing its production budget, materials usage and materials purchases budget for the forthcoming period. The following information is known:

Budgeted sales	2,300 units
Current inventory of finished goods	400 units
Required closing inventory of finished goods	550 units

Each unit of the product uses 6 kg of material X and details of this are as follows:

Current inventory of X	2,000 kg
Required closing inventory of X	2,600 kg

What is the production volume required for the forthcoming period to meet the sales demand?

A   3,050 units

B   2,450 units

C   2,300 units

D   2,150 units

248 A company makes three products, X, Y and Z. The following information is available:

	X	Y	Z
Budgeted production (units)	200	400	300
Machine hours per unit	5	6	2

Variable overheads	$2.30 per machine hour
Fixed overheads	$0.75 per machine hour

What is the overhead budget?

A $12,200

B $12,000

C $11,590

D $10,980

The following information should be used for questions 249, 250 and 251

A toy manufacturer produces two products, a clockwork clown and a wind-up train. Standard cost data for the products are as follows:

	Clockwork clown	Wind-up train
Direct materials ($5 per kg)	2 kg	1 kg
Direct labour ($8 per hour)	18 minutes	30 minutes
Budgeted sales	450	550

Budgeted inventories are as follows:

Finished goods

Opening inventory	20	50
Closing inventory	30	40

Raw materials

Opening inventory	50 kg
Closing inventory	60 kg

249 What is the total direct material usage budget?

A 1,540 kg

B 1,470 kg

C 1,460 kg

D 1,440 kg

250 What is the total direct material purchases budget?

A $7,350

B $7,300

C $7,250

D $7,200

251 What is the total direct labour budget?

A $3,264

B $3,280

C $3,290

D $3,296

252 A job requires 2,400 actual labour hours for completion but it is anticipated that idle time will be 20% of the total time required. If the wage rate is $10 per hour, what is the budgeted labour cost for the job, including the cost of the idle time?

A $19,200

B $24,000

C $28,800

D $30,000

253 What is a continuous budget?

(i) Prepared in advance for the period in question

(ii) Updated regularly by adding further periods

(iii) Also known as a rolling budget

(iv) Always prepared for a full year in advance

A (i), (ii) and (iii)

B (i), (iii) and (iv)

C (i), (iii) and (iv) only

D (i), (ii) and (iv)

254 Vincent is preparing a cash budget for July. His credit sales are as follows.

	$
April (actual)	40,000
May (actual)	30,000
June (actual)	20,000
July (estimated)	25,000

His recent debt collection experience has been as follows.

Current month's sales	20%
Prior month's sales	60%
Sales two months prior	10%
Cash discounts taken	5%
Irrecoverable debts	5%

How much may Vincent expect to collect from credit customers during July?

A $18,000

B $20,000

C $21,000

D $24,000

255 DRF's projected revenue for 20X9 is $28,000 per month. All sales are on credit. Receivables' accounts are settled 50% in the month of sale, 45% in the following month, and 5% are written off as irrecoverable debts after two months.

What are the budgeted cash collections for March?

A $24,500

B $26,600

C $28,000

D $32,900

256 A company anticipates that 10,000 units of product z will be sold during January. Each unit of z requires 2 litres of raw material w. Actual stocks as of 1 January and budgeted inventories as of 31 January are as follows.

	1 January	31 January
Product z (units)	14,000	12,000
Raw material w (litres)	20,000	15,000

1 litre of w costs $4.

If the company pays for all purchases in the month of acquisition, what is the cash outlay for January purchases of w?

A $84,000

B $80,000

C $44,000

D $12,000

257 A company has a two-month receivables' cycle. It receives in cash 45% of the total gross sales value in the month of invoicing. Irrecoverable debts are 20% of total gross sales value and there is a 10% discount for settling accounts within 30 days.

What proportion of the first month's sales will be received as cash in the second month?

A 25%

B 30%

C 35%

D 55%

258 Spears makes gross sales of $40,000 per month, of which 10% are for cash, the rest on credit.

Experience shows that the credit sales are received as follows:

Receivables paying
within one month   40%
within two months   50%
Settlement discounts (for payment within one month)   4%

What will be the total expected cash receipts in any month?

A $35,824

B $36,400

C $38,560

D $40,000

259 Selected figures from a firm's budget for next month are as follows.

Sales	$450,000
Gross profit on sales	30%
Decrease in trade payables over the month	$10,000
Increase in cost of inventory held over the month	$18,000

What is the budgeted payment to trade payables?

A $343,000

B $323,000

C $307,000

D $287,000

PAPER F2/FMA : MANAGEMENT ACCOUNTING

260 A company has a current cash balance of $7,000, trade receivables of $15,000 and trade payables of $40,000. The company can sell goods costing $50,000 for $70,000 next month. One half of all sales are collected in the month of sale and the remainder in the following month. All purchases are made on credit and paid during the following month. Inventory levels will remain constant during the month. General cash expenses will be $60,000 during the month.

What is the cash balance at the end of the month?

- A $25,000 overdrawn
- B $26,000 overdrawn
- C $33,000 overdrawn
- D $43,000 overdrawn

261 Which of the following would NOT be included in a cash budget?

- (i) Depreciation
- (ii) Provisions for doubtful debts
- (iii) Wages and salaries

- A All three
- B (i) and (ii) only
- C (i) and (iii) only
- D (ii) and (iii) only

262 The following details have been extracted from the payables' records of X Limited:

Invoices paid in the month of purchase	25%
Invoices paid in the first month after purchase	70%
Invoices paid in the second month after purchase	5%

Purchases for July to September are budgeted as follows:

July	$250,000
August	$300,000
September	$280,000

For suppliers paid in the month of purchase, a settlement discount of 5% is received.

What amount is budgeted to be paid to suppliers in September?

- A $278,500
- B $280,000
- C $289,000
- D $292,500

263 Galway Ltd budgeted to make sales of $1,500, $1,800 and $2,800 in its first three months of operation.

25% of its sales are expected to be for cash and another 25% of total sales will also be collected in the same month by offering a 10% discount; 40% will be collected in the following month, and the remainder the month after that.

How much cash did Galway Ltd budget to receive in its third month of operation?

   A $1,800

   B $2,200

   C $2,270

   D $2,800

264 **Budgeted production overhead expenditure for April and May is as follows:**

April $93,000
May $87,000

One third of the production overhead expenditure is fixed cost, including depreciation of production machinery of $8,000 per month.

Payments for variable production overhead expenditure are made 50% in the month they are incurred and 50% in the month following that in which they are incurred.

Payments for fixed production overhead expenditure are made in the month following that in which they are incurred.

How much would be shown in the cash budget for May in respect of payments for fixed production overhead and variable production overhead?

	Fixed ($)	Variable ($)
A	23,000	60,000
B	31,000	60,000
C	23,000	62,000
D	31,000	62,000

FLEXIBLE BUDGETS

265 **What is a flexible budget?**

   A   a budget for semi-variable overhead costs only

   B   a budget which, by recognising different cost behaviour patterns, is designed to change as volume of activity changes

   C   a budget for a twelve month period which includes planned revenues, expenses, assets and liabilities

   D   a budget which is prepared for a rolling period which is reviewed monthly, and updated accordingly

PAPER F2/FMA : MANAGEMENT ACCOUNTING

266 **What is a purpose of a flexible budget?**

A   to cap discretionary expenditure

B   to produce a revised forecast by changing the original budget when actual costs are known

C   to control resource efficiency

D   to communicate target activity levels within an organisation by setting a budget in advance of the period to which it relates

267 **What is a fixed budget?**

A   a budget for a single level of activity

B   a budget used when the mix of products is fixed in advance of the budget period

C   a budget which ignores inflation

D   an overhead cost budget

268 **Which of the following statements are correct?**

(i)   A fixed budget is a budget that considers all of an organisation's costs and revenues for a single level of activity.

(ii) A flexible budget is a budget that is produced during the budget period to recognise the effects of any changes in prices and methods of operation that have occurred.

(iii) Organisations can use budgets to communicate objectives to their managers.

A   (i) and (ii) only

B   (i) and (iii) only

C   (ii) and (iii) only

D   All of them

269 Oswald Press produces and sells textbooks for schools and colleges. The following budgeted information is available for the year ending 31 December 20X6:

	Budget	Actual
Sales (units)	120,000	100,000
	$000	$000
Sales revenue	1,200	995
Variable printing costs	360	280
Variable production overheads	60	56
Fixed production cost	300	290
Fixed administration cost	360	364
Profit	120	5

What does the flexed budget show?

A   a profit of $10,000

B   a loss of $10,000

C   a profit of $100,000

D   a loss of $100,000

SECTION A-TYPE QUESTIONS : **SECTION 1**

270 Which of the following statements is true?

A   A fixed budget is a budget that remains the same from one accounting period to the next

B   A fixed budget is produced for one product for different levels of activity

C   A flexible budget is designed to change as activity levels change

D   A fixed budget is useful when comparing budget figures with actual figures

271 The following budgeted information comes from the accounting records of Smith

	Original budget
Sales units	1,000
	$
Sales revenue	100,000
Direct material	40,000
Direct labour	20,000
Variable overhead	15,000
Fixed overhead	10,000
Profit	15,000

In a period where the actual sales were 1,200 units, what would be the budgeted flexed profit?

A $17,000

B $20,000

C $22,000

D $35,000

272 When budgeting, what are variable costs conventionally deemed to do?

A   Be constant per unit of output

B   Vary per unit of output as production volume changes

C   Be constant in total when production volume changes

D   Vary in total, from period to period when production is constant

273 F Ltd makes a single product for which the budgeted costs and activity for a typical month are as follows:

Budgeted production and sales	15,000 units
Budgeted unit costs	$
Direct materials	30
Direct labour	46
Variable overheads	24
Fixed overheads	80
	180

The standard selling price of the product is $220 per unit. During October only 13,600 units were produced.

What is the total budget cost allowance contained in the flexed budget for October?

[ ]

274 The following extract is taken from the overhead budget of Y Ltd:

Budgeted activity   50%   75%
Budgeted overhead $100,000 $112,500

What would the budgeted overhead cost be for an activity level of 80%?

A $115,000

B $120,000

C $160,000

D $360,000

275 Globe Ltd. has the following original budget and actual performance for product Bean for the year ending 31 December.

	Budget	Actual
Volume sold (litres)	4,000	5,000
	$000	$000
Sales revenue	1,500	1,950
Less costs:		
Direct materials	36	45
Direct labour	176	182
Fixed Overheads	89	90
Operating profit	1,199	1,633

What is the total production cost of the flexed budget?

$ [ ]

CAPITAL BUDGETING

276 The details of an investment project are as follows:

Cost of asset bought at the start of the project	$80,000
Annual cash inflow	$25,000
Cost of capital	5% each year
Life of the project	8 years

What is the present value of the project?

A   −$120,000

B $120,000

C $81,575

D   −$81,575

277 A company is planning to open a new store in a new geographic location. An initial site evaluation has taken place at a cost of $5,000 and a store location has been found. The new store can be rented for $9,500 per annum. It will require refurbishment at a cost of $320,000.

Which of the following costs are relevant for an NPV calculation?

(i) $5,000

(ii) $9,500

(iii) $320,000

A   (i) only

B   (i) and (ii)

C   (ii) and (iii)

D   (iii) only

278 B Company is deciding whether to launch a new product. The initial outlay and the forecast possible annual cash inflows are shown below:

Year 0	(60,000)
Year 1	23,350
Year 2	29,100
Year 3	27,800

The company's cost of capital is 8% per annum.

Assume the cash inflows are received at the end of the year and that the cash inflows for each year are independent.

What is the expected net present value to the nearest $ for the product?

$ ☐

279 An education authority is considering the implementation of a CCTV (closed circuit television) security system in one of its schools. Details of the proposed project are as follows:

Life of project	5 years
Initial cost	$75,000
Annual savings:	
Labour costs	$20,000
Other costs	$5,000
NPV at 15%	$8,800

What is the internal rate of return for this project?

A 16%

B 18%

C 20%

D 22%

280 The following measures have been calculated to appraise a proposed project

The internal rate of return is 12%

The return on capital employed is 16%

The payback period is 4 years

Which of the following statements is correct?

A the payback is less than 5 years so the project should go ahead

B the IRR is lower than the return on capital employed so the project should not go ahead

C the IRR is greater than the cost of capital so the project should go ahead

D The IRR is positive so the project should go ahead

281 CC Company is considering an investment of $300,000 which will earn a contribution of $40,000 each year for 10 years at today's prices. The company's cost of capital is 11% per annum.

What is the net present value of the project?

A ($64,440)

B $23,556

C $64,440

D $235,560

SECTION A-TYPE QUESTIONS : SECTION 1

282 Sandwich Queen is looking to expand its restaurant facilities to increase its seating capacity a further 40%. Results for the current year are:

	$000	$000
Food sales	200	
Drink sales	170	
		370
Food costs	145	
Drink costs	77	
Staff costs	40	
Other costs	20	
		282
Cash flow		88

Sales and variable costs will increase in line with the seating capacity increase. The other costs are 40% fixed. An extra employee will be required to serve the extra seating capacity. There are currently 4 employees on an equal wage.

What is the relevant annual net cash flow to the nearest $000 of the proposed expansion?

$ ☐

283 JAH Company is about to invest $400,000 in machinery and other capital equipment for a new product venture. Cash flows for the first three years are estimated as follows

Year	$000
1	210
2	240
3	320

JAH Company requires a 17% return for projects of this type. What is the NPV of this venture?

A   –$154,670

B $45,010

C $220,450

D $154,670

284 A company has determined that the net present value of an investment project is $17,706 when using a 10% discount rate and $(4,317) when using a discount rate of 15%.

What is the internal rate of return of the project to the nearest 1%?

☐ %

KAPLAN PUBLISHING

PAPER F2/FMA : MANAGEMENT ACCOUNTING

285 A company is considering an investment of $400,000 in new machinery. The machinery is expected to yield incremental profits over the next five years as follows:

Year	Profit ($)
1	175,000
2	225,000
3	340,000
4	165,000
5	125,000

Thereafter, no incremental profits are expected and the machinery will be sold. It is company policy to depreciate machinery on a straight line basis over the life of the asset. The machinery is expected to have a value of $50,000 at the end of year 5.

What is the payback period of the investment in this machinery?

A   0.9 years

B   1.3 years

C   1.5 years

D   1.9 years

286 **What is an interest rate that includes the effect of compounding known as?**

A   Nominal interest

B   Simple interest

C   Compound interest

D   Effective interest

287 **Which of the following statements are true about IRRs?**

(i)   IRR considers the time value of money

(ii)   if the IRR exceeds the companies cost of capital the NPV at the company's cost of capital should be positive

(iii) it is possible for one investment to have 2 IRRs

A   (i) only

B   (i) and (ii) only

C   (ii) and (iii) only

D   (i), (ii) and (iii)

288 **What is the effective annual rate of interest of 2.1% compounded every three months?**

A   6.43%

B   8.40%

C   8.67%

D   10.87%

86   KAPLAN PUBLISHING

SECTION A-TYPE QUESTIONS : **SECTION 1**

289 A bank offers different bank accounts with different interest rates:

Bank account 1 = 10% interest per year, interest calculated quarterly

Bank account 2 = 12% interest per year, interest calculated monthly

Bank account 3 = 1.2% interest per month

Bank account 4 = 3% interest per quarter

Which account gives the highest annual effective interest rate?

- A   1
- B   2
- C   3
- D   4

BUDGETARY CONTROL AND REPORTING

290 In a responsibility accounting system which of the following costs is most likely to appear on the performance report for the manager of a purchasing department?

- A   Cost of direct labour
- B   Rent of machinery
- C   Repairs to machinery
- D   Cost of materials

291 In a responsibility accounting system for which of the following should the production line manager be held responsible?

- A   Raw material prices and labour wage rates
- B   Raw material usage and labour wage rates
- C   Raw material prices and labour hours worked
- D   Raw material usage and labour hours worked

292 What term describes: 'the forecasting of differences between actual and planned outcomes, and the implementation of action, before the event, to avoid such differences'?

- A   Feedforward control
- B   Variance analysis
- C   Budgeting
- D   Feedback control

293 Martin Mags produces and sells industry magazines. The following budgeted information is available for the year ending 31 December 20X6:

	Budget	Flexed budget	Actual
Sales (units)	120,000	100,000	100,000
	$000	$000	$000
Sales revenue	1,200	1,000	995
Variable printing costs	360	300	280
Variable production overheads	60	50	56
Fixed production cost	300	300	290
Fixed administration cost	360	360	364
Profit/(Loss)	120	(10)	5

What are the total expenditure and volume variances?

	Expenditure variance	Volume variance
A	$15,000 favourable	$130,000 adverse
B	$95,000 adverse	$115,000 favourable
C	$115,000 adverse	$95,000 favourable
D	$130,000 adverse	$15,000 favourable

294 What is the volume variance?

A   The difference between the flexible budget and the actual results

B   The difference between the fixed budget and the flexible budget

C   The difference between the fixed budget and the actual results

D   The difference between the original budget and the actual results

295 Which of the following statements are correct?

(i)   An adverse variance increases profit

(ii) A favourable variance increases profit

(iii) A favourable variance will arise when actual revenue is greater than budgeted revenue

(iv) An adverse variance will arise when actual costs are greater than budgeted costs

Options:

A   (i) only

B   (ii) only

C   (i), (iii) and (iv)

D   (ii), (iii) and (iv)

SECTION A-TYPE QUESTIONS : SECTION 1

296 Complete the table below by calculating the missing figures.

Use minus signs where appropriate and put A into the table to denote an adverse variance and F to denote a favourable variance.

	Budgeted $	Actual $	Variance value $	A/F
RECEIPTS				
Cash sales	4,200	3,800	400	A
Credit sales	42,100	48,000	5,900	F
Total receipts	46,300	51,800	5,500	F
PAYMENTS				
Cash purchases	500	1,200	700	A
Credit purchases	42,200	35,100	7,100	A
Labour costs	2,500	3,200	700	A
Capital expenditure	8,000	6,000	2,000	F
General expenses	4,000	3,800	200	F
Total payments				
Net cash flow				

BEHAVIOURAL ASPECTS OF BUDGETING

297 Which of the following statements about imposed budgets are correct?

(i) Imposed budgets are likely to set realistic targets because senior management have the best idea of what is achievable in each part of the business.

(ii) Imposed budgets can be less effective than budgets set on a participative basis, because it is difficult for an individual to be motivated to achieve targets set by someone else.

(iii) Imposed budgets are generally quicker to prepare and finalise than participative budgets.

A (i) and (ii) only

B (i) and (iii) only

C (ii) and (iii) only

D (iii) only

298 Which of the following is an NOT an advantage of top-down budgeting?

- A   It is less time consuming
- B   It reduces budgetary slack
- C   It is more likely to motivate managers
- D   Budgets will be closer to the company's objectives

299 In the context of budget preparation what does the term 'goal congruence' mean?

- A   the alignment of budgets with objectives using feed-forward control
- B   the setting of a budget which does not include budget bias
- C   the alignment of corporate objectives with the personal objectives of a manager
- D   the use of aspiration levels to set efficiency targets.

300 Which of the following is a disadvantage of participation in standard setting?

- A   Morale and performance are supressed
- B   Staff may try to incorporate budget padding
- C   Decision making will not improve
- D   Budget requirements are not clearly communicated to staff

301 Which of the following best describes 'budgetary slack'?

- A   The difference between what has been set as a budgetary objective and what has been achieved for the period.
- B   The demotivating impact of a budgetary target that has been set too high.
- C   The deliberate over-estimation of expenditure and/or under-estimation of revenues in the budgetary planning process.
- D   Accumulated favourable variances reported against a specific item of budgeted expenditure.

302 One of the purposes of a budget is to set targets to motivate managers and optimise their performance. Which of the following is most likely to motivate managers?

- A   The participation of managers in the budget setting process
- B   Imposed budgets
- C   The inclusion of budgetary slack
- D   Easy budget targets

SYLLABUS AREA D – STANDARD COSTING

STANDARD COSTING SYSTEMS

303 When considering setting standards for costing which of the following would NOT be appropriate?

- A The normal level of activity should always be used for absorbing overheads
- B Average prices for materials should be used, encompassing any discounts that are regularly available
- C The labour rate used will be the rate at which labour is paid
- D Average material usage should be established based on generally-accepted working practices

304 What are performance standards that have remained unchanged over a long period of time known as?

- A ideal standards
- B current standards
- C basic standards
- D attainable standards

305 What are performance standards that allow for efficient but not perfect operating conditions known as?

- A ideal standards
- B current standards
- C basic standards
- D attainable standards

306 Which of the following statement are true and which are false?

Statement	True	False
A variance is the difference between budgeted and actual cost.		
A favourable variance means actual costs are less than budgeted.		
An adverse variance means that actual income is less than budgeted.		

PAPER F2/FMA : MANAGEMENT ACCOUNTING

VARIANCE CALCULATIONS AND ANALYSIS

307 A company uses standard marginal costing. Last month the standard contribution on actual sales was $10,000 and the following variances arose:

Total variable costs variance	$2,000 adverse
Sales Price variance	$500 favourable
Sales volume contribution variance	$1,000 adverse

What was the actual contribution for last month?

$ ☐

308 A company uses standard marginal costing. Last month, when all sales were at the standard selling price, the standard contribution from actual sales was $50,000 and the following variances arose:

Total variable cost variance	$3,500 Adverse
Total fixed costs variance	$1,000 favourable
Sales volume contribution variance	$2,000 favourable

What was the actual contribution for last month?

A $46,500

B $47,500

C $48,500

D $49,500

309 The following information relates to labour costs for the past month:

Budget	Labour rate	$10 per hour
	Production time	15,000 hours
	Time per unit	3 hours
	Production units	5,000 units
Actual	Wages paid	$176,000
	Production	5,500 units
	Total hours worked	14,000 hours

There was no idle time.

What were the labour rate and efficiency variances?

	Rate variance	Efficiency variance
A	$26,000 adverse	$25,000 favourable
B	$26,000 adverse	$10,000 favourable
C	$36,000 adverse	$2,500 favourable
D	$36,000 adverse	$25,000 favourable

SECTION A-TYPE QUESTIONS : SECTION 1

310 The following details relate to product T, which has a selling price of $44.00:

	$/unit
Direct materials	15.00
Direct labour (3 hours)	12.00
Variable overhead	6.00
Fixed overhead	4.00
	37.00

During April 20X6, the actual production of T was 800 units, which was 100 units fewer than budgeted. The budget shows an annual production target of 10,800, with fixed costs accruing at a constant rate throughout the year. Actual overhead expenditure totalled $8,500 for April 20X6.

Overheads are absorbed on the basis of units produced.

What were the overhead variances for April 20X6?

	Expenditure $	Volume $
A	367 A	1,000 A
B	500 A	400 A
C	100 A	1,000 A
D	100 A	400 A

311 A company operates a standard marginal costing system. Last month its actual fixed overhead expenditure was 10% above budget resulting in a fixed overhead expenditure variance of $36,000.

What was the actual expenditure on fixed overheads last month?

A $324,000

B $360,000

C $396,000

D $400,000

312 FGH has the following budgeted and actual data:

Budgeted fixed overhead cost	$120,000
Budgeted production (units)	20,000
Actual fixed overhead cost	$115,000
Actual production (units)	21,000

What is the fixed overhead volume variance?

A   is $4,500 adverse

B   is $5,500 favourable

C   is $6,000 favourable

D   is $10,500 favourable

KAPLAN PUBLISHING

313 A company budgeted to make 30,000 units of a product P. Each unit was expected to take 4 hours to make and budgeted fixed overhead expenditure was $840,000. Actual production of product P in the period was 32,000 units, which took 123,000 hours to make. Actual fixed overhead expenditure was $885,600.

What was the fixed overhead capacity variance for the period?

A $21,000 favourable

B $21,000 adverse

C $35,000 adverse

D $56,000 favourable

314 QRL uses a standard absorption costing system. The following details have been extracted from its budget for April 20X7:

Fixed production overhead cost $48,000
Production (units)   4,800

In April 20X7 the fixed production overhead cost was under-absorbed by $8,000 and the fixed production overhead expenditure variance was $2,000 adverse.

What was the actual number of units produced?

A   3,800

B   4,000

C   4,200

D   5,400

315 A company has a higher than expected staff turnover and as a result staff are less experienced than expected.

As an indirect result of this, are the labour rate variance and material usage variance likely to be adverse or favourable?

	Labour rate	Material usage
A	Favourable	Favourable
B	Adverse	Favourable
C	Favourable	Adverse
D	Adverse	Adverse

316 A company is obliged to buy sub-standard materials at lower than standard price because nothing else is available.

As an indirect result of this purchase, are the materials usage variance and labour efficiency variance likely to be adverse or favourable?

	Materials usage	Labour efficiency
A	Favourable	Favourable
B	Adverse	Favourable
C	Favourable	Adverse
D	Adverse	Adverse

317 Fawley's direct labour cost data relating to last month were as follows:

Standard labour cost of actual hours worked	$116,000
Standard hours worked	30,000
Standard rate per hour	$4
Labour rate variance	$5,800 favourable
Labour efficiency variance	$4,000 favourable

What is the actual rate of pay per hour (to 2 decimal places)?

$ ☐

318 Michel has the following results.

10,080 hours actually worked and paid costing $8,770

If the rate variance is $706 adverse, the efficiency variance $256 favourable, and 5,000 units were produced, what is the standard production time per unit?

- A 1.95 hours
- B 1.96 hours
- C 2.07 hours
- D 2.08 hours

319 An extract from the standard cost card for product CJ is as follows:

Direct labour (0.5 hours × $12) $6

710 units of CJ were produced in the period and staff worked 378 hours at a total cost of $4,725. Of these hours 20 were lost due to a material shortage.

What is the labour efficiency variance?

- A $516 favourable
- B $36 favourable
- C $36 adverse
- D $516 adverse

PAPER F2/FMA : MANAGEMENT ACCOUNTING

320 A company makes a single product. The following details are from the cost card for the product:

Direct labour   10 hours at $5 per hour
Variable overhead   10 hours at $1.50 per hour

The actual results for the last period are:

500 units produced
Labour   4,800 hours
Variable overheads $7,700

What are the variable overhead expenditure and efficiency variances?

	Expenditure	Efficiency
A	$300 A	$500 F
B	$300 F	$500 A
C	$500 A	$300 F
D	$500 F	$300 A

321 A company uses standard absorption costing. The following data relate to last month:

	Budget	Actual
Sales and production (units)	1,000	900
	Standard	Actual
	$	$
Selling price per unit	50	52
Total production cost per unit	39	40

What was the adverse sales volume profit variance last month?

$ _____ Adv

322 A company operates a standard marginal costing system. Last month actual fixed overhead expenditure was 2% below budget and the fixed overhead expenditure variance was $1,250.

What was the actual fixed overhead expenditure for last month?

A $61,250
B $62,475
C $62,500
D $63,750

323 Under absorption costing the sales volume variance is calculated by multiplying the difference in sales volumes multiplied by?

A   Standard contribution per unit
B   Standard cost per unit
C   Standard profit per unit
D   Standard selling price per unit

SECTION A-TYPE QUESTIONS : SECTION 1

324 A business uses marginal costing to calculate variances. If they were to use absorption costing the current method of calculating the sales volume variance would be?

- A Higher or the same
- B Lower or the same
- C The same
- D Different but not able to say higher or lower

The following information relates to questions 325 and 326

The standard direct material cost for a product is $50 per unit (12.5 kg at $4 per kg). Last month the actual amount paid for 45,600 kg of material purchased and used was $173,280 and the direct material usage variance was $15,200 adverse.

325 What was the direct material price variance last month?

- A $8,800 adverse
- B $8,800 favourable
- C $9,120 adverse
- D $9,120 favourable

326 What was the actual production last month?

- A 3,344 units
- B 3,520 units
- C 3,952 units
- D 4,160 units

327 A new machine is purchased which is more expensive, but requires less labour to operate per unit.

What is the impact on the fixed overhead variances?

	Expenditure variance	Volume variance
A	Adverse	Adverse
B	Adverse	Favourable
C	Favourable	Favourable
D	Favourable	Favourable

328 D — $1,080 adverse

329 C — (ii) and (iii) only

330 D — $5,916 adverse

331 1,950 kg

SECTION A-TYPE QUESTIONS : SECTION 1

332 The following information relates to a month's production of product CN:

	Budget	Actual
Units produced	600	580
Input of material P (kg)	1,500	1,566
Cost of material P purchased and input	$25,500	$25,839

What is the price variance for material P?

A $783 favourable

B $339 adverse

C $1,189 favourable

D $1,972 adverse

333 A company uses a standard absorption costing system. Last month budgeted production was 8,000 units and the standard fixed production overhead cost was $15 per unit. Actual production last month was 8,500 units and the actual fixed production overhead cost was $17 per unit.

What was the total adverse fixed production overhead variance for last month?

A $7,500

B $16,000

C $17,000

D $24,500

334 A company is reviewing actual performance to budget to see where there are differences. The following standard information is relevant:

	$ per unit
Selling price	50
Direct materials	4
Direct labour	16
Fixed production overheads	5
Variable production overheads	10
Fixed selling costs	1
Variable selling cost	1
Total costs	37
Budgeted sales units	3,000
Actual sales units	3,500

What was the favourable sales volume variance using marginal costing?

A $9,500

B $7,500

C $7,000

D $6,500

335 A company uses variance analysis to control costs and revenues.

Information concerning sales is as follows:

Budgeted selling price	$15 per unit
Budgeted sales units	10,000
Budgeted profit per unit	$5
Actual sales revenue	$151,500
Actual units sold	9,800

What is the sales volume profit variance?

A $500 favourable

B $1,000 favourable

C $1,000 adverse

D $3,000 adverse

336 A company operates a standard absorption costing system. The standard fixed production overhead rate is $15 per hour.

The following data relate to last month:

Actual hours worked	5,500
Budgeted hours	5,000
Standard hours for actual production	4,800

What was the fixed production overhead capacity variance?

A $7,500 adverse

B $7,500 favourable

C $10,500 adverse

D $10,500 favourable

337 Direct labour cost data relating to last month is as follows:

Actual hours worked	28,000
Total direct labour cost	$117,600
Direct labour rate variance	$8,400 adverse
Direct labour efficiency variance	$3,900 favourable

To the nearest thousand hours, what were the standard labour hours for actual production last month?

A   31,000 hrs

B   29,000 hrs

C   27,000 hrs

D   25,000 hrs

338 Which of the following variances would you find within an absorption costing system and which in a marginal costing system?

	Absorption costing	Marginal costing
Sales volume contribution variance		
Fixed overhead capacity variance		
Fixed overhead volume variance		
Sales volume profit variance		
Fixed overhead efficiency variance		

RECONCILIATION OF BUDGETED AND ACTUAL PROFIT

339 The budgeted contribution for last month was $43,900 but the following variances arose:

	$
Sales price variance	3,100 adverse
Sales volume contribution variance	1,100 adverse
Direct material price variance	1,986 favourable
Direct material usage variance	2,200 adverse
Direct labour rate variance	1,090 adverse
Direct labour efficiency variance	512 adverse
Variable overhead expenditure variance	1,216 favourable
Variable overhead efficiency variance	465 adverse

What is the actual contribution for last month? $ ☐

340 Below is a statement of variances for a business:

Sales price variance	$1,500F
Sales volume variance	$2,100A
Materials price variance	$4,200A
Materials usage Variance	$1,500F
Labour rate variance	$900F
Labour efficiency Variance	$450A
Fixed overhead expenditure variance	$1,750F
Fixed overhead volume variance	$1,800A

The budgeted profit for the period was $250,000 what was the actual profit?

A $247,100

B $248,300

C $251,700

D $252,900

341 Below is a statement of variances for a business:

Sales price variance	$200F
Sales volume variance	$350F
Materials price variance	$250F
Materials usage Variance	$120A
Labour rate variance	$450A
Labour efficiency Variance	$800A
Fixed overhead expenditure variance	$600F
Fixed overhead volume variance	$860A

The actual profit for the period was $7,170 what was the budget profit?

A $6,340

B $5,240

C $9,100

D $8,000

342 Below is a statement of variances for a business, including the budgeted and actual profit.

What is the missing value for the Labour rate variance?

Budget profit	$19,000
Sales price variance	$1,200A
Sales volume variance	$2,000F
Materials price variance	$3,500F
Materials usage Variance	$4,200A
Labour rate variance	$
Labour efficiency Variance	$1,500A
Fixed overhead expenditure variance	$1,500F
Fixed overhead volume variance	$750A
Actual profit	$21,100

SYLLABUS AREA E – PERFORMANCE MEASUREMENT

PERFORMANCE MEASUREMENT OVERVIEW

343 Which of the following are elements of a mission statement?

   (i)   Purpose
   (ii) Strategy
   (iii) Values
   (iv) Culture

   A   All of them
   B   (i) and (ii) only
   C   (ii) only
   D   (ii) and (iv) only

344 An organisation is divided into a number of divisions, each of which operates as a profit centre. Which TWO of the following would be useful measures to monitor divisional performance?

   A   Contribution
   B   Controllable profit
   C   Return on investment
   D   Residual income

345 When measuring performance which of the following could impact the overall results for the business?

   (i)   A new competitor
   (ii) A change in local government
   (iii) An increase in interest rates
   (iv) A change in national government

   A   (i) and (iv)
   B   none of them
   C   (ii) and (iv)
   D   All of them

346 Which of the following performance measurements could be a result of government legislation?

- A Carbon footprint
- B Retention of customers
- C Return on Capital employed
- D Capacity ratio

PERFORMANCE MEASUREMENT – APPLICATION

347 In the last year a division's controllable return on investment was 25% and its controllable profit was $80,000. The cost of finance appropriate to the division was 18% per annum.

What was the division's controllable residual income in the last year?

- A $5,600
- B $22,400
- C $74,400
- D $76,400

348 A government body uses measures based upon the 'three Es' to the measure value for money generated by a publicly funded hospital. It considers the most important performance measure to be 'cost per successfully treated patient'.

Which of the three E's best describes the above measure?

- A Economy
- B Effectiveness
- C Efficiency
- D Externality

349 A government is looking at assessing hospitals by reference to a range of both financial and non-financial factors, one of which is survival rates for heart by-pass operation.

Which of the three E's best describes the above measure?

- A Economy
- B Effectiveness
- C Efficiency
- D Externality

350 Which of the following measures would not be appropriate for a cost centre?

- A Cost per unit
- B Contribution per unit
- C Comparison of actual labour cost to budget labour cost
- D Under or over absorption of overheads

351 A government is looking at assessing state schools by reference to a range of both financial and non-financial factors, one of which is average class sizes.

Which of the three E's best describes the above measure?

A   Economy

B   Effectiveness

C   Efficiency

D   Externality

352 **For operational purposes, for a company operating a fleet of delivery vehicles, which of the following would be most useful?**

A   Cost per mile run

B   Cost per driver hour

C   Cost per tonne mile

D   Cost per kg carried

353 A division has a residual income of £240,000 and a net profit before imputed interest of £640,000.

If it uses a rate of 10% for computing imputed interest on its invested capital, what is its return on investment (ROI) to the nearest whole number?

A   4%

B   10%

C   16%

D   27%

354 JKL Inc budgeted to make 1,000 units in May using 2,000 hours of direct labour. Actual output was 1,100 units which took 2,300 hours.

What is the production/volume ratio?

A   91%

B   105%

C   110%

D   115%

355 RL Inc budgeted to make 200 units in June with a standard labour usage of 0.6 hours per unit. Actual output was 180 units which took 126 hours.

What is the efficiency ratio?

A   86%

B   90%

C   105%

D   116%

356 CAP Inc budgeted to make 50 units in July with a standard labour usage of 1.2 hours per unit. Actual output was 49 units which took 61 hours.

What is the capacity ratio?

- A 96%
- B 98%
- C 100%
- D 102%

357 HH plc monitors the % of total sales that derives from products developed in the last year. Which part of the balanced scorecard is this measure classified under?

- A Financial perspective
- B Customer perspective
- C Internal perspective
- D Learning perspective

358 Which of the following KPIs would be used to assess the liquidity of a company?

- (i) Return on capital employed
- (ii) Gross profit percentage
- (iii) Acid test ratio
- (iv) Gearing ratio

- A (i) and (ii) only
- B (iii) only
- C (iv) only
- D (iii) and (iv) only

359 K Class has calculated the following indictors

- (i) Return on capital employed
- (ii) Training costs as a percentage of total costs

Which of the balanced scorecard perspectives would these measures relate to?

	(i)	(ii)
A	Financial	Financial
B	Financial	Internal
C	Internal	Learning and growth
D	Financial	Learning and growth

SECTION A-TYPE QUESTIONS : SECTION 1

360 Area 27 are a pizza delivery company and have asked you to suggest some performance indicators that could be used to measure the customer perspective and the internal perspective of the balanced scorecard. Which of the following would be appropriate?

	Customer	Internal
A	Number of customer complaints	Time taken from order to delivery pizza
B	Cost per pizza	Cost of time spent on training
C	Number of late deliveries	Profit per pizza
D	Cost of delivery vehicles	Gross profit percentage

Use the following information for Questions 361 – 367.

Extracts from a company's accounts show the following balances:

	£000		£000
Inventories	150	Revenue	2,700
Receivables	300	Cost of sales	1,300
Cash	25	Gross profit	1,400
Payables	230	Admin costs	500
Overdraft	90	Distribution costs	350
		Operating profit	550
		Finance cost	75

361 Which of the following is the company's current ratio, calculated to the nearest two decimal places?

- A 1.48
- B 1.41
- C 1.96
- D 1.02

362 Which of the following is the company's quick ratio, calculated to the nearest two decimal places?

- A 1.41
- B 1.02
- C 1.48
- D 1.30

KAPLAN PUBLISHING 107

363 Which of the following is the receivables' payment period in days (to the nearest day)?

- A   41 days
- B   84 days
- C   78 days
- D   45 days

364 Which of the following is the payables' payment period in days (to the nearest day)?

- A   31 days
- B   65 days
- C   60 days
- D   35 days

365 Which of the following is the inventory holding period (to the nearest day)?

- A   4 days
- B   10 days
- C   24 days
- D   42 days

366 What is the return on sales for the company?

- A   52%
- B   39%
- C   20%
- D   25%

367 What is the interest cover of the company?

- A   4.67 times
- B   5.67 times
- C   7.33 times
- D   6.50 times

SECTION A-TYPE QUESTIONS : **SECTION 1**

Use the following information for Questions 368 – 372.

Extracts from a company's accounts show the following:

	£000	£000
Non-Current assets		30,000
Current assets		
Inventory	22,000	
Trade receivables	12,506	
Cash	5,006	
		39,512
Total assets		69,512
Equity		
Share capital		100
Revaluation reserve		12,000
Retained earnings		26,412
Non-current liabilities		
Loans		16,000
Current liabilities		
Trade payables		15,000
Total equity and liabilities		69,512

Additional Notes	£000
Revenue	64,323
Profit before interest and taxation	27,657

368 What is the gearing ratio (total debt/equity) of the company?

  A 44.3%

  B 41.5%

  C 60.6%

  D 57.1%

369 Which of the following is the company's current ratio, calculated to the nearest two decimal places?

  A 2.63

  B 1.27

  C 1.61

  D 1.17

370 Which of the following is the company's quick ratio, calculated to the nearest two decimal places?

  A 0.83

  B 1.27

  C 1.17

  D 2.57

KAPLAN PUBLISHING 109

PAPER F2/FMA : MANAGEMENT ACCOUNTING

371 Which of the following is the ROCE of the company (return on capital employed)?

- A 72%
- B 92%
- C 47%
- D 51%

372 What are the receivable days of the company (to the nearest whole day)?

- A 14 days
- B 18 days
- C 71 days
- D 90 days

Use the following information for Questions 373 – 378.

Extracts from a company's accounts show the following:

Statement of profit or loss	£000	Statement of financial position	£000	£000
Revenue	2,250	Non-current assets		700
Cost of sales	1,000	Current assets		
Gross profit	1,250	Inventory	150	
Distribution costs	275	Trade receivables	240	
Administrations	150	Cash	100	
Operating profit	825			490
Finance cost	80	Long term loans		200
Profit before Tax	745	Trade payables		275
Tax	90			
Profit for the year	655			

373 What is the gross profit margin?

- A 55.6%
- B 36.7%
- C 33.1%
- D 29.1%

374 What is the return on sales?

- A 55.6%
- B 36.7%
- C 33.1%
- D 29.1%

SECTION A-TYPE QUESTIONS : **SECTION 1**

375 What is the current ratio?

- A 1.2
- B 0.9
- C 1.4
- D 1.8

376 What are the receivable days?

- A 88 days
- B 80 days
- C 70 days
- D 39 days

377 What are the payable days?

- A 100 days
- B 80 days
- C 143 days
- D 45 days

378 What is the inventory turnover in days?

- A 24 days
- B 55 days
- C 44 days
- D 66 days

379 A division has a residual income of $50,000 and a net profit before imputed interest of $80,000.

If it uses a rate of 10% for computing imputed interest on its invested capital, what is its return on investment (ROI) to the nearest whole number?

- A 4%
- B 10%
- C 16%
- D 27%

KAPLAN PUBLISHING

380 A division of a company has capital employed of $2m and its return on capital is 12%. It is considering a new project requiring capital of $500,000 and is expected to yield profits of $90,000 per annum. The company's interest rate is 10%.

If the new project is accepted, what will the residual income of the division be?

A $40,000

B $80,000

C $30,000

D $330,000

381 The following information relates to a small production unit during a period:

Budgeted hours   9,500 hours
Actual hours worked   9,200 hours
Standard hours of work produced   9,300 hours

What is the efficiency ratio for the period?

A   97%

B   98%

C   99%

D   101%

382 A company makes a product for which the standard labour time is 2 hours per unit. The budgeted production hours for a given week were 820. During the week the production staff were able to produce 380 units of product. Staff worked and were paid for 800 hours. During the week 20 production hours were lost due to a shortage of material.

What is the efficiency ratio?

A   95.00%

B   95.12%

C   97.44%

D   97.50%

383 A company has calculated that its activity ratio is 103.5% and that its efficiency ratio is 90%.

What is the capacity ratio?

A   86.96%

B   93.15%

C   115.00%

D   193.50%

384 How is the activity (production volume) ratio calculated?

A   Actual hours ÷ Budgeted hours

B   Budgeted hours ÷ Actual hours

C   Standard hours for actual output ÷ Actual hours

D   Standard hours for actual output ÷ Budgeted hours

385 The direct labour capacity ratio for a period was 104%.

What could have caused this?

A   Actual hours worked being greater than budgeted hours

B   Actual hours worked being less than budgeted hours

C   Standard time for actual output being greater than budgeted hours

D   Standard time for actual output being less than budgeted hours

386 Green division is one of many divisions in the Colour group. At its year-end, the non-current assets invested in Green were $30 million, and the net current assets were $5 million.

Included in this total was a new item of plant that was delivered three days before the year end. This item cost $4 million and had been paid for by Colour, which had increased the amount of long-term debt owed by Green by this amount. The profit earned in the year by Green was $6 million before the deduction of $1.4 million of interest payable to Colour. What is the most appropriate measure of ROI for the Green division?

A   13.1%

B   14.8%

C   17.1%

D   19.4%

387 Division M has produced the following results in the last financial year:

		$000
Net profit		360
Capital employed:	Non-current assets	1,500
	Net current assets	100

For evaluation purposes all divisional assets are valued at original cost. The division is considering a project which will increase annual net profit by $25,000, but will require average inventory levels to increase by $30,000 and non-current assets to increase by $100,000. There is an 18% capital charge on investments.

Given these circumstances, will the evaluation criteria of Return on Investment (ROI) and Residual Income (RI) motivate Division M management to accept this project?

	ROI	RI
A	Yes	Yes
B	Yes	No
C	No	Yes
D	No	No

388 Which TWO of the following performance indicators could be used to measure the quality of a service?

    A   Number of customer complaints

    B   Customer retention

    C   Overtime worked

    D   Number of sick days

389 Which balanced scorecard perspective would the performance indicator 'Training costs as a % of total costs' come under?

    A   Financial

    B   Customer

    C   Learning and growth

    D   Internal

390 A company wants to measure performance under the 'Internal' perspective of the balanced scorecard. Which of the following would be an appropriate measure?

    A   ROI

    B   Warranty claims

    C   New products developed

    D   Labour capacity ratio

391 Which TWO of the following would be a suitable measure of resource utilisation for a private sector college?

	Tick
Average class size	
Tutor grading by students	
Pass rates	
Percentage room occupancy	

SECTION A-TYPE QUESTIONS : SECTION 1

392 A business is concerned that not all the employees are making the best use of their time. Consider the following information:

	Budget operations	Actual operations	Budget employees	Actual employees
Department A	800	1,000	4	5
Department B	700	660	5	3
Department C	1,200	1,050	8	7
Department D	300	400	4	5

Which department is making the best use of the employees' time when compared to budget?

A   A
B   B
C   C
D   D

COST REDUCTIONS AND VALUE ENHANCEMENT

393 Which two of the following could be used to control costs?

	Tick
Setting targets for cost centre managers	
Reducing the cost budget	
Cost variance analysis	
Increasing sales volume	

394 Value analysis looks to do which of the following?

	Tick
Control costs	
Reduce costs	
Improve sales	
Increase the value of the product	

KAPLAN PUBLISHING

395 Which of the following is defined as 'the body of knowledge concerned with the analysis of the work methods and the equipment used in performing a job, the design of an optimum work method and the standardisation of proposed work methods'?

- A Work study
- B Work measurement
- C Job study
- D Method measurement

396 Which of the following relates to Value analysis and which to Value engineering?

	Value analysis	Value engineering
Reviews current products to reduce costs		
Reviews products at the design stage to reduce costs		

397 Which of the following techniques would be useful for controlling costs?

- (i)   Actual versus flexed budget
- (ii) Variance analysis
- (iii) Trend of costs analysis

- A (i) and (ii) only
- B (i) and (iii) only
- C (ii) and (iii) only
- D (i), (ii) and (iii)

MONITORING PERFORMANCE AND REPORTING

398 Copenhagen is an insurance company. Recently there has been concern that too many quotations have been sent to clients either late or containing errors.

The department concerned has responded that it is understaffed, and a high proportion of current staff has recently joined the firm. The performance of this department is to be carefully monitored.

Which of the following non-financial performance indicators would NOT be an appropriate measure to monitor and improve the department's performance?

- A Percentage of quotations found to contain errors when checked
- B Percentage of quotations not issued within company policy of three working days
- C Percentage of department's quota of staff actually employed
- D Percentage of budgeted number of quotations actually issued

SECTION A-TYPE QUESTIONS : **SECTION 1**

399 A company wants to encourage an investment centre to make new investments. Performance measurement using which of the following KPIs would achieve this?

  A ROI

  B ROCE

  C RI

  D IRR

400 Why would a company want to encourage the use of non-financial performance indicators?

  A To encourage short termism

  B To look at the fuller picture of the business

  C To enable results to be easily manipulated to the benefit of the manager

  D To prevent goal congruence

401 Which of the following is not a type of benchmarking?

  A Internal

  B Strategic

  C International

  D Functional

402 In a responsibility accounting system which of the following costs is least likely to appear on the performance report for the foreman of a production department?

  A Cost of direct labour

  B Rent of machinery

  C Repairs to machinery

  D Cost of materials used

403 In a responsibility accounting system for which of the following should the purchasing manager be held responsible?

  A Raw material prices

  B Raw material usage

  C Labour hours worked

  D Labour wage rates

KAPLAN PUBLISHING

117

404 The operating statement used by an organisation to measure the performance of its divisions is structured as follows.

	$	$	$
External sales		X	
Internal transfers		X	
Variable cost of sales	(X)		
Other variable divisional costs	(X)		
		(X)	
Contribution		X	
Depreciation on controllable non-current assets	(X)		
Other controllable fixed costs	(X)		
		(X)	
Controllable operating profit			X
Depreciation on other divisional non-current assets	(X)		
Other traceable divisional costs	(X)		
		(X)	
Traceable divisional profit		X	
Apportioned head office cost		(X)	
Divisional net profit			X

Which of the following would provide the best basis for measuring the performance of a manager of an investment centre?

A   Contribution

B   Controllable operating profit

C   Traceable divisional profit

D   Divisional net profit

405 Classify the following as either a measure of effectiveness, efficiency or economy according to the 3Es framework for an NHS hospital

	Effectiveness	Efficiency	Economy
Have the waiting lists been reduced?			
What was the average cost per patient treated?			
Have mortality rates gone down?			
Did the hospital spend more or less on drugs this year?			
What was the average spend per bed over the period?			
Did the hospital spend more or less on nurses' wages?			

406 YU is a charity based in country K which aims to offer value for money. It has been set up to manage an area of woodland on behalf of the local population.

YU aims to have around 3,000 visitors to the woodland every year, but in the last year it has only had around half of this number. YU has spent more on advertising than in previous years, but has moved from using leaflets to radio advertisements. While YU was able to buy a large amount of radio advertising, YU's directors were unaware that the chosen station had relatively low numbers of listeners.

With reference to value for money, the low number of visitors indicates that YU has failed with regards to _____1_____ over the past year. Its poor use of its advertising budget also indicates a lack of _____2____.

Which of the options below can be used to fill in the missing words in gaps 1 and 2?

Note that each term can be used more than once.

- A   Effectiveness
- B   Economy
- C   Ethics
- D   Efficiency
- E   Expertise

407 Which of the following statements are correct?

- A   Non-financial performance indicators can be used easily to compare one organisation to another
- B   Financial performance indicators encourage a long-term view of performance
- C   Financial performance indicators provide all the analysis of progress needed
- D   Non-financial performance indicators are difficult to determine

408 How can short-termism be prevented?

- A   Focus performance measurement on financial performance only
- B   Focus performance measurement on non-financial performance only
- C   Focus performance measurement on both financial and non-financial performance
- D   Create budgets for more than one year at a time.

409 The management process which involves comparison of competences with best practice within and outside the organisation is known as?

- A   Balanced scorecard
- B   Benchmarking
- C   Productivity
- D   Resource analysis

410 VG is planning to introduce a new benchmarking procedure within its organisation, but is unsure which type of benchmarking would be most appropriate. It is aware that each type of benchmarking has certain drawbacks.

VG has identified that _____1_____ benchmarking is often difficult to undertake as it is difficult to convince the other party to share information about their operations.

_____2_____ benchmarking is unlikely to suggest any truly innovative solutions and is typically only useful where the organisation feels that conformity of service is crucial to its operations.

Finally, _____3_____ benchmarking often fails to provide data on the benchmarking company's core functions as it requires the organisation to benchmark itself against an organisation in a different industry.

Which of the options below can be used to fill in the missing words in gaps 1 and 2?

A   Functional

B   Internal

C   Competitive

411 KV operates a van rental company through a chain of around 35 stores. It has received a number of complaints from customers about the service they have received. KV's investigation has revealed that different stores are offering radically different levels of service to customers.

KV is the current market leader in the van rental market, with a market share which is significantly ahead of its nearest rival. KV's managers are still keen to ensure their market share does not fall and have decided to undertake a benchmarking process to help the business standardise the level of service it offers to customers across its business.

Which type of benchmarking would be most appropriate for KV to adopt?

A   Functional

B   Strategic

C   Competitive

D   Internal

Section 2

SECTION B-TYPE QUESTIONS

BUDGETING

412 L Co wants to be able to predict their overhead costs with more accuracy. The company accountant has analysed costs for the past six months:

Note: perform all calculations to the nearest $

	Production level (units)	Overhead costs ($)
January	10	3,352
February	10.5	3,479
March	12	3,860
April	9	3,098
May	9.5	3,225
June	10.25	3,416

Further analysis has revealed:

$\Sigma x = 61.25$ $\Sigma y = 20,430$ $\Sigma xy = 209,903$ $\Sigma x^2 = 630.56$

Required:

(a) Use regression analysis to identify the variable cost per unit. **(2 marks)**

(b) Which graph shows best the relationship between production levels and overhead costs for L Co?

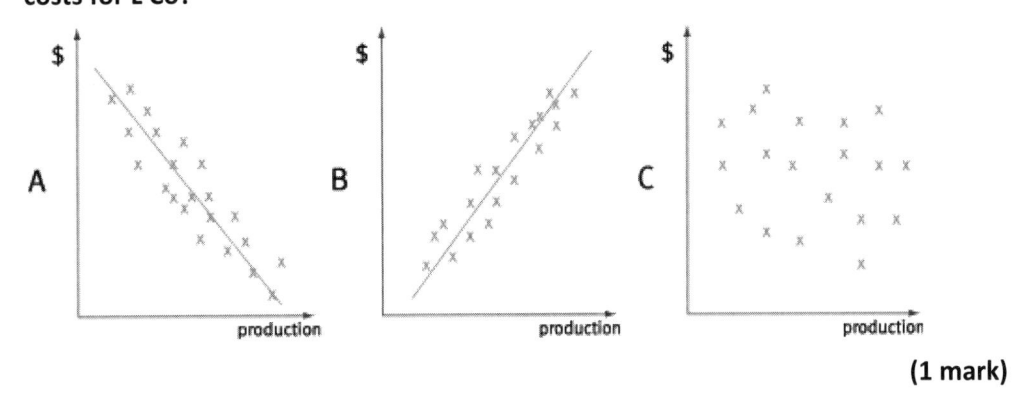

(1 mark)

(c) Further analysis has shown that there is a price index applicable to the overhead costs:

	Production level (units)	Overhead costs ($)	Index
January	10	3,352	100
February	10.5	3,479	101
March	12	3,860	102
April	9	3,098	104
May	9.5	3,225	105
June	10.25	3,416	106

Required:

Using high low analysis, calculate the variable cost per unit in June's prices. (3 marks)

(d) Within time series analysis, which TWO of the following are concerned with long term movements/fluctuations in variables?

A Seasonal variations

B Cyclical variations

C Random variations

D The Trend

(2 marks)

(e) Which one of the following options about the Paasche and Laspeyre indices is correct?

	Paasche index	Laspeyre index
A	Underestimates the effect of inflation	Uses base data to weight the index
B	Overestimates the effect of inflation	Uses base data to weight the index
C	Underestimates the effect of inflation	Uses current data to weight the index
D	Overestimates the effect of inflation	Uses current data to weight the index

(2 marks)

(Total: 10 marks)

413 Daps Co makes spades and forks. The following budgeted information is available:

	Month one	Month two
Fork production	220 units	240 units
Spade production	170 units	180 units

Each fork uses 1.5 kg of steel, and each spade uses 2 kg of steel.

No finished goods inventory is held, but Daps Co's raw material inventory policy is to hold enough material to cover half of the next month's production requirements.

A spreadsheet for the material purchases budget is being prepared for month one:

	A	B
		kgs
1	Steel required for production	Gap 1
2	Opening inventory	Gap 2
3	Closing inventory	Gap 3
4	Material purchases	

Required:

(a) Calculate the figure that should be entered into:

    (i) Gap 1   (2 marks)

    (ii) Gap 2   (2 marks)

    (iii) Gap 3   (1 mark)

(b) State the formula that should be entered into cell B4   (1 mark)

(c) Are the following statements true or false?

Statement one: The master budget includes the capital expenditure budget.

Statement two: Continuous budgets are also known as rolling budgets.

Statement three: Scenario planning is mainly used in the short term.

Statement four: The mission of an organisation is the target to be met in the medium term.   (2 marks)

(d) Which TWO of the following are the main aims of budgeting?

    A   Controlling costs

    B   Identifying objectives

    C   Evaluating manager's performance

    D   Introducing budgetary bias   (2 marks)

(Total: 10 marks)

414 Mr Grob started trading in 20X3, selling one product, wheelbarrows, on credit to small retail outlets. The following budgeted information for 20X4 has been gathered:

	January 20X4	February 20X4	March 20X4
Credit sales	$12,000	$15,000	$21,000

Receivables have recently been settling their debts 50% in the month following sale, and 50% two months after sale. A prompt payment discount of 3% is offered to those receivables paying within one month.

The gross profit margin is expected to be 25%. Due to an anticipated continued increase in sales, Mr Grob intends to increase inventory levels in March 20X4 by $2,000, and it is intended that the payables balance is increased by $3,000 to ease cash flow in the same month.

PAPER F2/FMA : MANAGEMENT ACCOUNTING

Required:

(a) Calculate the budgeted cash that will received in March 20X4. (3 marks)

(b) Calculate the budgeted payment to suppliers in March 20X4 (3 marks)

(c) Calculate the chain base index for sales in February 20X4 and March 20X4 (2 marks)

(d) The following incomplete statement has been made.

The product life cycle has (gap 1) stages. Mr Grob's business is in the (gap 2) phase of the product lifecycle.

Required:

Select the correct words to complete the sentence.

Gap 1

A   Four

B   Five (1 mark)

Gap 2

A   Introduction

B   Growth (1 mark)

(Total: 10 marks)

415 J Co is considering investing in a new machine costing $18,750, payable immediately. The scrap value will be zero, and the machine will be depreciated on a straight line basis. Output would be 1,000 units per year for each of the six years of the machine's life. Each unit earns a contribution of $5.

Required:

(a) Assuming that the cash flows arise evenly throughout the year, calculate the payback period in years and months. (2 marks)

(b) The management of J Co have heard about the concept of the time value of money.

Required:

(i) Complete the gaps in the following statement:

The time value of money means that $1 now is worth (GAP 1) than $1 in the future. The reasons for this are risk, (Gap 2) and potential for earning a return e.g. interest. (2 marks)

(ii) Using a discount rate of 8%, and assuming that the cash flows arise at the end of a year, calculate the discounted payback period. (2 marks)

(c) Using a discount factor of 8%, calculate the net present value of purchasing the new machine. (2 marks)

124   KAPLAN PUBLISHING

(d) Are the following statements about investment appraisal true or false?

Statement one: If the cost of capital increased to 10%, the net present value of purchasing the new machine would decrease.

Statement two: The payback method of investment appraisal is a useful method to consider time risk.

	Statement 1	*Statement 2*
A	True	False
B	True	True
C	False	False
D	False	True

(2 marks)

(Total: 10 marks)

STANDARD COSTING

416 Cabrinda Co manufactures bulbs. The following figures are available:

- 500 kg of direct materials were actually purchased
- The standard cost per kg is $2.25, leading to a standard cost of actual purchases of $1,125
- The direct materials price variance is $125 favourable
- The direct materials usage variance is $45 adverse

Required:

(a) From the information provided calculate

  (i) The actual price paid per kg for the direct material (2.5 marks)

  (ii) The standard quantity that should have been used for actual production.

  (2.5 marks)

(b) Which of the following is likely to lead to the variances stated above?

  A lower quality direct material has been purchased

  B higher quality direct material has been purchased (1 mark)

(c) The following graph shows the standard price and quantity and the actual and price and quantity relating to the direct material for the manufacture of the bulbs.

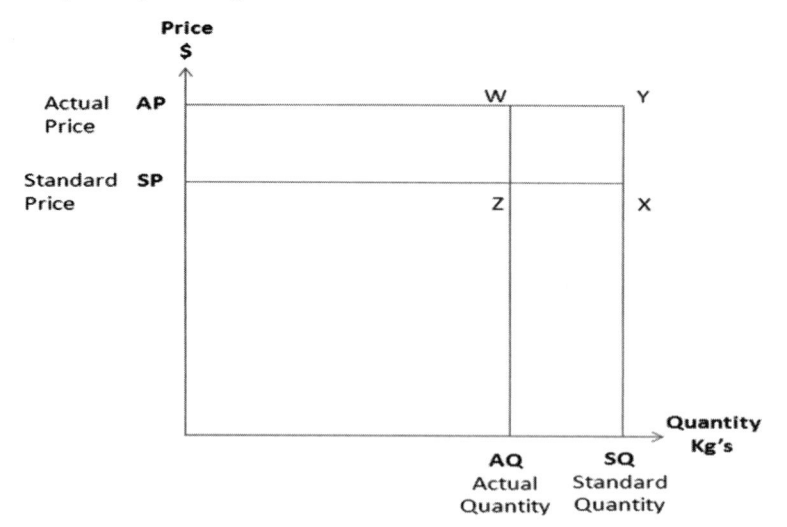

Required:

Which area correctly represents the direct material price variance?

A   APWZSP

B   APYXSP

C   AQWYSQ

D   AQZXSQ   (2 marks)

(d) The following spreadsheet has started to be completed for direct materials, with a ✓ showing where data has been entered.

	A	B	C
1		Standard	Actual
2	Production in units	✓	✓
3	Kg's per unit	✓	
4	Cost per kg ($)	✓	✓
5	Total kg's purchased		C6/C4
6	Total material cost		✓

Required:

What will be the formula for the materials usage variance?

A   (C5xC4)−(B2xB3xB4)

B   (C5xB4)−(B2xB3xB4)

C   (C5xC4)−(C2xB3xC4)

D   (C5xB4)−(C2xB3xB4)   (2 marks)

(Total: 10 marks)

SECTION B-TYPE QUESTIONS : SECTION 2

417 The following is a proforma operating statement for Wick Co, a company manufacturing candles.

$

Budgeted profit

Sales volume variance

Standard profit on actual sales

Sales price variance

	Favourable ($)	Adverse ($)
Cost variances		
Materials price		
Materials usage		
Labour rate		
Labour efficiency		
Variable overhead rate		
Variable overhead efficiency		
Fixed overhead expenditure		
Fixed overhead capacity		
Fixed overhead efficiency		

Total

Actual profit

(a) Which of the following THREE statements are correct?

A Wick Co uses standard profit per unit to calculate the sales volume variance.

B The fixed overhead expenditure variance is the same figure as the over or under absorption of fixed overheads

C Wick Co absorbs fixed overheads on an hourly basis.

D The efficiency variances will all either be favourable or adverse   (2 marks)

(b) The following information is available for Wick Co for month 1

Budgeted
   Fixed overheads $20,000 to be absorbed at $10/hr
   Time to make one unit   4 hours

Actual
   Fixed overheads $23,000
   Time taken to make 550 units 2,475 hours

PAPER F2/FMA : MANAGEMENT ACCOUNTING

Required:

Calculate the fixed overhead:

(i) Expenditure variance and state if it is favourable or adverse (2 marks)

(ii) Capacity variance and state if it is favourable or adverse. (2.5 marks)

(iii) Efficiency variance and state if it is favourable or adverse. (2.5 marks)

(c) Is the following statement true/false?

'A favourable fixed overhead capacity variance is likely to arise if a new machine is bought to replace an unreliable one.'

A True

B False (1 mark)

(Total: 10 marks)

418 Bogh Co manufactures wooden picture frames.

The company's information system produces an operating statement, and on the basis of the variances calculated, managers are assessed and bonuses paid.

The standard material cost for each picture frame is $8. This is made up:

| Wood | 0.5 kg @ $10 per kg | $5 |
| Glass | 0.25 kg @ $12 per kg | $3 |

In July, Bogh manufactured 300 picture frames, and purchased:

| Wood | 170 kg | $2,040 |
| Glass | 70 kg | $860 |

Required:

(a) Using the information above, calculate:

(i) The total materials price variance and state if it is adverse or favourable.
0 (2.5 marks)

(ii) The total materials usage variance and state if it is adverse or favourable (2.5 marks)

(b) The managers have now been told that although the levels of glass inventory did not change during July, wood inventory rose by 15 kg.

Which manager will need to have this fact accounted for in their performance appraisal?

A Purchasing manager

B Production manager (1 mark)

SECTION B-TYPE QUESTIONS : SECTION 2

(c) In the following graph, which area arises because both the material quantity and price are above standard levels?

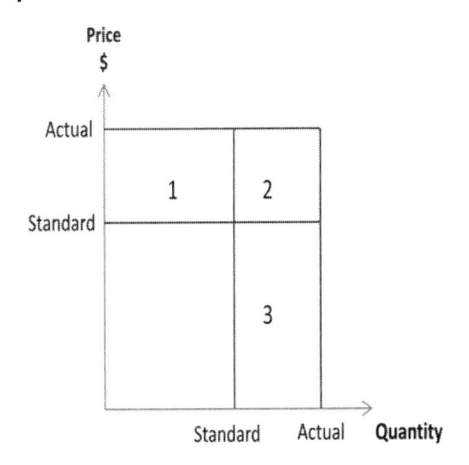

- A Area 1 only
- B Area 2 only
- C Area 2 and 3
- D Area 1 and 2

(2 marks)

(d) Are the following statements true or false?

Statement one: A flexed budget cannot be produced for non-manufacturing costs such as sales commission.

Statement two: All costs can be controlled in the long term.

	Statement one	*Statement two*
A	True	True
B	True	False
C	False	True
D	False	False

(2 marks)

(Total: 10 marks)

KAPLAN PUBLISHING 129

419 An operating statement has been partially completed for a company that makes pies and pasties:

	$
Budgeted contribution	5,075
Sales volume variance	175 (F)
Standard contribution on actual sales	5,250
Sales price variance	750 (A)
	4,500

	Favourable ($)	Adverse ($)
Cost variances		
Materials price		700
Materials usage	600	
Labour rate		724
Labour efficiency	650	
Variable overhead rate		
Variable overhead efficiency		
GAP 1		
Fixed overhead expenditure		
Total		

Required:

(a) For the following variances, state whether it is true or false that the variance stated above could be caused by better quality ingredients being purchased for the pies:

  (i) Sales volume (1 mark)

  (ii) Materials price (1 mark)

  (iii) Labour rate (1 mark)

  (iv) Materials usage (1 mark)

  (v) Sales price (1 mark)

(b) What should the title be in Gap 1? (1 mark)

(c) Using the following information, calculate the variable overhead rate and efficiency variances, and state if they are favourable or adverse.

Actual production was 1,500 units which were completed in 3,620 hours at a variable overhead cost of $11,000.

The budget was that each pie would take 2.5 hours to make and the variable overhead absorption rate would be $3 per hour. (4 marks)

(Total: 10 marks)

PERFORMANCE MEASUREMENT

420 Tel Co manufactures televisions and sells them to large retailers. Due to high staff turnover, no liquidity ratios have been calculated for the year ahead.

The bank is concerned about the forecast increase in Tel Co's overdraft to $40,500 at 30 November 20X4, and has suggested that the ratios be calculated. The following forecast information is available for the year ended 30 November 20X4:

	$
Revenue	343,275
Cost of sales	284,000
Purchases	275,000
Closing Inventory	35,000
Receivables	37,400
Payables	35,410

Required:

(a) For Tel Co for the year ended 30 November 20X2 calculate:

    (i) The inventory holding period   (1.5 marks)

    (ii) The receivables collection period   (1.5 marks)

    (iii) The payables period   (1.5 marks)

    (iv) The current ratio   (1.5 marks)

Perform your calculations for (i), (ii) and (iii) to the nearest day and assume that there are 365 days in a year

Perform your calculation for part (iv) to 3 decimal places.

(b) Tel Co's quick ratio is 0.49. If they sell half of their inventory to pay off part of the bank overdraft, what will happen to their quick ratio?

    A   Stay the same

    B   Increase

    C   Decrease   (2 marks)

(c) In an attempt to improve their liquidity position, Tel Co is considering offering an early settlement discount to its customers. Which TWO of the following outcomes may occur as a result of offering the early settlement discount?

    A   Sales increase

    B   Bad debts increase

    C   Administration cost decrease

    D   Receivables decrease   (2 marks)

(Total: 10 marks)

421 Drive Co is a diverse business, one division of which runs a courier business using a fleet of small vans. The following information has been produced by the manager of the division for the year ended 30 June 20X4:

Revenue	$500,000
Gross profit	$120,000
Operating profit	$50,000
Loan (8% per year)	$60,000
Asset turnover	4

Required:

(a) Using the information provided, calculate (perform your calculations to 2 decimal places):

   (i) Interest cover (1.5 marks)

   (ii) Return on capital employed (ROCE) (2.5 marks)

   (ii) Gearing (2 marks)

(b) The manager of the courier division is retiring this year and his bonus is being paid based on the ROCE percentage of the division.

Which TWO of the following actions could the manager of the courier division have taken in order to improve his bonus?

   A   Delay repairs to the fleet of vans.

   B   Understate the closing inventory of fuel held in the depot.

   C   Include all the revenue for an uncompleted new contract.

   D   Overstate the bad debt provision (2 marks)

(c) The management of Drive Co would like to introduce some more operational measures for performance evaluation.

Which of the following measures would be most useful?

   A   cost per tonne mile

   B   cost per driver hour

   C   van idle time percentage

   D   driver idle time percentage (2 marks)

(Total: 10 marks)

422 Mal Co currently sells 25 styles of sports watches. The market has remained static with an overall revenue of $50 million.

Mal Co is always trying to bring out new designs and colours to try and increase market share or at least maintain it. In order to not fall behind their competitors, Mal Co tries to bring new products to the market quickly. Therefore Mal Co undertakes market research one year, and the results of that market research are incorporated in the new styles/colours that are launched the next year.

Historically, Mal Co have measured their performance by looking for an increase in the revenue and net profit figures and ensuring that there is cash in the bank. A new financial manager has been appointed who is keen to increase the range of performance measures used by Mal Co.

The following data is available:

	Year ended 31 October 20X3	Year ended 31 October 20X4
Revenue	$5.75 million	$6 million
Number of styles	22	25
Net profit	$345,000	$348,000
Market research costs	$200,000	$150,000

Required:

(a) Calculate:

    (i) Net profit percentage for 20X4   (1.5 marks)

    (ii) Market share for 20X4   (1.5 marks)

    (iii) Increase in revenue   (1.5 marks)

    (iv) Revenue per style of watch for 20X4   (1.5 marks)

    (v) Increase in sales per $ of market research   (2 marks)

(b) Mal Co are considering setting up another division selling expensive watches. The two divisions would be run as profit centres, with head office costs being allocated to each division. Managers' bonuses will be dependent on the divisions meeting their targets. Targets that are being considered are:

    (i) Gross profit percentage

    (ii) Contribution

    (iii) Net profit for the division

    (iv) Return on capital employed.

Which of the targets should be used to assess the performance of the divisional manager and provide motivation?

    A   (i) only

    B   (i) and (ii) only

    C   (i), (ii) and (iii) only

    D   All of them   (2 marks)

(Total: 10 marks)

423 Grub Co is a fast food restaurant. Historically they have always relied upon financial measures of performance, concentrating on ratios such as the number of burgers sold and the profit made per burger sold.

Grub Co is now considering implementing a balanced scorecard approach.

Required:

(a) Complete the following statements about the balanced scorecard approach, choosing from the options available:

Before a balanced scorecard approach can be considered, an organisation needs to first have (gap1). The balanced scorecard approach focuses on (gap 2)

Gap 1

A key performance indicator's agreed with management

B a mission statement

C operational plans in place (1 mark)

Gap 2

A short term improvements for the business.

B the long term success of the business. (1 mark)

(b) For each of the following measures, state if they are measuring the financial, customer, internal, or learning perspective of Grub Co's balanced scorecard:

(i) Profit made per burger (1 mark)

(ii) Time taken from the customer ordering food to food being passed to the customer (1 mark)

(iii) Percentage of employees with higher level food hygiene certificates. (1 mark)

(iv) Percentage of burgers cooked but not sold as they are inedible. (1 mark)

(c) The following explanation of benchmarking is incomplete:

There are four types of benchmarking, being (gap 1), competitive, functional and strategic. Comparing the results of Grub Co with McDonalds would be a form of (gap 2) benchmarking

State the words that fill the gaps. (2 marks)

(d) Select the option that has the steps in a systematic benchmarking exercise in the correct order:

A analysis→ planning→ action→ review

B review→ planning→ action→ analysis

C planning→ analysis→ action→ review

D analysis→ action→ review→ planning (2 marks)

(Total: 10 marks)

Section 3

FREE TEXT QUESTIONS (PAPER BASED EXAM ONLY)

A: THE NATURE, SOURCE AND PURPOSE OF MANAGEMENT INFORMATION

424 Explain the difference between management and financial accounting.

425 State the three levels at which planning is undertaken within an organisation.

426 List the eight characteristics of good information.

427 Define a direct cost and an indirect cost. Give an example of each for a book publisher.

428 Define a semi-variable cost and explain how this type of cost changes in relation to changes in the level of activity.

B: COST ACCOUNTING TECHNIQUES

429 Explain what is meant by a marginal cost.

430 Define an overhead cost.

431 By what basis would you apportion the following cost?

   (i) Rent

   (ii) Power

   (iii) Depreciation

   (iv) Cost of canteen facility

   (v) Machine maintenance labour

   (vi) Supervision

432 Explain how a predetermined overhead absorption rate is calculated.

433 Explain why an under- or over-absorption of overhead may occur.

434 Explain what is meant by a' normal loss'.

435 Distinguish between an abnormal loss and an abnormal gain.

436 Define job costing.

437 Define batch costing.

C: BUDGETING

438 What is the difference between a budget and a forecast?

439 Explain what is meant by the principal budget factor

440 Explain what is meant by a flexible budget

441 State two advantages and two disadvantages of a flexible budget.

442 Explain what is meant by a flexed budget

D: STANDARD COSTING

443 Explain what is meant by standard costing

444 Explain what is meant by a standard cost

445 Describe four types of standard.

446 Explain what is meant by a standard hour.

447 Give five possible sources of information from which a standard materials price may be estimated.

448 Explain what is meant by a cost variance?

449 What would an adverse materials price variance and a favourable materials usage variance indicate and what might this be caused by?

450 What does an adverse variable overhead efficiency variance indicate and what might be the cause?

451 What is the relationship between the labour efficiency variance and the variable overhead efficiency variance? Why might the monetary value be different?

452 Explain briefly the possible causes of

(i) A favourable material usage variance;

(ii) A favourable labour rate variance;

(iii) An adverse sales volume contribution variance.

453 Explain the meaning and relevance of interdependence of variances when reporting to managers.

E: PERFORMANCE MEASUREMENT

454 A balanced scorecard measures performance from four perspectives: customer satisfaction, growth, financial success and process efficiency.

Briefly explain these processes.

455 Explain the meaning of responsibility accounting.

456 Discuss one potential problem that might be experienced as a result of using ROI to appraise the performance of the divisions.

Recommend one alternative performance measure that could be used to address this problem.

457 Explain why it might be preferable for Managers not to be involved in setting their own budgets when meeting the budget is used as a basis for performance measurement.

458 Explain the meaning of the term 'critical success factors' in a business giving examples of such factors.

459 Briefly discuss the strengths and weaknesses of ROI and RI as methods of assessing the performance of divisions.

460 Explain two factors that should be considered when designing divisional performance measures.

461 Describe the three elements of VFM

462 What is the difference between internal and functional benchmarking?

463 What are the problems of only using financial performance indicators for measuring the performance of a company?

Section 4

ANSWERS TO SECTION A-TYPE QUESTIONS

SYLLABUS AREA A – THE NATURE, SOURCE AND PURPOSE OF MANAGEMENT INFORMATION

ACCOUNTING FOR MANAGEMENT

1   D

2   A

Reginald is only responsible for costs

3   A

Cost accounting can be used for inventory valuation to meet the requirements of both internal reporting and external financial reporting.

4   B

Cost accounting is not part of financial accounting.

5   A

Qualitative data is normally non-numerical. Information comes from both internal and external sources. Operational information is usually short-term (current) in nature. Quantitative data will be as accurate as possible.

6   C

The manager of a profit centre needs to know about the profits of the centre, i.e. revenues and costs. (Revenues only are appropriate for a revenue centre; costs only for a cost centre; and revenues, costs and assets employed for an investment centre.)

7   C

Lowering a selling price, presumably to increase sales volume, is a short-term decision/plan. The measures in A, B and D are not planning decisions at all: they are all monitoring/control activities.

8

	Management accounts	Financial accounts
Prepared yearly		✓
For internal use	✓	
Contains future information	✓	

9 B

Strategic planning is carried out by senior managers and is concerned with long-term planning. Both quantitative and qualitative information is used.

10 D

(i) ROCE compares profit to capital employed and is not a suitable measure for a profit centre as the manager does not have responsibility for capital employed.

(ii) Cost centres are found in all organisations.

(iii) The manager of a revenue centre is only responsible for revenues, not costs.

11

	YES	NO
Control	✓	
Plan	✓	
Co-ordinate	✓	
Make decisions	✓	
Motivate	✓	

12 A

The mixing and pouring departments are cost centres. The paint is not poured into tins until after the colour adding department so a litre tin would not be a suitable cost unit.

SOURCES OF DATA

13 B

The information should be sufficiently accurate given time and cost constraints. Managers should be made aware of the degree of accuracy of the information.

14 C

15 C

This is the definition of systematic sampling.

ANSWERS TO SECTION A-TYPE QUESTIONS : SECTION 4

16 **B**

Simple random sampling always eliminates selection bias but does not guarantee a representative sample.

17 **D**

Accountant first stratifies the invoices according to value and then selects randomly. Sampling method is stratified.

18 **D**

Option A is not random – it is a systematic sample.

Option B selects only those who are in a class – so it is NOT random.

Option C, again, is not random as it only selects from 10% of colleges (and therefore does not include home study, or the other 90%).

19 **B**

Secondary data is used for one purpose, although it was originally collected for another purpose.

20

	Primary	Secondary
Data collected outside a polling station regarding voters choices	×	
An internet search for the cheapest fuel available in the area		×
Government statistics on the levels of unemployment		×
Data collected by observation on the number of cars flowing through a junction during peak travel hours	×	

21 **D**

22 **C and D**

23 **D**

Useful management information does not necessarily have to be presented in report format, supported by calculations or communicated in writing.

24 **D**

Data consists of numbers, letters, symbols, raw facts, events and transactions which have been recorded but not yet processed into a form which is suitable for making decisions. Information is data which has been processed in such a way that it has a meaning to the person who receives it, who may then use it to improve the quality of decision making.

25 B

Information is processed data. The distinction is that data is unprocessed whereas information is processed.

26 A

External information is obtained from sources outside the organisation. Statistics relating to the consumer price index come from the government. Information about price lists, production volumes and discounts to customers comes from sources within the organisation.

27 A

All of the others have been processed in some way and are information.

28 C

Primary data is data which is used solely for the purpose for which it was collected.

29 D

Information from the Institute of Directors, the tax authorities (e.g. HM Revenue and Customs in the UK) and a government department (national minimum wage) are all examples of external information – i.e. information from an external source.

PRESENTING INFORMATION

30 D

A simple bar chart would show five bars illustrating the different salaries in different regions.

31 C

The sales revenue is dependent on the money spent on advertising. The more advertising that is done the higher the sales revenue should be. Not vice versa

32 63°

241/1,384 × 360 = 62.69° = 63°

33 B

45°/360° × $800,000 = $100,000

34 D

A bar chart is a good way of illustrating total sales month by month. The length of the bar each month is a measure of total sales. The bar can be divided into three parts, to show the amount of sales achieved for each of the three products. This is called a component bar chart.

ANSWERS TO SECTION A-TYPE QUESTIONS : SECTION 4

35   A

36   D

37

	True	False
Area 3 shows the best performance in Q3	✓	
Area 2 sales are consistent quarter on quarter		✓
Q4 has the largest volume of sales across all areas	✓	
Area 1 shows the best performance in Q2	✓	

COST CLASSIFICATION

38   D

Options B and C would begin from 0 and are clearly incorrect. Option A would be similar to the graph given except it would be flat at the top due to the maximum annual charge.

39   A

Variable cost per unit = [($274,000 − $250,000) ÷ (15,000 − 12,000)] = $8

Total fixed cost above 11,000 units = [$274,000 − (15,000 × $8)] = $154,000

Total fixed cost below 11,000 units = (10 ÷ 11) × $154,000 = $140,000

Total cost for 10,000 units = [(10,000 × $8) + $140,000] = $220,000

40   B

As the royalty relates to every unit produced, it is therefore classified as a direct expense.

41

Division	Cost centre	Profit centre	Investment centre
Car sales		✓	
Motorbike sales			✓
Manufacturing	✓		
Finishing			✓

42   B

Inventory is valued at full production cost which includes direct material, direct labour and production overheads.

KAPLAN PUBLISHING

43 A

Supervisor's wages are usually classified as a step cost because a supervisor may be responsible for supervising up to a specific number of workers. However, if output increases such that additional direct labour is required, then an extra supervisor will be required. Rates do step up in cost but that is in relation to time not output i.e. the rates may increase year on year.

44 C

C is the correct answer because a manager is not a cost object but may be linked to a cost centre in a responsibility accounting system.

45 B

Answers A, C and D are incorrect, leaving B as the only possible answer. Depreciation of fixtures is an overhead cost, and could be production, administration or selling and distribution overheads, depending on the nature of the fixtures.

46 D

The cost of the ingredients is a direct material cost.

47 A and B

The prime cost is the total of all direct costs which will include direct expenses as well as direct labour and materials.

48 C

The inventory valuation will be unchanged. Finished goods are valued at the total production cost and the rent of the warehouse would be classed as a distribution cost.

49

Cost	Fixed	Variable	Semi-variable
Director's salary	✓		
Wood		✓	
Rent of factory	✓		
Phone bill – includes a line rental			✓
Factory workers wage		✓	

50 A

The graph shows a reduction in unit variable costs beyond certain output levels. Only Answer A is consistent with this cost behaviour pattern.

ANSWERS TO SECTION A-TYPE QUESTIONS : SECTION 4

51

Cost	Code
Salary of trainee IT consultant	B100
Planning costs to renew lease of the office	C200
Wages of the office manager	B200
Cleaning materials used by cleaner	A200

52

Cost	Materials	Labour	Expenses
Designer skirts	✓		
Heating costs			✓
Depreciation of fixtures and fittings			✓
Cashier staff salaries		✓	

53 B

Managers are not usually classified as direct labour.

54 C

Item B describes the costs of an activity or cost centre. Item A describes cost units. Item D describes budget centres. A cost centre is defined as 'a production or service location, function, activity or item of equipment for which costs are accumulated'.

55 $187,000

	$
Total cost of 18,500 hours	251,750
Total cost of 17,000 hours	246,500
Variable cost of 1,500 hours	5,250

Variable cost per machine hour = $5,250/1,500 machine hours = $3.50.

	$
Total cost of 17,000 hours	246,500
Less variable cost of 17,000 hours (× $3.50)	59,500
Balance = fixed costs	187,000

56 A

The cost is direct as it can be directly attributed to a job. It is an expense because it is invoiced to the company and not a payroll cost.

KAPLAN PUBLISHING 145

3PAPER F2/FMA : MANAGEMENT ACCOUNTING

57 A

	Cost per unit ($) (125 units)	Cost per unit ($) (180 units)
T1	8.00	7.00
T2	14.00	14.00
T3	19.80	15.70
T4	25.80	25.80

Cost types T2 and T4 are variable and T1 and T3 are semi-variable.

58

Cost	Direct	Indirect
Machine operators wages	✓	
Supervisors wages		✓
Resin for golf balls	✓	
Salesmen's salaries		✓

59 A

	$
Total cost of 15,100 square metres	83,585
Total cost of 12,750 square metres	73,950
Variable cost of 2,350 square metres	9,635

Variable cost is $9,635/2,350 square metres = $4.10 per square metre.

Fixed costs can be found by substitution:

	$
Total cost of 12,750 square metres	73,950
Variable cost of 12,750 square metres (× $4.10)	52,275
Fixed costs	21,675

So for 16,200 square metres:

Overheads = $21,675 + (16,200 × $4.10)

= $88,095

60 A

ANSWERS TO SECTION A-TYPE QUESTIONS : SECTION 4

61 B

	$
Total cost of 10,000 units	400,000
Total cost of 5,000 units	250,000
Variable cost of 5,000 units	150,000

Therefore the variable cost per unit = $150,000/5,000 units = $30 per unit.

62 C

	Units		$
Total cost of	20,000	=	40,000
Total cost of	4,000	=	20,000
Therefore variable cost of	16,000	=	20,000

Variable cost per unit = $20,000/16,000 units = $1.25 per unit.

63 D

Graph D is consistent with the cost behaviour for total materials given.

Graph A implies that there is a certain range of activity (just above 15,000 units) when total materials cost is constant.

Graph B implies that total materials cost falls beyond 15,000 units of activity.

Graph C implies that the lower cost per unit for materials applies only to units purchased in excess of 15,000.

64

Cost	Production	Administration	Distribution
Purchases of plastic to make pens	✓		
Managing director's bonus		✓	
Depreciation of factory machinery	✓		
Salaries of factory workers	✓		
Insurance of sales team cars			✓

65 A

For the first 10 hours of calls only the fixed line rental is charged therefore the answer cannot be B or D, which show no costs until a number of hours have passed. Graph C shows a variable cost is charged from nil to a maximum number of hours which is incorrect. The answer is A.

KAPLAN PUBLISHING

66 C

Use the two levels of production above 1,100 units per month for the high-low analysis as at these levels fixed costs are the same.

Units	Total cost ($)
1,400	68,200
1,200	66,600
200	1,600

Variable cost per unit = ($1,600 ÷ 200) = $8

Total fixed cost (above 1,100 units) = [$68,200 – (1,400 × $8)] = $57,000

Total cost for 1,000 units = [($57,000 – $6,000) + (1,000 × $8)] = $59,000

67

Cost	Direct	Indirect
Bricks	✓	
Plant hire for long term contract	✓	
Builders' wages	✓	
Accountants' wages		✓

SYLLABUS AREA B – COST ACCOUNTING TECHNIQUES

ACCOUNTING FOR MATERIALS

68 **$4,350**

{[Buffer Inventory + (EOQ ÷2)] × Annual holding cost per component}

= [700 units + (1500 units ÷ 2)] × $3.00 = $4,350

69 **C**

Materials inventory account

	$000s		$000s
Opening inventory	15	Issued to production	165
Payables for purchases	176	Returned to suppliers	8
Returned to stores	9	Written off	4
		Closing balance (balancing item)	23
	200		200

70 **D**

Option A: A stores ledger account records details of receipts and issues

Option B: A stores requisition will also detail quantity required

Option C: Lead time is the time between placing an order and receiving goods

71 **B**

Perpetual inventory involves recording, as they occur, receipts, issues and the resulting balances of individual items of inventory, in either quantity, or quantity and value.

72 **B**

Indirect materials are overhead costs so debit production overhead. An issue of materials is a credit from the material control account

73

	Materials Requisition	Purchase Requisition	Goods received note	Goods returned note
Material returned to stores from production				✓
Form completed by the stores department detailing inventory requirements		✓		
Materials returned to supplier				✓
	Materials Requisition	Purchase Requisition	Goods received note	Goods returned note
Form completed by stores on receipt of goods			✓	
Form completed by production detailing inventory requirements.	✓			

74 C

A goods requisition note (materials requisition) will be raised by the production department requesting that the stores department obtain material from suppliers. A purchase order will then be raised by the purchasing department and sent to the supplier. Delivery notes and goods received notes are used when supplies are delivered.

75 $131,000

Materials inventory account

	$000s		$000s
Opening inventory	23	Issued to production	144
Purchases (bal fig)	131		
Returned to stores	5		
		Closing balance	15
	159		159

76 B

Standard costs are used to help control the costs of purchases. Regular stocktakes and physical security help to minimise losses from stores.

ANSWERS TO SECTION A-TYPE QUESTIONS : SECTION 4

77   A

In times of rising prices FIFO will give a higher valuation of the closing inventory as the older lower prices will be issued to production.

Opening inventory + units purchased	440
Units sold	(290)
Closing inventory (units)	150
FIFO Closing inventory: 150 units @ $2.78	$417

AVCO	Weighted average cost		$
	100 units @ $2.52		252
	140 units @ $2.56		358
	200 units @ $2.78		556
	440		1,166
Average cost per unit	1,166/440		$2.65
Closing inventory: 150 units @ $2.65			$397.50
FIFO higher by (417 – 397.50)			$19.50

78   B

- If prices have fallen during the year, AVCO will give a higher value of closing inventory than FIFO, which values goods for resale at the latest prices.
- Where the value of closing inventory is higher, profits are higher.

79   B

	Items	Unit value	
		$	$
Opening inventory	6	15	90
January: purchases	10	19.80	198
	16	18	288
February: sales	(10)	18	(180)
	6	18	108
March: purchases	20	24.50	490
	26	23	598
March: sales	(5)	23	(115)
	21	23	483

KAPLAN PUBLISHING

	$
Sales (15 × $30)	450
Cost of sales	
Opening Inventory	90
Purchases	688
Closing Inventory	(483)
	(295)
Gross profit	155

80 **$1,110**

Date		Units	Unit value $	Inventory value $
1 October	Opening inventory	60		720
8 October	Purchase 40 units at $15	40		600
14 October	Purchase 50 units at $18	50		900
		150	14.80	2,220
21 October	Sold 75 units: cost	(75)	14.80	(1,110)
31 October	Closing inventory	75	14.80	1,110

81 **D**

The closing inventory of 12 items (15 − 5 + 10 − 8) comprise

	$
10 items at $3.50 each	35.00
2 items at $3 each	6.00
Cost on a FIFO basis is	41.00

82 **A**

When prices are rising, FIFO will give a higher valuation for closing inventory, because the closing inventory will consist of the most recently-purchased items. Higher closing inventory means lower cost of sales and higher profit.

83 **A**

The formula for the EOQ has the holding cost as the denominator. If this increases, the EOQ will be lower. A lower EOQ means that more orders will have to be placed each year; therefore, the total annual ordering cost will increase.

84 C

		$
Purchase costs	(20,000 units × $40)	800,000
Order costs	(20,000/500 orders × $25/order)	1,000
Holding costs	(500/2 average units × $4/unit)	1,000
Total costs		802,000

85 7,800

Maximum usage × maximum lead time = 520 × 15 = 7,800 units

86 B

Average inventory = ROQ/2 + minimum inventory

= 100/2 + 20 = 70 chairs

87 D

The economic batch quantity determines the batch size for products manufactured internally. The EBQ is the batch size which minimises the total of inventory holding costs and batch set-up costs.

88

Characteristic	FIFO	LIFO	AVCO
Potentially out of date valuation on issues.	✓		
The valuation of inventory rarely reflects the actual purchase price of the material.			✓
Potentially out of date closing inventory valuation.		✓	
This inventory valuation method is particularly suited to inventory that consist of liquid materials e.g. oil.			✓
This inventory valuation method is particularly suited to inventory that has a short shelf life e.g. dairy products.	✓		
This inventory valuation method is suited to a wheat farmer who has large silos of grain. Grain is added to and taken from the top of these silos.		✓	
In times of rising prices this method will give higher profits.	✓		
In times of rising prices this method will give lower profits.		✓	
In times of rising prices this method gives a middle level of profits compared to the other two.			✓
Issues are valued at the most recent purchase cost.		✓	
Inventory is valued at the average of the cost of purchases.			✓
Inventory is valued at the most recent purchase cost.	✓		

3 PAPER F2/FMA : MANAGEMENT ACCOUNTING

89 B

Economic batch quantity = $\sqrt{\dfrac{2C_oD}{C_h\left(1-\dfrac{D}{R}\right)}}$

$= \sqrt{\dfrac{2(1,500)(40,000)}{25\left(1-\dfrac{40,000}{100,000}\right)}} = \sqrt{\dfrac{120\text{million}}{15}} = \sqrt{8,000,000}$

= 2,828 units.

90 A and C

The EOQ model distinguishes between holding costs (A and C) and ordering costs B and D)

91 C

Annual holding cost = {[Buffer inventory + (EOQ ÷2)] × Annual holding cost per component}

= {[500 + (2000 ÷2)] × 2} = 3,000

92 $4.49

Let Co = ordering cost

185 = √{[2 × Co × (4 × 2,000)] ÷ [0.05 × 42]}

185 = √(16,000 × Co ÷ 2.1)

Co = 185^2 × 2.1 ÷ 16,000 = $4.49

Note that the period for demand must be the same as that given for holding cost. As holding cost is given as an annual figure quarterly demand must be converted to annual demand by multiplying by 4.

93

Statement	True	False
In periods of rising prices, FIFO gives a higher valuation of closing inventory than LIFO or AVCO.	✓	
In periods of falling prices, LIFO gives a higher valuation of issues of inventory than FIFO or AVCO.		✓
AVCO would normally be expected to produce a valuation of closing inventory somewhere between valuations FIFO and LIFO.	✓	
FIFO costs issues of inventory at the most recent purchase price.		✓
AVCO costs issues of inventory at the oldest purchase price.		✓
LIFO costs issues of inventory at the oldest purchase price.		✓
FIFO values closing inventory at the most recent purchase price.	✓	
LIFO values closing inventory at the most recent purchase price.		✓
AVCO values closing inventory at the latest purchase price.		✓

ANSWERS TO SECTION A-TYPE QUESTIONS : **SECTION 4**

94   C

Using the formula given: EOQ = √[(2 × 120 × 48,000) ÷ (0.10 × 80)] = 1,200 units

95   A

	$
Purchasing cost (48,000 × $80)	3,840,000
Ordering cost (48,000 ÷ 1,200) × $120	4,800
Holding costs [(1,200 ÷ 2) × $80 × 0.10]	4,800
Total cost	3,849,600

96   C

	$
Purchasing cost (48,000 × $80 × 0.99)	3,801,600
Ordering cost (48,000 ÷ 2,000) × $120	2,880
Holding costs [(2,000 ÷ 2) × $80 × 0.99 × 0.10]	7,920
Total cost	3,812,400

Annual total saving = $(3,849,600 – 3,812,400) $37,200

97   C

Order quantity = 750 units

		$
Order cost	600 × 12 × 8.75/750 =	84
Holding cost	0.1 × 2.24 × 750/2 =	84
Purchase cost	600 × 12 × 2.24 =	16,128
Total cost		16,296

Order quantity = 2,000 units

		$
Order cost	600 × 12 × 8.75/2,000 =	31.50
Holding cost	0.1 × 2.24 × 0.95 × 2,000/2 =	212.80
Purchase cost	600 × 12 × 2.24 × 0.95 =	15,321.60
		15,565.90

Change in cost = $16,296 – $15,566 = saving of $730.

98 C

Annual production rate = 500 × 50 = 25,000

Using the economic batch quantity formula given,

2,000 = √{(2 × setup cost × 5,000)/(1.5 × (1–5,000/25,000))}

$2,000^2$ = 2 × setup cost × 5,000/1.5 × 0.8

Setup cost = $2,000^2$ × 1.5 × 0.8 /2 × 5,000

Setup cost = $480

99 A

The sales process may begin with an enquiry from a potential customer. The customer then places the order. When the order is delivered, the customer is sent an invoice. The customer is then required to pay the invoice within the credit period allowed.

100 C

A purchase originates with a requisition for goods, by either the stores department or a user department. The buying department negotiates purchase terms and issues a purchase order to send to the supplier. The supplier processes the order and delivers the goods. A delivery note is provided with the goods when delivered. The stores department then produces its own document to record the goods received (the goods received note), which includes additional details such as the code for the item of inventory. The supplier sends the invoice when the goods are delivered. Invoices received from suppliers are called purchase invoices.

When the invoice has been checked and confirmed as correct, a cheque requisition might be prepared, for a senior manager to sign, asking the relevant section of the accounts department to prepare a cheque and send it to the supplier.

101 A

Option B describes a purchase requisition note. Option C describes a delivery note. Option D describes a material requisition note.

102 A and C

103 B

A material requisition note is a document used internally for requisitioning a quantity of inventory from the stores.

104 A and B

An invoice is matched to a goods received note and a purchase order before payment is made.

105 A

The introduction of buffer inventory would increase average stockholding. So (iii) is correct. Total holding cost would increase but holding costs per unit should stay the same or may even decrease so (i) is incorrect. The Economic Order Quantity is dependent on the cost of ordering per order, annual demand and unit holding costs, none of which should change so EOQ should not be affected. Total ordering cost should not be affected.

106 A

The EOQ calculation does not include safety inventory.

107 C

A materials returned note is used to record materials sent back to stores from production. A materials requisition note is a request from production to stores for material. A goods received note is produced by the stores department to record the receipt of goods into stores and a delivery note is provided by the supplier when goods are delivered.

108 D

The price should be checked against a copy of the purchase order, or possibly against an official price list from the supplier. The purchase order should show the price the buyer has negotiated, including any discount. The quantity ordered might not be the same as the quantity delivered, so the quantity on the invoice should be checked against the goods received note. The goods received note is preferable to the delivery note, because the delivery note might be signed quickly, before the stores department has had time to check for faulty items or to carry out a detailed count of the items delivered.

ACCOUNTING FOR LABOUR

109 A

Statement (i) is correct, because extra spending would be incurred to pay the additional temporary staff. Statement (ii) is incorrect, because total spending on labour is unaffected when spare capacity is utilised and idle time reduced. Statement (iii) is also incorrect, because total labour costs will not be increased by switching labour from working on one product to working on another product. However, there is an opportunity cost in switching labour. This is the total contribution forgone by no longer producing and selling the original product. This opportunity cost would be a relevant cost in evaluating a decision to switch the labour from one product to the other. Even so, as worded, statement (iii) is incorrect.

110 B

Unless the overtime can be traced to a specific product or job, it will be treated as an indirect production cost and absorbed into units using the normal absorption basis.

111 B

The employee took 44 hours to perform 94 operations. The standard time allowed per operation is 37.5 minutes, giving a standard time of (94 × [37.5/60]) = 58.75 hours to perform 94 operations. The time saved is therefore (58.75 − 44) = 14.75 hours. The bonus payable will be:

(time taken/time allowed) × time saved × hourly rate

= (44/58.75) × 14.75 × $6.50 = $71.80 (rounded).

The gross wage for Week 24 will therefore be (44 hours × $6.50) + $71.80 = $357.80.

112 A

Direct labour costs are credited to wages and salaries and debited to work-in-progress.

113

Cost	Direct	Indirect
Basic pay for production workers	✓	
Supervisors wages		✓
Bonus for salesman		✓
Production workers overtime premium due to general pressures.		✓
Holiday pay for production workers		✓
Sick pay for supervisors		✓
Time spent by production workers cleaning the machinery		✓

114 $300,000

(4,800 units × 5 hours × $10 per hour) ÷ 0.80 = $300,000

115 C

If direct labour is working at below the agreed productivity level, this will lead to lower output than planned. This could have been caused by factors which resulted in idle time, such as (ii) and (iii) but would not lead to idle time.

116 B

40 × $15 = $600. Note that the basic element of overtime is classified as a direct cost. The normal treatment of overtime premium is for it to be treated as an indirect cost.

117 B

Average employment during the year was (5,250 + 5,680)/2 = 5,465

The labour turnover rate = 360/5,465 × 100 = 6.6%

118 D

Expected hours to make actual output/actual hours = 192/180 × 100% = 106.7%

119 D

Actual hours/budget hours = 180/185 × 100% = 97.3%

120 C

Expected hours to make actual output/budget hours = 192/185 × 100 = 103.8%

121

Payment method	Basic rate	Overtime premium	Overtime payment
This is the amount paid above the basic rate for hours worked in excess of the normal hours.		✓	
This is the total amount paid per hour for hours worked in excess of the normal hours.			✓
This is the amount paid per hour for normal hours worked.	✓		

122 B

	$
600 units at $0.40	240.00
50 units at $0.50	25.00
10 units at $0.75	7.50
For 660 units	272.50

123 B

Piecework is an incentive-based pay scheme, because employees are paid more for producing more, and so have an incentive to be more productive. A day rate scheme, in which employees receive a basic rate of pay, does not offer any incentive to be more productive.

124 A

(500 × 0.50) + (100 × 0.55) + (20 × 0.60) = $317

125

Payment method	Time-rate	Piecework	Piece-rate plus bonus
Labour is paid based solely on the production achieved.		✓	
Labour is paid extra if an agreed level of output is exceeded.			✓
Labour is paid according to hours worked.	✓		

KAPLAN PUBLISHING

3PAPER F2/FMA : MANAGEMENT ACCOUNTING

126   C AND D

A timesheet and a job card are used to allocate labour costs to cost units. An attendance record card is used for payroll purposes and an employee record card details all of the information relating to an employee.

127   D

Grade B labour costs are an indirect labour cost. Grade A labour costs are direct costs for the basic pay, but overtime premium is treated as an indirect cost if the overtime hours are worked as general overtime. If overtime is worked for a specific purpose, such as a customer order, the cost of the overtime premium paid to direct labour is treated as a direct cost. The direct labour cost for the week is therefore:

	$
30 hours worked in overtime	
Cost of basic pay, Grade A labour (30 × $10)	300
Cost of overtime premium for hours on specific order (10 × 50% of $10)	50
	350

128   D

Good units = 512 – 17 – 495

200 units at $0.15 + 295 units at $0.20 = $89

129   C

Labour turnover ratio = 8/55 × 100% = 14.55%

ACCOUNTING FOR OVERHEADS

130 $58,540

Reapportion service cost centre K first as it does work for service cost centre J but not vice versa.

	G	H	J	K
Overhead cost ($)	40,000	50,000	30,000	18,000
Reapportion K	9,000	7,200	1,800	(18,000)
			31,800	
Reapportion J		9,540	(31,800)	
		$58,540		

131   C

An absorption rate is used to determine the full cost of a product or service. Answer A describes overhead allocation and apportionment. Absorption does not control overheads, so answer D is not correct.

132 D

X = 46,000 + 0.1Y

Y = 30,000 + 0.2X

X = 46,000 + 0.1(30,000 + 0.2X) = 46,000 + 3,000 + 0.02X

0.98X = 49,000 and X = 50,000

Y = 30,000 + 0.2(50,000) = 40,000

P = 95,000 + 0.4(50,000) + 0.3(40,000) = 127,000

Alternatively use the repeated distribution method as follows;

	P	Q	X	Y
Overhead cost ($)	95,000	82,000	46,000	30,000
Reapportion X	18,400	18,400	(46,000)	9,200
Reapportion Y	11,760	23,520	3,920	(39,200)
Reapportion X	1,568	1,568	(3,920)	784
Reapportion Y	235	470	78	(784)
Reapportion X	31	31	(78)	16
Reapportion Y	5	9	2	(16)
Rounding	1	1		
	$127,000			

133 B

	$
Actual expenditure	56,389
Absorbed cost (12,400 × 1.02 × $4.25)	53,754
Total under-absorption	2,635

134 A

Under- or over-absorption is determined by comparing the actual overhead expenditure with the overhead absorbed.

135 D

Fixed production overheads are over-absorbed when actual expenditure is less than budget and/or actual production volume is higher than budget.

136 D

Over-absorbed overheads increase profit, and so are recorded as a credit entry in either an over-absorbed overhead account or directly as a credit in the statement of profit and loss. The matching debit entry could be either in the WIP account or the production overhead control account, depending on the costing system used.

137 C

Indirect labour is a costing concept. The double entry is:

Wages control		Overhead control	
	Indirect labour × (overheads)	Indirect labour × (wages)	

138 $18.00

Machining hours	=	(4,000 × 0.5 hour) + (4,000 × 1.0 hour)
	=	6,000 hours
Assembly hours	=	(4,000 × 0.2 hour) + (4,000 × 0.25 hour)
	=	1,800 hours
Machining absorption rate	=	$\dfrac{\$120{,}000}{6{,}000 \text{ hours}}$
	=	$20 per hour
Assembly absorption rate	=	$\dfrac{\$72{,}000}{1{,}800 \text{ hours}}$
	=	$40 per hour
Fixed overhead per unit of Pye	=	(0.5 hour × $20) + (0.2 hour × $40)
	=	$18

139 D

Cost apportionment is concerned with sharing costs according to benefit received.

140 B

	$
Actual overheads	694,075
Under recovery	(35,000)
Overhead absorbed	659,075

OAR = $\dfrac{\$659{,}075}{32{,}150}$

= $20.50

ANSWERS TO SECTION A-TYPE QUESTIONS : SECTION 4

141 B

	$
Actual overheads	245,600
Over-absorption of overheads	6,400
Overheads absorbed	252,000

Absorption rate = $252,000/45,000 hours = $5.60 per direct labour hour.

142 $14.00

	$
Actual overhead	138,000
Over-absorbed overhead	23,000
Therefore amount of overhead absorbed	161,000

Hours worked = 11,500.

Therefore absorption rate per hour = $161,000/11,500 hours = $14 per hour.

143 C

Let the overhead apportioned from service department C be $C.

Let the overhead apportioned from service department D be $D.

$\quad$ C = 3,200 + 0.20D .....(1)

$\quad$ D = 4,600 + 0.10 C ....(2)

Substitute (1) in (2)

$\quad$ D = 4,600 + 0.10 (3,200 + 0.20D)

$\quad$ D = 4,600 + 320 + 0.02D

$\quad$ 0.98D = 4,920

$\quad$ D = 5,020.

Substitute in (1)

$\quad$ C = 3,200 + 0.20 (5,020)

$\quad$ C = 4,204.

Total overhead for department X = 5,000 + 0.50C + 0.20D

$\quad$ = 5,000 + 0.50 (4,204) + 0.20 (5,020)

$\quad$ = 5,000 + 2,102 + 1,004

$\quad$ = 8,106.

Note: You could have reached the same answer by using the repeated distribution method.

KAPLAN PUBLISHING

3PAPER F2/FMA : MANAGEMENT ACCOUNTING

144 B

Fixed overhead absorption rate = $36,000/18,000 = $2 per direct labour hour.

Variable overhead absorption rate = $9,000/18,000 = $0.50 per direct labour hour.

	$	$
Overheads absorbed:		
Fixed (20,000 × $2)		40,000
Variable (20,000 × $0.50)		10,000
Total overhead absorbed		50,000
Overheads incurred:		
Fixed	39,000	
Variable	12,000	
Total overhead incurred		51,000
Under-absorbed overhead		1,000

145 B

$(\$3,000 \times \frac{700}{8,000}) + (\$11,000 \times \frac{80}{400}) + (\$7,000 \times \frac{20}{70}) = \$(262.50 + 2,200 + 2,000) = \$4,462.50$

146 C

$60 \times \frac{12}{120} + 100 \times \frac{8}{100} = \$14$

ABSORPTION AND MARGINAL COSTING

147 C

Total variable cost	= $(4 + 5 + 3 + 3) = $15
Contribution per unit	= $20 – $15 = $5
Total contribution earned	= $5 × 800 = $4,000

148 D

If a sales value of $100 per unit is assumed then the original and revised situations will be:

	Original	Revised
	$	$
Selling price	100	110
Variable cost/unit	60	60
Contribution/unit	40	50

Fixed costs do not affect contribution and if sales volume is unchanged then the overall change in contribution can be measured using the contribution per unit:

$\frac{(50 - 40)}{40} \times 100 = 25\%$

ANSWERS TO SECTION A-TYPE QUESTIONS : SECTION 4

149 12,500 UNITS

Absorption costing profit = $2,000 > Marginal Costing profit = $(3,000)

Therefore Production > Sales by $5,000

$5,000 = OAR × number of units change in inventory

$5,000 = $2 × number of units change in inventory

Therefore number of units change in inventory = $\dfrac{\$5,000}{\$2}$ = 2,500

If Sales = 10,000 units, therefore Production = Sales + 10,000 units = 12,500 units.

150 B

Contribution per unit = $(10 – 6) = $4.

	$
Total contribution (250,000 × $4)	1,000,000
Fixed overheads (200,000 × $2)	400,000
Profit	600,000

151 B

Fixed production overhead per unit = $48,000/12,000 units = $4.

Sales volume is less than production volume by 280 units.

In absorption costing, this means that some fixed overheads will be carried forward in the closing inventory value. Fixed overheads in this addition to inventory = 280 units × $4 = $1,120.

In marginal costing, all fixed overheads incurred in a period are charged as an expense against profit. Marginal costing profit would therefore be lower than the absorption costing profit by $1,120.

152 $56,850

As inventory decreases over the period, the cost of sales will be higher with absorption costing, since they will include fixed overhead in the opening inventory now sold. The extra cost of sales (and thus reduction in profit) = (8,500 – 6,750) × $3 = $5,250.

This means that since profit will be lower with absorption costing by $5,250, the absorption costing profit will be $(62,100 – 5,250) = $56,850.

153 C

There was an increase in inventory in the period; therefore the absorption costing profit is higher than the marginal costing profit (because a larger amount of fixed overhead is carried forward in the closing inventory value).

	$
Marginal costing profit	72,300
Less: fixed costs in opening inventory (300 units × $5)	(1,500)
Add: fixed costs in closing inventory (750 units × $5)	3,750
Absorption costing profit	74,550

154

	Marginal costing	Absorption costing
The cost of a product includes an allowance for fixed production costs.		✓
The cost of a product represents the additional cost of producing an extra unit.	✓	

155 B

Production volume exceeded sales volume, so the profit with absorption costing is higher than the profit with marginal costing.

Fixed overheads in inventory = $30,000/750 = $40 per unit, therefore total fixed overhead in closing inventory (absorption costing) = 250 units × $40 = $10,000. Profit with marginal costing is therefore lower by $10,000.

156 D

		$000
Variable production cost of boats	45/750 × 700	42
Fixed production costs (absorbed)	30/750 × 700	28
Production costs of 700 boats		70
Closing inventory of 100 boats		(10)
Production cost of 600 sold		60
Under-absorbed overhead	30–28	2
Variable selling costs	5/500 × 600	6
Fixed selling costs		25
		93
Profit		15
Sales revenue	90/500 × 600	108

ANSWERS TO SECTION A-TYPE QUESTIONS : SECTION 4

157 B

In an absorption costing system, the fixed cost per unit would be $3,000/15,000 units = $0.20 per unit.

Budgeted profit with marginal costing   = Contribution – Fixed costs

= $26,000 – $3,000 = $23,000.

By switching to absorption costing, in a period when inventory levels increase by 2,000 units, absorption costing profit would be higher by 2,000 units × fixed cost per unit, i.e. by 2,000 × $0.20 = $400.

Absorption costing profit = $23,000 + $400 = $23,400.

158 A

Total contribution will increase as sales volume increases, but the contribution per unit will be constant as long as the sales price and variable cost per unit are unchanged. Overhead is not absorbed to product unit so there is no under/over absorption of overhead. Marginal costing does provide useful information for decision making because it highlights contribution, which is a relevant cash flow for decision-making purposes.

159 C

Increase in inventory of 34,000 – 31,000 = 3,000 units.

Difference in profits of $955,500 – $850 500 = $105,000

OAR = $105,000/3,000 = $35 per unit

Level of activity = $1,837,500/£35 = 52,500 units

160 A

Profit figures only differ if inventory changes in the period.

161 B

Suppose we start with the following situation.

	$ per unit
Selling price	100
Variable cost	(60)
Contribution	40

Sales 1,000 units; total contribution $40,000

A, B and C would have the following effects.

	A $ per unit	B $ per unit
Selling price	100	110
Variable cost	(54)	(60)
Contribution	46	50
Total contribution	$46,000	$50,000

C : Total contribution = $40,000 × 1.1

= $44,000

Fixed costs are irrelevant since we are concerned with *contribution*.

162 $78.10

Inventory is valued at full production cost i.e. both fixed and variable production costs.

$(33.00 + 45.10) = $78.10

COST ACCOUNTING METHODS

163 C

	Job 812 $
Direct materials	60
Direct labour	40
Direct expenses	20
Prime cost	120
Production overheads ($40 ÷ 8) × $16	80
Non-production overheads (0.6 × $120)	72
Total cost – Job 812	272

164 D

Statement A is correct. Job costs are identified with a particular job, whereas process costs (of units produced and work in process) are averages, based on equivalent units of production.

Statement B is also correct. The direct cost of a job to date, excluding any direct expenses, can be ascertained from materials requisition notes and job tickets or time sheets.

Statement C is correct, because without data about units completed and units still in process, losses and equivalent units of production cannot be calculated.

Statement D is incorrect, because the cost of normal loss will usually be incorporated into job costs as well as into process costs. In process costing this is commonly done by giving normal loss no cost, leaving costs to be shared between output, closing inventory and abnormal loss/gain. In job costing it can be done by adjusting direct materials costs to allow for normal wastage, and direct labour costs for normal reworking of items or normal spoilage.

165 D

	Job 1 $	Job 2 $	Total $
Opening WIP	8,500	0	8,500
Material in period	17,150	29,025	46,175
Labour for period	12,500	23,000	35,500
Overheads (see working)	43,750	80,500	124,250
	81,900	132,525	214,425

Working

Total labour cost for period = $(12,500 + 23,000 + 4,500) = $40,000

Overhead absorption rate = $140,000/$40,000 = 3.5 times the direct labour cost.

166 C

	Job 3 $
Opening WIP	46,000
Labour cost for period	4,500
Overheads (3.5 × $4,500)	15,750
Total production costs	66,250
Profit (50%)	33,125
Selling price of 2,400 boards	99,375

Selling price of one board = $99,375/2,400 = $41.41

3PAPER F2/FMA : MANAGEMENT ACCOUNTING

167 **$21,150**

This can be calculated as a balancing figure in the process account.

Process account

	kg		$		kg		$
Input (balance)	3,000		21,150	Output	2,800	(× 7.50)	21,000
Abnormal gain	100	(× 7.50)	750	Normal loss	300	(× 3)	900
			21,900				21,900

Alternatively:

	$
Cost of output (2,800 × 7.50)	21,000
Scrap value of normal loss (300 × 3)	900
	21,900
Less: Value of abnormal gain (100 × 7.50)	(750)
Cost of input	21,150

168 **B**

	Units
Input	13,200
Less: Normal loss (13,200 × 10/110)	1,200
Expected output	12,000

	$
Process costs	184,800
Less: scrap value of normal loss (1,200 × $4)	4,800
Cost of good output	180,000

Cost for each expected unit of output = $180,000/12,000 = $15.

Finished units of output, and also abnormal loss and abnormal gain units will be valued at this amount.

169 **$11.60**

Cost per unit = net process costs/expected output

= (9,000 + 13,340 − 300)/2,000 − 100

= $22,040/1,900 = $11.60.

170 A

	$
Opening WIP	1,710
Completion of opening WIP (300 × 0.40 × $10)	1,200
Units started and completed in the month	
(2,000 – 300) × $10	17,000
Total value (2,000 units)	19,910

171 C

	Materials equivalent units
Opening inventory completed (400 × 0%)	0
Units started and finished in the period (800 – 400)	400
Closing inventory (600 × 75%)	450
Total equivalent units produced in the period	850

172 $77,616

Sales value of production:

Product W: (12,000 × 10) = $120,000

Product X: (10,000 × 12) = $120,000

Therefore joint production costs are apportioned W:X in the ratio 1:1

Amount apportioned to product X is (776,160 ÷ 2) = $388,080

20% of X's production is in closing inventory @ (0.2 × 388,080) = $77,616

173 D

	Units
J: (6,000 – 100 + 300) =	6,200
K: (4,000 – 400 + 200) =	3,800
	10,000

Joint costs apportioned to J: (6,200 ÷ 10,000) × $110,000 = $68,200

PAPER F2/FMA : MANAGEMENT ACCOUNTING

174 C

Total sales revenue = ($18 × 10,000) + ($25 × 20,000) + ($20 × 20,000) = $1,080,000

Joint costs to be allocated = $277,000 − ($2 × 3,500)

= $270,000

Allocation rate = ($270,000/1,080,000) = 0.25 of sales revenue.

Joint costs allocated to product 3 = 0.25 × ($20 × 20,000)

= $100,000

= ($100,000/20,000 units) $5 per unit

175 C

		$
Prime cost		6,840.00
Fixed overhead	$300,000/60,000 × 156	780.00
		7,620.00
Profit	20% × 7,620.00	1,524.00
Job price		9,144.00

176 D

Abnormal loss units are valued as one equivalent unit of cost, the same as units of good production. This cost is credited to the process account and debited to the abnormal loss account. The scrap value of abnormal loss is then credited to the abnormal loss account (with the matching debit to bank).

177 A

		kg
Input		12,750
Output	Normal loss	510
	Finished goods	12,700
		13,210
Abnormal gain		460

178 A

	kg
Material input	2,500
Normal loss (10%)	(250)
Abnormal loss	(75)
Good production achieved	2,175

179 C

Direct labour hours = $400 ÷ $8 = 50 hours

	$
Prime cost (300 + 400)	700
Production overheads (50 × $26)	1,300
Total production cost	2,000
Non-production overheads (1.20 × 700)	840
Total cost	2,840

180 B

Finished output = (20,000 + 110,000 − 40,000) = 90,000 units.

Closing WIP = 40,000 units 50% complete = 20,000 equivalent units.

Cost per equivalent unit (in $000) = $132,000/(90,000 + 20,000)

= $1,200 per equivalent unit/finished car.

181 B

The total value of WIP will increase. The number of equivalent units will increase which will cause the cost per unit to decrease.

182 C

Normal loss is 10% of input = 20 kg.

Actual loss = 50 kg

Abnormal loss = 50 − 20 = 30 kg

Equivalent units of output:

	Total	Materials	Conversion
Finished output	150	150	150
Abnormal loss	30	30	15
Total EUs	180	180	165

Cost per equivalent unit:

Material cost = 200 × $4 = $800

Labour and overheads cost = 100 × $15 + $1,000 = $2,500

Materials = $800/180 = $4.44

Conversion = $2,500/165 = $15.15

Total cost of completed unit = $(4.44 + 15.15) = $19.59

183 10,200 EU

Flow of units

2,000 + 12,000 = 11,000 (bal) + 3,000

Units started and finished = 11,000 – 2,000	=	9,000
Closing WIP = 3,000 × 20%	=	600
Opening WIP = 2,000 × 30%	=	600
		10,200

184 C

Cost per unit = ($1,200 + $3,500 – $30)/(200 – 30) = $27.47 per kg

$27.47 × 190 = $5,219

185 A

Process costing is used for companies producing large quantities of similar products (homogeneous output) and these are valued at average cost.

186 A

	$
Direct materials 120 kg @ $4 per kg	480
Direct labour: 3 hours @ $10 per hour	30
20 hours @ $5 per hour	100
Hire of machine: 2 days @ $100 per day	200
Overhead 23 hours @ $8 per hour	184
	994
Price charged	942
Loss	(52)

187 C

		$
Prime cost		6,840.00
Fixed overhead	$300,000/60,000 × 156	780.00
		7,620.00
Profit	20% × 7,620.00	1,524.00
Job price		9,144.00

188 B

Basic hours = 110 × $8 = $880

Overtime hours = 110 – (3 × 30) = 20 hours

Overtime premium = 20 × 8 × 0.25 = $40

Total direct labour cost = $880 + $40 = $920

189 D

A service industry is an industry not involved in agriculture, mining, construction or manufacturing. Transport industries are service industries.

190 A and C

Services are usually (but not always) associated with labour and labour costs, low material costs and relatively high indirect costs. Service costing also makes use of composite cost units, such as the cost per guest/day, cost per patient/day, cost per passenger/mile and so on.

191 D

A charitable foundation will be a not-for-profit organisation.

192 B

Average cost per occupied bed per day

$$= \frac{\text{Total cost}}{\text{Number of beds occupied}}$$

$$= \frac{\$100{,}000 + \$5{,}000 + \$22{,}500}{6{,}450 \times 2} = \$9.88$$

or 127,500/(200 × 2 + 30) × 30 = $9.88

193 B

	Company A	Company B
Cost per:	$	$
Millions of units sold	208	104
Thousand consumers	750	625
$m of sales	33,333	20,000

The cost per unit sold, per consumer and per $m of sales are all higher for Company A than for Company B indicating that Company A is less efficient than Company B.

194 B

$$\text{Room occupancy \%} = \frac{\text{Total number of rooms occupied daily}}{\text{Rooms available to be let}} \times 100\%$$

$$= \frac{200 + 30}{240 + 40} \times 100\% = 82.1\%$$

195 C

A service is intangible and inventory cannot be held. Services generally have a high level of fixed costs and there are often difficulties in identifying a suitable cost unit.

ALTERNATIVE COSTING PRINCIPLES

196 A

ABC is fairly complicated, is a form of absorption (not marginal) costing and is particularly useful when fixed overheads are high and not primarily volume driven.

197

	Internal failure costs	External failure costs	Inspection costs	Prevention costs
Cost of the a customer service team		✓		
Cost of equipment maintenance				✓
Cost of operating test equipment			✓	

A customer service team deals with customer queries and complaints from outside the organisation, typically after goods have been delivered to the customer. The costs of this team arise from quality failures and are preventable. They are external failure costs. Maintenance is intended to prevent machine breakdowns and so to prevent quality failures, and they are therefore prevention costs. Test equipment is used for inspection.

198 C

External failure costs are those incurred due to poor quality of goods delivered to customers; therefore this includes compensation costs.

Appraisal costs are those incurred in the measuring of quality of output; therefore this includes test equipment running costs.

199 B

	$
Sales revenue: 600 units × $450	450
Return required: 20% × $450	90
	———
Target cost per unit:	360

200 D

A product's life cycle costs are very inclusive; none of these would be excluded.

201 A

Value analysis involves identify why and how customers value a product to enable cost savings to be made without compromising the value to the customer.

202 B

ANSWERS TO SECTION A-TYPE QUESTIONS : **SECTION 4**

SYLLABUS AREA C – BUDGETING

NATURE AND PURPOSE OF BUDGETING

203 B

The main purposes of budgeting are to plan and control. Budgets also usually give authority to spend up to the budget limit. Budgets are not primarily used for decision making.

204 D

The budget committee is made up from senior managers of each function in the organisation.

205 D

A budget manual will include all of the options.

206 C

STATISTICAL TECHNIQUES

207 A

As advertising will hopefully generate sales, advertising is the independent variable and sales revenue the dependent; i.e. advertising is x and sales revenue is y.

		$
High	Sales revenue from $6,500 of advertising	225,000
Low	Sales revenue from $2,500 of advertising	125,000
	Sales revenue from $4,000 of advertising	100,000

Sales revenue for each $1 of advertising = $100,000/$4,000 = $25.

	$
Sales revenue from $6,500 of advertising	225,000
Sales revenue from $6,500 of advertising (x $25)	162,500
Sales revenue with no advertising	62,500

This gives a function of sales revenue = $62,500 + $25x, where x is the spending on advertising.

208 C

In the formula C = 1,000 + 250P, 1,000 represents the weekly fixed costs and 250 the variable cost per unit.

209 2.04

$C = F + Vx$

$14,520 = 7,788 + V(3,300)$

$6,732 = 3,300V$

$V = 2.04$

210 A

Coefficient of determination = r^2 = 0.6 × 0.6 = 0.36 = 36%

211 A

$$a = \frac{\Sigma y}{n} - \frac{b \Sigma x}{n}$$

$$a = \frac{183,000}{5} - \frac{4,200 \times 21}{5} = [36,600 - 17,640] = 18,960.$$

If there are 2 salesmen in the month, expected costs will be: 18,960 + (4,200 × 2) = 27,360

212 A

This question is a simple test of your understanding of the meaning of the elements in a regression analysis formula. Statements (i) and (ii) are correct, but statement (iii) is wrong. The total value of x multiplied by the total value of y would be written as Σx Σy, not as Σxy.

213 0.69

You should use the formulae provided in the examination (formulae sheet)

$$b = \frac{(11 \times 13,467) - (440 \times 330)}{(11 \times 17,986) - (440)^2} = \frac{2,937}{4,246} = 0.6917 = 0.69$$

214 B

Σx = Σ Advertising expenditure = 100,000

Σy = Σ Sales revenue = 600,000

n = number of pairs of data = 5

215 A

216 B

Σy = 17,500 + 19,500 + 20,500 + 18,500 + 17,000 = 93,000

Σx = 300 + 360 + 400 + 320 + 280 = 1,660

a = (93,000 ÷ 5) − (29.53 × 1,660 ÷ 5) = 8,796.04

ANSWERS TO SECTION A-TYPE QUESTIONS : SECTION 4

217 B

+1 represents perfect positive correlation.

−1 represents perfect negative correlation.

The nearer to 0 the correlation coefficient the less correlation between the variables.

218 A

$$b = \frac{n \Sigma xy - \Sigma x \Sigma y}{n \Sigma x^2 - (\Sigma x)^2}$$

= [(5 × 23,091) − (129 × 890)] ÷ [(5 × 3,433) − (129^2)] = 1.231

$$a = \frac{\Sigma y}{n} - b \frac{\Sigma x}{n}$$

= (890 ÷ 5) − [(1.231 × 129) ÷ 5] = 146 (nearest whole number)

219 B

The correlation coefficient must be between +1 and −1.

220 C

221 A

Quarter	'Real' sales
1	$\frac{109}{100}$ × 100 = 109.0
2	$\frac{120}{110}$ × 100 = 109.1
3	$\frac{132}{121}$ × 100 = 109.1
4	$\frac{145}{133}$ × 100 = 109.0

The 'real' series is approximately constant and keeping up with inflation.

222 C

Current cost = $5 × 430 ÷ 150 = $14.33

KAPLAN PUBLISHING

3PAPER F2/FMA : MANAGEMENT ACCOUNTING

223 B

	P0	P1	Q1	P1Q1	P0Q1
Flour	0.25	0.30	10,000	3,000	2,500
Eggs	1.00	1.25	5,000	6,250	5,000
Milk	0.30	0.35	10,000	3,500	3,000
Potatoes	0.05	0.06	10,000	600	500
				13,350	11,000

$$= \frac{13,350}{11,000} \times 100 = 121.36$$

224 C

	P0	P1	Q0	P1Q0	P0Q0
Flour	0.25	0.30	8,000	2,400	2,000
Eggs	1.00	1.25	4,000	5,000	4,000
Milk	0.30	0.35	10,000	3,500	3,000
Potatoes	0.05	0.06	6,000	360	300
				11,260	9,300

$$= \frac{11,260}{9,300} \times 100 = 121.08$$

225 C

See table below (226)

226 D

See table below

	Sales volume (units)	Trend	Variation
January	172,100		
February	149,600		
March	165,800	166,040	−240
April	182,600	171,040	11,560
May	160,100	176,040	−15,940
June	197,100	181,040	16,060
July	174,600	186,040	−11,440
August	190,800	191,040	−240
September	207,600	196,040	11,560
October		201,040	−15,940
November		206,040	16,060
December	199,600	211,040	−11,440

ANSWERS TO SECTION A-TYPE QUESTIONS : SECTION 4

227 D

228 A

($2,000 × 120 ÷ 160) = $1,500

229 B

(5,000 + 23 × 4,000 − 1,500) = 95,500

230 A

y = 3,000 + (150 × 3)

y = 3,450

Actual − trend = variation

3,500 − 3,450 = +50

231 C

y = 3,000 + (150 × 15)

y = 5,250

Trend + variation = actual

5,250 + 50 = 5,300

232 C

Development, Introduction, and Decline

233 A

	P_0	P_1	Q_0	$P_1 Q_0$	$P_0 Q_0$
F	11	12	21	252	231
G	22	26	56	1,456	1,232
H	18	18	62	1,116	1,116
I	20	22	29	638	580
J	22	23	31	713	682
				4,175	3,841

$= \dfrac{4,175}{3,841} \times 100 = 108.7$

KAPLAN PUBLISHING

3PAPER F2/FMA : MANAGEMENT ACCOUNTING

234 C

	P_0	P_1	Q_1	P_1Q_1	P_0Q_1
F	11	12	25	300	275
G	22	26	52	1,352	1,144
H	18	18	79	1,422	1,422
I	20	22	35	770	700
J	22	23	36	828	792
				4,672	4,333

$$= \frac{4,672}{4,333} \times 100 = 107.8$$

235 B and C

A database (rather than a spreadsheet) contains records and files and is most suitable for storing large volumes of data

236 C

The formula for correlation is $r = \dfrac{n\Sigma xy - (\Sigma x)(\Sigma y)}{\sqrt{\{n\Sigma x^2 - (\Sigma x)^2\}\{n\Sigma y^2 - (\Sigma y)^2\}}}$

Here n is 7 and to construct the formula we need to identify the appropriate totals from row 11.

A and D are wrong because they use n = 6.

B is wrong because it lacks the square root required for the bottom of the formula.

237 B

All are said to be advantages of spreadsheet software with the exception of (i) security.

A computer-based approach exposes the firm to threats from viruses, hackers and general system failure.

238 D

Budgeted production for a period = budgeted sales for the period – opening inventory of finished goods for the period + closing inventory of finished goods for the period.

Sales	F3
(Opening Inventory)	(10% F3)
Closing Inventory	10% F4
Production	90% F3 + 10% F4

Or [(0.9*F3) + (0.1*F4)]

239 B

Using graphics is usually done using the chart wizard not the format cells option.

ANSWERS TO SECTION A-TYPE QUESTIONS : **SECTION 4**

BUDGET PREPARATION

240 94,400

Units required	100,000
Less: opening inventory	(14,000)
Add: closing inventory required (14,000 × 0.6)	8,400
	94,400

241 B

The production budget is the sales budget **minus** opening inventory of finished goods **plus** closing inventory of finished goods.

242 B

4,500/0.9 = 5,000 litres.

Note that opening and closing inventories are relevant to the material purchases budget, not the material usage budget.

243 A

The material usage budget is the material requirement for the units produced.

244 C

		$
Product A	1,750 units × 3 hours/unit × $7 /hour	36,750
Product B	5,000 units × 4 hours/unit × $7 /hour	140,000
		176,750

245 D

A principal budget factor is defined as the factor acting as the constraint on the overall level of activity in a period. It is often sales demand, but could be a key production resource or cash.

246 D

If 1X and 2Y are sold, this earns $250. Call this a batch.

The company wants to earn $100,000.

$100,000/250 = 400 batches.

This is 400 X and 800 Y

KAPLAN PUBLISHING

247 B

	Units
Budgeted sales	2,300
Current inventory	(400)
Closing inventory required	550
Production	2,450

248 A

Machine hours required:

X	1,000 hours
Y	2,400 hours
Z	600 hours
Total	4,000

Overhead budget:

Variable: 4,000 × $2.30 = $9,200

Fixed: 4,000 × $0.75 = $3,000

Total = $(9,200 + 3,000) = $12,200

249 C

	Clockwork clown	Wind-up train	Total
Budgeted sales	450	550	
+ Closing inventory	30	40	
– Opening inventory	(20)	(50)	
Production budget	460	540	
Material usage	× 2 kg	× 1 kg	
Material usage budget	920 kg	540 kg	1,460 kg

250 A

Total material usage	1,460 kg
+ Closing inventory	60
– Opening inventory	(50)
Total material purchases	1,470 kg
Material purchases budget = 1,470 × $5	$7,350

ANSWERS TO SECTION A-TYPE QUESTIONS : SECTION 4

251 A

	Clockwork clown	Wind-up train
Budgeted sales	450	550
+ Closing inventory	30	40
– Opening inventory	(20)	(50)
Production budget	460	540
Labour	× 18/60	× 30/60
	138 hours	270 hours

Total   408 hours × $8 = $3,264

252 D

Paid hours including idle time = 2,400 × 100/80 = 3,000

Budgeted labour cost = 3,000 hours × $10 = $30,000

253 A

A continuous budget does not have to be prepared for a whole year; the budget period could be a month or a quarter.

254 B

	$
July's sales $25,000 × 20%	5,000
June's sales $20,000 × 60%	12,000
May's sales $30,000 × 10%	3,000
	20,000

255 B

	$
February sales 45% × $28,000	12,600
March sales 50% × $28,000	14,000
	26,600

KAPLAN PUBLISHING

256 C

	Units
Sales of Z	10,000
Opening inventory	(14,000)
Reduction in inventory	12,000
Production	8,000

	Litres
Usage at 2 litres per Z	16,000
Opening inventory	(20,000)
Closing inventory	15,000
Purchases	11,000

Therefore cash cost is 11,000 × $4 = $44,000.

257 B

Consider sales of $100

Cash receipt in month of sale = 45% × 100 = $45

This is after a discount of 10%, so must represent 45/0.9 = $50 of sales value

Irrecoverable debts = 20% of any month's sales = $20

The receipts in month 2 must be the rest of the sales = 100 – 50 – 20 = $30

$$\$30/\$100 \times 100 = 30\%$$

258 A

	$
Cash sales 10% of $40,000	4,000
Receivables	
$36,000 × 40% × 96%	13,824
$36,000 × 50%	18,000
	35,824

259 A

Payment = $(450,000 × 70% + 18,000 + 10,000) = $343,000

260 D

	$
Opening balance	7,000
Receipts from payables	
Re previous month's sales (= opening receivables)	15,000
Re this month's sales (= half this month's sales)	35,000
Payments to payables (= opening payables)	(40,000)
Expenses	(60,000)
Bank overdraft	(43,000)

261 B

Depreciation and the provision for doubtful debts are not cash flow items and so would not be included in a cash budget.

262 C

The amount budgeted to be paid to suppliers in September is $289,000.

		$
25% of September purchases	25% × $280,000, less 5% discount (i.e. x 95%)	66,500
70% of August purchases	70% × $300,000	210,000
5% of July purchases	5% × $250,000	12,500
Total payments		289,000

263 B

The cash received in the third month of trading was $2,200

	$
Cash sales in month 3: (25% of $2,800)	700
Cash from credit sales in month 3: (25% of $2,800, less 10%)	630
Cash from credit sales in month 2: (40% of $1,800)	720
Cash from credit sales in month 1: (10% of $1,500)	150
	2,200

264 A

The amount to be shown in the cash budget for May in respect of payments for fixed production overhead is $23,000.

Cash to be paid in May for April fixed overhead

= $(93,000/3) − $8,000 depreciation

= $23,000

The amount to be shown in the cash budget for May in respect of payments for variable production overhead is $60,000.

Cash to be paid in May for April variable overhead = $(93,000 × 2/3)/2 = $31,000

Cash to be paid in May for May variable overhead = $(87,000 × 2/3)/2 = $29,000

$60,000

FLEXIBLE BUDGETS

265 B

Option C is a fixed budget and option D is a rolling budget. Option A is incorrect as a flexible budget includes all costs.

266 C

A flexible budget helps to control resource efficiency by providing a realistic budget cost allowance for the actual level of activity achieved. Control action can therefore be more effective because the effects of any volume change have been removed from the comparison.

267 A

A fixed budget is a budget prepared for a planned single level of activity. It does not ignore inflation (option C is incorrect) and it includes direct costs as well as overhead costs (option D is incorrect). A fixed budget can be prepared for a single product as well as a mix of products (option B is incorrect).

268 B

Statement (i) is correct. A fixed budget is prepared for a single level of activity.

Statement (ii) is incorrect. A flexible budget is prepared during the budget period but it recognises only the effects of changes in the volume of activity.

Statement (iii) is correct. A major purpose of the budgetary planning exercise is to communicate an organisation's objectives to its managers.

ANSWERS TO SECTION A-TYPE QUESTIONS : SECTION 4

269 B

Flexed budget:

	Budget	Flexed Budget	Actual
Sales (units)	120,000	100,000	100,000
	$000	$000	$000
Sales revenue	1,200	1,000	995
Variable printing costs	360	300	280
Variable production overheads	60	50	56
Fixed production cost	300	300	290
Fixed administration cost	360	360	364
Profit/(Loss)	120	(10)	5

270 C

271 B

	Original Budget	Flexed Budget
Sales units	1,000	1,200
	$	$
Sales revenue	100,000	120,000
Direct material	40,000	48,000
Direct labour	20,000	24,000
Variable overhead	15,000	18,000
Fixed overhead	10,000	10,000
Profit	15,000	20,000

272 A

Variable costs are conventionally deemed to be constant per unit of output.

273 $2,560,000

Total variable cost per unit = Direct material + Direct labour + Variable overheads

Total variable cost per unit = 30 + 46 + 24 = $100

Flexed for 13,600 units = $1,360,000

Total fixed costs for the period = $80 × 15,000 units = 1,200,000

Total cost for 13,600 units = $1,360,000 + $1,200,000 = $2,560,000

KAPLAN PUBLISHING 189

274 A

VC per unit = (112,500 − 100,000)/(75 − 50) = $500

Fixed cost in total = 100,000 − (500 × 50) = $75,000

Total overhead for 80% activity = $75,000 + (500 × 80) = $115,000

275 $354,000

(36,000 + 176,000)/4,000 × 5,000 = 265,000

265,000 + 89,000 = $354,000

CAPITAL BUDGETING

276 C

	$	AF	$
Outflow	(80,000)	1.000	(80,000)
Cash inflow $25,000 each year for 8 years	25,000	6.463	161,575
Present value of project			$81,575

277 C

The $9,500 and $320,000 are future incremental cash flow figures so are relevant. The $8,000 is sunk (past) cost so it is not a relevant cost.

278 $8,634

Year	Cash inflow/(outflow)	Discount factor @ 8%	Present value $
0	(60,000)	1.000	(60,000)
1	23,350	0.926	21,622
2	29,100	0.857	24,939
3	27,800	0.794	22,073
Net present value			8,634

279 C

Try 20%

Year	Cash $	20%	PV $
0	(75,000)		(75,000)
1 – 5	25,000	2.991	74,775
			(225)

$$\text{IRR} = 15 + \frac{8,800}{(8,800 - -225)} \times 5$$

$$\text{IRR} = 15 + \frac{8,800}{9,025} \times 5$$

IRR = 19.88% therefore 20% to the nearest 1%

280 C

Statement A is not correct as there is no company policy to confirm the payback is appropriate. Statement B is not correct as the IRR and ROCE are not comparable. Statement D is not correct as the IRR is always a positive whether the project is acceptable or not.

Statement C is correct as the IRR must be greater than the cost of capital (the discount rate) used to appraise the project as the project has a return therefore a positive NPV at the company's cost of capital so the project should go ahead.

281 A

Year	Cash $	11%	PV $
0	(300,000)		(300,000)
1 – 10	40,000	5.889	235,560
			(64,440)

282 $44,000

	Current $000	$000		Expansion $000	$000
Food sales	200		× 40%	80	
Drink sales	170		× 40%	68	
		370			148
Food costs	145		× 40%	58	
Drink costs	77		× 40%	31	
Staff costs	40		40/4 × 1	10	
Other costs	20		× 60% × 40%	5	
		282			104
Cash flow		88			44

283 D

Year	Cash ($000)	17% discount factor	Present value ($000)
0	(400)	1.000	(400.00)
1	210	0.855	179.55
2	240	0.731	175.44
3	320	0.624	199.68
			154.67

284 14%

$$10 + \frac{\$17,706}{(\$17,706 - -\$4,317)} \times (15-10) = 14\%$$

285 C

Depreciation is not a cash flow so needs to be added back to profit to calculate cash flows.

Depreciation on straight line basis = ($400,000 − $50,000)/5 = $70,000 per year

Year	Profit ($)	Cash flow ($)	Cumulative cash flow ($)
0		(400,000)	(400,000)
1	175,000	245,000	(155,000)
2	225,000	295,000	140,000

Payback period = 1 + 155/295 years = 1.5 years to nearest 0.1 years

286 D

287 D

288 C

Using the formula $[(1.021)^4 - 1] \times 100 = 8.67\%$

289 C

$(1 + 0.1/4)^4 - 1 \times 100 = 10.38\%$

$(1 + 0.12/12)^{12} - 1 \times 100 = 12.68\%$

$(1 + 0.012)^{12} - 1 \times 100 = 15.39\%$

$(1 + 0.03)^4 - 1 \times 100 = 12.55\%$

ANSWERS TO SECTION A-TYPE QUESTIONS : **SECTION 4**

BUDGETARY CONTROL AND REPORTING

290   D

291   D

The production-line manager does not control prices or rates

292   A

Feedforward control compares the budgeted outcome with the current best forecast of what actual results will be. For example, suppose that the budgeted sales for the year are 1,000 units. After six months, actual sales for the year to date might be 450 units, and the current estimate of what actual sales will be for the year might be 900 units. Using feedforward control, management will identify a difference of 100 units in sales (1,000 – 900 units) and try to take measures for increasing sales up to the 1,000 target by the end of the year, by selling 550 units in the second half of the year.

293   A

The expenditure variance is measured by the difference between the flexed budget and the actual cost.

The expenditure variance is $15,000 favourable.

The volume variance is measured by the difference between the original budget and the flexed budget.

The volume variance is $130,000 adverse.

294   B

The volume variance is the difference between the fixed and flexible budget.

295   D

296

	Budgeted $	Actual $	Variance value $	A/F
RECEIPTS				
Cash sales	4,200	3,800	400	A
Credit sales	42,100	48,000	5,900	F
Total receipts	46,300	51,800	5,500	A
PAYMENTS				
Cash purchases	500	1,200	700	A
Credit purchases	28,000	35,100	7,100	A
Labour costs	2,500	3,200	700	A
Capital expenditure	8,000	6,000	2,000	F
General expenses	4,000	3,800	200	F
Total payments	43,000	49,300	6,300	A
Net cash flow	3,300	2,500	800	A

BEHAVIOURAL ASPECTS OF BUDGETING

297 C

Statement (i) is incorrect. Managers at an operational level are more likely to know what is realistically achievable than a senior manager imposing budget targets from above. Statement (ii) is arguably correct: participation in budgeting could improve motivation. Statement (iii) is correct: imposed budgets should be much quicker to prepare, because less discussion time and negotiation time is required than with participative budget-setting.

298 C

Top-down budgeting are imposed budgets so are less likely to motivate managers. Bottom–up budgeting involve more participation from managers, therefore they are more likely to motivate managers.

299 C

Where there is goal congruence, managers who are working to achieve their own personal goals will automatically also be working to achieve the organisation's goals. Although the use of aspiration levels to set targets (option D) is likely to help in the achievement of goal congruence, it is not of itself a definition of the term.

ANSWERS TO SECTION A-TYPE QUESTIONS : SECTION 4

300 B

A is incorrect as participation in the budget procedure should improve morale and thus improve performance. C is incorrect as more knowledge at base level will improve decision making. D is incorrect as the staff themselves can be involved in the budget process so will have input and knowledge of the budget.

301 C

Budgetary slack is also called budget bias. Budget holders may sometimes try to obtain a budget that is easier to achieve. They may do this either by bidding for expenditure in excess of what they actually need or, in the case of sales budgets, by deliberately setting easy revenue targets.

302 A

Managers are more likely to be motivated to achieve the target if they have participated in setting the target. Participation can reduce the information gap that can arise when targets are imposed by senior management. Imposed targets are likely to make managers feel demotivated and alienated and result in poor performance. Participation however can cause problems; in particular, managers may attempt to negotiate budgets that they feel are easy to achieve which gives rise to 'budget padding' or budgetary slack, this can result in budgets that are unsuitable for control purposes. If targets are too easy then managers will not need to be motivated to achieve their goals.

SYLLABUS AREA D – STANDARD COSTING

STANDARD COSTING SYSTEMS

303 C

The standard labour rate should be the expected rate/hour, but allowing for standard levels of idle time. For example, if the work force is paid $9 per hour but idle time of 10% is expected, the standard labour rate will be $10 per hour, not $9.

304 C

This is a definition of 'basic standards'. Basic standards are not widely used in practice.

305 D

This is a definition of 'attainable standards'. Attainable standards are widely used in practice.

306

Statement	True	False
A variance is the difference between budgeted and actual cost.		✓
A favourable variance means actual costs are less than budgeted.	✓	
An adverse variance means that actual income is less than budgeted.	✓	

VARIANCE CALCULATIONS AND ANALYSIS

307 $8,500

Standard contribution on actual sales	$10,000
Add: favourable sales price variance	$500
Less: Adverse total variable costs variance	$(2,000)
Actual Contribution	**$8,500**

The standard contribution on actual sales has been obtained by adjusting the budgeted contribution by the sales volume contribution variance. Therefore, this variance should have been ignored in answering the question.

ANSWERS TO SECTION A-TYPE QUESTIONS : SECTION 4

308 A

Sales contribution on actual sales	$50,000
Less adverse total variable costs variance	$3,500
Actual contribution	$46,500

No adjustment is required for the favourable sales volume contribution variance: it would have already been added to the budgeted contribution to arrive at the standard contribution from actual sales given in the question. The total fixed costs variance, along with budgeted fixed costs, appears in a reconciliation statement below the actual contribution.

309 D

Ah × Ar =	$176,000	
	Rate variance	$36,000 A
Ah × Sr = 14,000 hrs × $10	$140,000	
	Efficiency variance	$25,000 F
Sh × Sr = 3 hrs × 5,500 units × $10	$165,000	

310 D

Expenditure variance:

Monthly budgeted production (10,800/12) = 900 units

Monthly budgeted expenditure
(Flexed budget) $
   Fixed costs (900 × $4)   3,600
   Variable costs (800 × $6)   4,800
   Total expected expenditure   8,400
   Actual expenditure   8,500

   Expenditure variance   100   (A)

Volume variance:

This only applies to fixed overhead costs:

Volume variance in units (900 – 800)	100 units (A)
Standard fixed overhead cost per unit	$4
Fixed overhead volume variance	$400 (A)

311 C

	$	
Expenditure variance	36,000	(A)
(= 10% of budgeted expenditure)		
Therefore budgeted expenditure 36,000/10 × 100	360,000	
Actual expenditure 36,000/10 × 110	396,000	

KAPLAN PUBLISHING   197

312 C

Fixed production overhead cost per unit = $120,000/20,000 units = $6 per unit.

Standard units ×	OAR	
21,000	$6	$126,000
Budget units ×	OAR	
20,000	$6	$120,000
	Volume variance	$6,000 F

313 A

Budgeted hours of work = 30,000 units × 4 hours = 120,000 hours.

Fixed overhead absorption rate/hour = $840,000/120,000 hours = $7/hour.

Actual hours ×	OAR	
123,000	$7	$861,000
Budget hours ×	OAR	
120,000	$7	$840,000
	Capacity variance	$21,000 F

314 C

Budgeted fixed overhead cost per unit = $48,000/4,800 units = $10.

	$	
Budgeted fixed overhead	48,000	
Expenditure variance	2,000	(A)
Actual fixed overhead	50,000	

	$
Actual fixed overhead	50,000
Under-absorbed fixed overhead	8,000
Absorbed overhead	42,000

Units produced = Absorbed overhead/Absorption rate per unit

= $42,000/$10 = 4,200 units.

315 C

Less experienced staff are likely to be paid at a lower rate and therefore the labour rate variance will be favourable.

Usage of materials is likely to be unfavourable as the staff are less experienced, thus there will be more wastage and a higher level of rejects.

316 D

Usage of materials is likely to be adverse as the materials are sub-standard, thus there will be more wastage and a higher level of rejects.

Time spent by the labour force on rejected items that will not become output leads to higher than standard time spent per unit of output.

317 $3.80

Ah × Ar = 29,000 × **$3.80**	$110,200		
		Rate variance	$5,800 F
Ah × Sr = 29,000 × $4	$116,000		
		Efficiency variance	$4,000 F
Sh × Sr = 30,000 × $4	$120,000		

318 D

Ah × Ar = 10,080 × $0.87	$8,770		
		Rate variance	$706 A
Ah × Sr = 10,080 × $0.80	$8,064		
		Efficiency variance	$256 F
Sh × Sr = **2.08** × 5,000 × $0.80	$8,320		

319 C

Standard hours ×	OAR		
710 × 0.5	$12	$4,260	
Actual hours ×	OAR		
378 – 20	$12	$4,296	
	Efficiency variance	$36 A	

320 C

Ah × Ar = 4,800 × $0.87	$7,700		
		Expenditure variance	$500 A
Ah × Sr = 4,800 × $1.50	$7,200		
		Efficiency variance	$300 F
Sh × Sr = 500 × 10 × $1.50	$7,500		

321 $1,100

(Budgeted quantity – Actual quantity) × standard profit per unit

(1,000 – 900) × ($50 – $39) = $1,100

322 A

Fixed overhead expenditure variance = Actual cost – Budgeted cost = $1,250 A

Actual overhead = Budgeted cost – 2%

2% = $1,250

Actual overhead = 1,250/2 × 98 = $61,250

PAPER F2/FMA : MANAGEMENT ACCOUNTING

323 C

324 A

The sales volume variance under marginal costing is based on standard contribution per unit and under absorption costing is based on standard profit per unit. Standard contribution is either greater than or the same as standard profit depending on the value of fixed costs. Therefore the variance will either be higher or the same.

325 D

See working below (326)

326 A

Aq × Ap =	$173,280
	Price variance **$9,120 F**
Aq × Sp = 45,600 ×$ 4	$182,400
	Usage variance $15,200 A
Sq × Sp = **3,344 units** × 12.5 kg × $4	$167,200

327 B

The purchase of the new machine is likely to result in improved efficiency but higher depreciation costs.

328 D

Standard hours ×	OAR	
3,700 × 1.5	$2.40	$13,320
Budget hours ×	OAR	
4,000 × 1.5	$2.40	$14,400
	Volume variance	$1,080 A

329 C

(i) will affect the sales price variance.

330 D

Aq × Sp = 1,566 × (76,500/1,500)	$79,866
	Usage variance $5,916 A
Sq × Sp = (580 × 1,500/600) × (76,500/1,500)	$73,950

331 1,950 KG

Aq × Sp = **1,650** × $2	$3,300	
	Usage variance	$300 A
Sq × Sp = 500 × 3 kg × $2	$3,000	

500 units did use	**1,650**
Less opening inventory	(100)
Plus closing inventory	400
Material purchases in kg	1,950

332 A

Aq × Ap =	$23,839
	Price variance $783 F
Aq × Sp = 1,566 × ($25,500/1,500)	$26,622

333 C

Expenditure variance = Budget cost − actual cost	= (8,000 × 15) − (8,500 × 17)
	= $24,500 A
Volume variance (8,500 − 8,000) × $15	= $7,500 F
Total variance	= $17,000 A

334 A

The standard contribution per unit is $(50 − 4 − 16 − 10 − 1) = $19.

Sales volume variance

= (Budgeted sales volume − actual sales volume) × Standard contribution per unit

= (3,000 − 3,500) × $19

= $9,500

335 C

Sales volume variance

= (Budgeted sales volume − actual sales volume) × Standard profit per unit

= (10,000 − 9,800) × $5

= $1,000 A

336 B

Actual hours ×	OAR	
5,500	$15	$82,500
Budget hours ×	OAR	
5,000	$15	$75,000
	Capacity variance	$7,500 F

337 B

Ah × Ar = 117,600
　　　　　　　　　　　Rate variance　$8,400 A
Ah × Sr = 28,000 × **$3.90**　$109,200
　　　　　　　　　　　Efficiency variance　$3,900 F
Sh × Sr = **29,000** × $3.90　$113,100

338

	Absorption costing	Marginal costing
Sales volume contribution variance		✓
Fixed overhead capacity variance	✓	
Fixed overhead volume variance	✓	
Sales volume profit variance	✓	
Fixed overhead efficiency variance	✓	

RECONCILIATION OF BUDGETED AND ACTUAL PROFIT

339　$38,635

	$
Budgeted contribution	43,900
Sales price variance	(3,100)
Sales volume contribution variance	(1,100)
Direct material price variance	1,986
Direct material usage variance	(2,200)
Direct labour rate variance	(1,090)
Direct labour efficiency variance	(512)
Variable overhead expenditure variance	1,216
Variable overhead efficiency variance	(465)
Actual contribution	38,635

ANSWERS TO SECTION A-TYPE QUESTIONS : **SECTION 4**

340 A

Budgeted profit	$250,000
Sales price variance	$1,500
Sales volume variance	($2,100)
Materials price variance	($4,200)
Materials usage Variance	$1,500
Labour rate variance	$900
Labour efficiency Variance	($450)
Fixed overhead expenditure variance	$1,750
Fixed overhead volume variance	($1,800)
Actual profit	$247,100

341 D

Actual profit	$7,170
Sales price variance	($200)
Sales volume variance	($350)
Materials price variance	($250)
Materials usage Variance	$120
Labour rate variance	$450
Labour efficiency Variance	$800
Fixed overhead expenditure variance	($600)
Fixed overhead volume variance	$860
Budgeted profit	$8,000

342 $2,750F

Budget profit	$19,000
Sales price variance	($1,200)
Sales volume variance	$2,000
Materials price variance	$3,500
Materials usage Variance	($4,200)
Labour efficiency Variance	($1,500)
Fixed overhead expenditure variance	$1,500
Fixed overhead volume variance	($750)
	$18,350
Actual profit	$21,100
Labour rate variance	$2,750F

KAPLAN PUBLISHING

SYLLABUS AREA E – PERFORMANCE MEASUREMENT

PERFORMANCE MEASUREMENT OVERVIEW

343 A

344 A and B

The manager of a profit centre can exercise control over revenues and controllable costs, but has no influence concerning the capital invested in the centre.
Contribution (A) would be a useful performance measure because a profit centre manager can exercise control over sales revenue and variable costs. Controllable profit (B) would also be useful as long as any overhead costs charged in deriving the profit figure are controllable by the profit centre manager. Apportioned central costs would not be deducted when calculating controllable profit. Return on investment (C), and residual income (D) would not be useful because they require a measure of the capital invested in the division.

345 D

346 A

PERFORMANCE MEASUREMENT – APPLICATION

347 B

Controllable assets = 80,000 ÷ 0.25 = $320,000

RI = $80,000 − ($320,000 × 0.18) = $80,000 − $57,600 = $22,400

348 C

Cost per patient is a measure of output related to input

349 B

Reducing mortality rates is likely to be a stated objective of the hospital and as such is a measure of output, or effectiveness

350 B

Contribution is calculated as sales revenue less variable costs. The manager of a cost centre will not be responsible for the revenue therefore this is not an appropriate measure.

351 C

Class sizes are the result of the number of pupils educated (output), the number of teachers employed (input) and how well the timetable is organised in using those teachers.

ANSWERS TO SECTION A-TYPE QUESTIONS : SECTION 4

352 C

Revenue is most likely to be based on the quantity delivered and the distance travelled. Cost per tonne miles gives a measure of both quantity and distance

353 C

RI = Net profit before interest − (10% × invested capital)

Therefore £240,000 = £640,000 − (10% × invested capital)

So 10% × invested capital = £400,000

Therefore invested capital = £4m

$$ROI = \frac{\text{Net profit before interest}}{\text{Invested capital}} = \frac{£640,000}{£4,000,000} \times 100 = 16\%$$

354 C

Actual output in standard hours = 1,100 × 2 = 2,200 hours

Budgeted production hours = 2,000 hours

Production/volume ratio = 2,200/2,000 = 1.1 or 110%

355 A

Actual output in standard hours = 180 × 0.6 = 108 hours

Actual production hours = 126 hours

Efficiency ratio = 108/126 = 0.857 or 86%

356 D

Actual production hours = 61 hours

Budgeted production hours = 50 × 1.2 = 60 hours

Capacity ratio = 61/60 = 1.017 or 102%

357 D

358 B

(i) and (ii) are financial indicators and (iv) is a risk indicator

359 D

360 A

361 A

(150 + 300 + 25)/(230 + 90) = 1.48

KAPLAN PUBLISHING

362 B

(300 + 25)/(230 + 90) = 1.02

363 A

(300/2,700) × 365 = 40.55 days

364 B

(230/1,300) × 365 = 64.58 days

365 D

(150/1,300) × 365 = 42.12 days

366 C

(550/2,700) × 100 = 20.3%

367 C

550/75 = 7.33 times

368 B

16,000/38,512 = 41.5%

369 A

(22,000 + 12,506 + 5,006)/15,000 = 2.63

370 C

(12,506 + 5,006)/15,000 = 1.17

371 D

27,657/(38,512 + 16,000) × 100 = 50.7%

372 C

12,506/64,323 × 365 = 70.97 days

373 A

(1,250/2,250) × 100 = 55.6%

374 B

(825/2,250) × 100 = 36.7%

ANSWERS TO SECTION A-TYPE QUESTIONS : SECTION 4

375 D

490/275 = 1.8

376 D

(240/2,250) × 365 = 39 days

377 A

(275/1,000) × 365 = 100 days

378 B

(150/1,000) × 365 = 55 days

379 D

RI = Net profit before interest − (10% × invested capital)

Therefore $50,000 = $80,000 − (10% × invested capital)

So 10% × invested capital = $30,000

Therefore invested capital = $300,000

ROI = 80,000/300,000 × 100 = 26.67 = 27% to the nearest whole number

380 B

Original profit	=	$2,000,000 × 12%	=	$240,000
New profit	=	$240,000 + $90,000	=	$330,000
New capital employed	=	$2,000,000 + $500,000	=	$2,500,000
Residual income	=	$330,000 − (10% × $2,500,000)	=	$80,000

381 D

Efficiency compares the standard hours produced with the hours actively worked

(9,300 hours ÷ 9,200 hours) × 100% = 101%.

382 C

383 C

Capacity ratio × Efficiency ratio = Activity ratio

Capacity ratio = 103.5/90 × 100% = 115%

384 D

This is the definition of the activity (PV) ratio.

385 A

The capacity ratio measures the number of hours actually worked compared to budget. A ratio that is greater than 100% means that more actual hours were worked than budget.

386 D

The most appropriate measure of ROI will include only assets available to earn profit during the year and will not include interest payable.

Thus ROI will be $6 million/($35 million – $4 million) = 19.4%

387 C

| ROI before project | = | 360/1,600 | = | 22.5% |
| ROI after project | = | 385/(1,600 + 130) | = | 22.3% |

Therefore management would reject this project, if ROI is used as an evaluation criterion.

| Residual value before project | = | 360 – (1,600 × 0.18) | = | $72,000 |
| Residual value after project | = | 385 – (1,730 × 0.18) | = | $73,600 |

Therefore management would accept this project if residual income is used as an evaluation criterion.

388 A and B

389 C

390 D

ROI = financial

Warranty claims = customer

New products = learning and growth

391

Average class size	✓
Tutor grading by students	
Pass rates	
Percentage room occupancy	✓

392 B

Calculate the average number of operations per employee:

	Budget	Actual
Department A	200	200
Department B	140	220
Department C	150	150
Department D	75	80

ANSWERS TO SECTION A-TYPE QUESTIONS : **SECTION 4**

COST REDUCTIONS AND VALUE ENHANCEMENT

393

Setting targets for cost centre managers	✓
Reducing the cost budget	Cost reduction
Cost variance analysis	✓
Increasing sales volume	Would lead to an increase in cost

394

Control costs	✓
Reduce costs	✓
Improve sales	VA looks at costs not sales
Increase the value of the product	The value of the product should not change if value analysis is applied correctly

395 A

396

	Value analysis	Value engineering
Reviews current products to reduce costs	✓	
Reviews products at the design stage to reduce costs		✓

397 D

All the techniques listed in the question could be used to monitor and control costs.

MONITORING PERFORMANCE AND REPORTING

398 D

Measuring the budgeted number of quotations actually issued would be monitoring the output and activity of the department but it would not be helpful in improving the department's performance in terms of the accuracy or speed of quotations in the scenario described.

399 C

400 B

401 C

KAPLAN PUBLISHING

PAPER F2/FMA : MANAGEMENT ACCOUNTING

402 B

Machine rental is more likely to be arranged at a higher level

403 A

The purchasing manager has some control of raw material prices

404 B

405

	Effectiveness	Efficiency	Economy
Have the waiting lists been reduced?	×		
What was the average cost per patient treated?		×	
Have mortality rates gone down?	×		
Did the hospital spend more or less on drugs this year?			×
What was the average spend per bed over the period?		×	
Did the hospital spend more or less on nurses' wages?			×

Effectiveness = links outputs with objectives, are the outputs achieving the objectives of the organisation.

Efficiency = links inputs to outputs, maximum output being achieved with the resources available

Economy = input measure, relationship between money spent and inputs

406 GAP 1 – EFFECTIVENESS, GAP 2 - EFFICIENCY

Effectiveness looks at results/outputs. The reduction in visitor numbers indicates poor effectiveness in YU. Inputs were constant (the same amount was spent on advertising as in previous years), suggesting YU was economical, but the medium used was less efficient than in previous years.

407 D

408 C

409 B

410 1 = COMPETITIVE, 2 = INTERNAL, 3 = FUNCTIONAL

411 D

Section 5

ANSWERS TO SECTION B-TYPE QUESTIONS

BUDGETING

412 (a) In the equation y = a + bx, b represents the variable cost per unit.

Using the formula b = [(6 × 209,903) − (61.25 × 20,430)]/[(6 × 630.56) − 61.25^2] = $254

(b) B

(c) The variable cost per unit = [($3,860 × 106/102) − ($3,098 × 106/104)]/(12 − 9) = $284

(d) B and D

(e) A

413 (a) (i) Steel required for production = 220 × 1.5 kg + 170 × 2 kg = 670 kg

(ii) Opening inventory = (220 × 1.5 kg + 170 × 2 kg) × 0.5 = 335 kg

(iii) Closing inventory = (240 × 1.5 kg + 180 × 2 kg) × 0.5 = 360 kg

(b) =B1 − B2 + B3

(c) (i) False

(ii) True

(iii) False

(iv) False

(d) A and C

414 (a) Cash received in March = $15,000 × 0.5 × 0.97 + $12,000 × 0.5 = $13,275

(b) Payment to suppliers in March = $21,000 × 0.75 + $2,000 − $3,000 = $14,750

(c) Chain base index in February $15,000/$12,000 × 100 = 125

Chain base index in March $21,000/$15,000 × 100 = 140

(d) Gap 1 B

Gap 2 B

PAPER F2/FMA : MANAGEMENT ACCOUNTING

415 (a) Payback period = $18,750/$5,000 = 3.75 years = 3 years 9 months.

(b) (i) Gap 1 more

Gap 2 inflation

(ii)

Year	Cash flow × DF	Cumulative cash flow
0	−18,750	−18,750
1	5,000 × 0.926 = 4,630	−14,120
2	5,000 × 0.857 = 4,285	−9,835
3	5,000 × 0.794 = 3,970	−5,865
4	5,000 × 0.735 = 3,675	−2,190
5	5,000 × 0.681 = 3,405	+1,215

As the cash flows arise at the end of the year payback will be 5 years

Alternative working

The project will payback when $18,750 = $5,000 × AF $_{1-n}$ @ 8%

AF$_{1-n}$ = 3.75

The annuity factor for 4 years is 3.312, and 5 years is 3.993. Therefore the payback must occur at 5 years as the cash flows arise at the end of the year.

(c) Net present value = $18,750 + ($5,000 × 4.623) = $4,365

(d) B

STANDARD COSTING

416 (a)

Aq × **Ap** = 500 × **2** (i) = 1,000

Price = 125F

Aq × Sp = 500 × 2.25 = 1,125

Usage = 45A

Sq × Sp = **480** (ii) × 2.25 = 1,080

(b) A

(c) A

(d) D

ANSWERS TO SECTION B-TYPE QUESTIONS : SECTION 5

417 (a) A, C and D

(b) (i) The expenditure variance is $23,000 – $20,000 = $3000 and is adverse

(ii) The capacity variance is (2,475 hours × $10) – $20,000 = $4,750 and is favourable

(iii) The efficiency variance is (550 units × 4 hours × $10) – (2,475 hours × $10) = $2,750 and is adverse

(c) A

418 (a)

Wood	Aq × Ap = 170 × 12	= 2,040	
Glass	Aq × Ap = 70 × 12.29	= 860	= 2,900

(i) Price = $360A

Wood	Aq × Sp = 170 × 10	= 1,700	
Glass	Aq × Sq = 70 × 12	= 840	= 2,540

(ii) Usage = $140A

Wood	Sq × Sp = 300 × 0.5 × 10	= 1,500	
Glass	Sq × Sp = 300 × 0.25 × 12	= 900	= 2,400

(b) B

(c) B

(d) C

419 (a) (i) True (better quality final product, sold more units)

(ii) True (better quality ingredients cost more)

(iii) False (nothing to do with the quality of ingredients)

(iv) True (less wastage in the preparation process)

(v) False (it is adverse, but better quality ingredients would imply a higher quality product and higher price)

(b) Actual contribution

(c)

Ah × **Ar** = 3,620 × 3.04 = 11,000

Rate = 140A

Ah × Sr = 3,620 × 3 = 10,860

Usage = 390F

Sh × Sr = 1,500 × 2.5 × 3 = 11,250

KAPLAN PUBLISHING

PERFORMANCE MEASUREMENT

420 (a) Liquidity ratios:

    (i) Inventory holding period = $35,000/$284,000 × 365 = 45 days

    (ii) Receivables collection period = $37,400/$343,275 × 365 = 40 days

    (iii) Payables period = $35,410/$275,000 × 365 = 47 days

    (iv) Current ratio = ($35,000 + $37,400)/($40,500 + $35,410) = 0.954

(b) B

New quick ratio = $37,400/($35,410 + $40,500 − $17,500) = 0.64

(c) A and D

421 (a) Calculations:

    (i) Interest cover = $50,000/0.08 × $60,000 = 10.42

    (ii) Asset turnover = revenue/capital employed

        4 = $500,000/CE therefore CE = $125,000

        ROCE = $50,000/$125,000 × 100 = 40.00%

        Or

        ROCE = asset turnover × operating profit margin = 4 × $50,000/$500,000 = 40.00%

    (iii) Gearing = debt/equity = $60,000/$125,000 = 48.00%

        Or

        Gearing = debt/debt + equity = $60,000/($60,000 + $125,000) = 32.43%

(b) A and C

(c) A

422 (a) Calculations

    (i) Net profit percentage = $348,000/$6,000,000 = 5.8%

    (ii) Market share $6,000,000/$50,000,000 = 12%

    (iii) Increase in revenue = $0.25m/$5.75m = 4.35%

    (iv) Revenue per style of watch = $6,000,000/25 = $240,000

    (v) Increase in sales per $ of market research = $250,000/$200,000 = 1.25

(b) B – net profit for the division would include the allocated head office expenses which are not controllable, and would therefore affect motivation. ROCE is calculated using net profit so this would be misleading as well.

ANSWERS TO SECTION B-TYPE QUESTIONS : SECTION 5

423 (a) Gap 1 B

Gap 2 B

(b) Perspectives

(i) Financial

(ii) Internal

(iii) Learning

(iv) Internal

(c) Gap 1 Internal

Gap 2 Competitive

(d) C

Section 6

ANSWERS TO FREE TEXT QUESTIONS

A: THE NATURE, SOURCE AND PURPOSE OF MANAGEMENT INFORMATION

424 Financial accounting is externally focused. It is concerned with the production of statutory accounts for an organisation. These reports are produced as a legal requirement and are published, to be used by parties external to the organisation such as investors, creditors, analysts, government bodies and the public.

Management accounting is **internally focused**. It is concerned with the provision of information to management to aid decision making. Unlike financial accounting, management accounting is not governed by rules and regulations. It is for internal use only and can be provided in any format. The aim of management accounting is to allow management to make the best decisions in the interest of the organisation in order to drive the business forward in the most successful way.

425 Planning is undertaken at three levels within an organisation: STRATEGIC, MANAGERIAL and OPERATIONAL.

426 The characteristics of good information can be remembered as ACCURATE:

- Accurate
- Complete
- Cost beneficial
- Understandable
- Relevant
- Authoritative
- Timely
- Easy to use

427 A direct cost is a cost which can be clearly identified with the cost object which is being costed. An indirect cost can be attributed to a batch of output, but cannot be directly attributable to a particular cost unit.

A direct cost for a book publisher would be paper. This would be classified as a direct material. An indirect cost could be the factory supervisor's salary. This could be classified as indirect labour.

428 A semi-variable cost is a cost which contains both fixed and variable components. The fixed part is unchanged by changes in the level of activity, but the variable component will change with the changes in the level of activity.

B: COST ACCOUNTING METHODS AND SYSTEMS

429 Marginal cost is the extra cost of making one additional unit.

430 An overhead cost is expenditure in labour, materials or services which cannot be economically identified with a specific saleable cost unit. Overheads are also referred to as indirect costs.

431 (i) Rent – Floor space

(ii) Power – Megawatt hours

(iii) Depreciation – Capital value

(iv) Cost of canteen facility – No. of workers

(v) Machine maintenance labour – Machine maintenance hours

(vi) Supervision – No. of workers.

432 A predetermined overhead absorption rate is calculated by dividing the budgeted costs by the budgeted level of activity.

433 An under- or over-absorption of overheads could occur due to two reasons:

1 The actual level of activity was different from the budgeted level of activity.

2 The actual overhead was different from the budgeted overhead.

434 A normal loss is the amount of loss that is expected from the operation of a process. This loss is expected and is based on past experience and is also considered unavoidable.

435 Abnormal loss and abnormal gain

The extent to which the actual loss exceeds the normal loss is referred to as the abnormal loss.

An abnormal gain is where the normal loss is less than expected, for example, if material input was 1,000 kgs and normal loss was 10%, if actual output was 950 kgs there would be an abnormal gain of 50 kgs and if actual output was 875 kgs then there would be an abnormal loss of 25 kgs.

436 Job costing is a form of specific order costing in which costs are attributed to individual jobs.

437 Batch costing is a form of specific order costing in which costs are attributed to batches of products.

C: BUDGETING

438 Budget and forecast

A forecast is a prediction of what is expected to happen, a budget is a quantified, formal plan that the organisation is aiming to achieve.

439 The principal budget factor is the limiting factor since this determines all other budgets.

In most companies, the level of demand determines the size and scale of the operation which is why many budgetary planning processes begin with the sales budget.

440 A flexible budget is a budget which, by recognising different cost behaviour patterns, is designed to change as volume of activity changes.

441 *Advantages*

(i) Fixed budgets make no distinction between fixed and variable costs,

(ii) Fixed budgets take no account of production shortfall.

Disadvantages

(i) Flexible budgets are more expensive to operate.

(ii) In many businesses, especially service industries, most costs are fixed over a budget period.

442 Flexed budget

An original budget is set at the beginning of the period based on the estimated level of activity. This is, then, flexed to correspond with the actual level of activity.

D: STANDARD COSTING

443 Standard costing is a control technique which compares standard costs and revenues with actual results to obtain variances which are used to improve performance.

444 A standard cost is the planned unit cost of the products, components or services produced in a period.

445 Types of standard

(i) A *basic standard* is a standard established for use over a long period from which a current standard can be developed,

(ii) An *ideal standard* is one which can be attained under the most favourable conditions, with no allowance for normal losses, waste or idle time,

(iii) An *attainable standard* is one which can be attained if a standard unit of work is carried out efficiently. Allowances are made for normal losses,

(iv) A *current standard* is based on current levels of performance. Allowances are made for current levels of loss and idle time, etc.

446 A standard hour is the amount of work achievable, at standard efficiency levels in an hour.

447 Sources of information

Standard materials price may be estimated from:

(i) Quotes/estimates from suppliers

(ii) Industry trends

(iii) Bulk discounts available

(iv) Quality of material

(v) Packaging and carriage inwards charges.

448 A cost variance is a difference between a planned, budgeted or standard cost and the actual cost incurred.

449 Materials variances

An adverse materials price variance and a favourable materials usage variance indicates that there is an inverse relationship between the two. This might be caused by purchasing higher quality material.

450 Variable overhead

It indicates that the work completed took longer than it should have done. It could be caused by employing semi-skilled workers instead of skilled workers who will take longer to complete the job.

451 Labour/overhead efficiency variance

The labour efficiency variance and the variable overhead efficiency variance will total the same number of hours. Their monetary value is likely to be different if their hourly rates are different.

452 (i) The material usage variance, being favourable, indicates that the amount of material used was less than expected for the actual output achieved. This could be caused by the purchase of higher quality materials, which resulted in less wastage than normal.

(ii) The labour rate variance, being favourable, indicates that the hourly wage rate paid was lower than expected. This could be due to employing a lower grade employee than was anticipated in the budget.

(iii) The sales volume contribution variance, being adverse, indicates that the number of units sold was less than budgeted. This may have been caused by an increased sales price which has reduced customer demand, or due to the actions of competitors.

453 Interdependence of variances is the term used to describe the situation when there is a single cause of a number of variances.

For example, the use of a higher grade of labour than was anticipated is likely to cause an adverse labour rate variance, a favourable labour efficiency variance, and possibly a favourable material usage variance (due to more experience of working with materials).

It is important that when variances are reported, the possibility that some of them may have a common cause should be acknowledged, and managers encouraged to work together for the benefit of the organisation.

E: PERFORMANCE MEASUREMENT

454 (i) Customer satisfaction perspective:

The customer perspective considers how the organisation appears to existing and new customers. It aims to improve quality of service to customers and looks at cost, quality, delivery, inspection, handling, etc.

(ii) Growth perspective:

The learning and growth perspective requires the organisation to ask itself whether it can continue to improve and create value. If an organisation is to continue having loyal, satisfied customers and make good use of its resources, it must keep learning and developing.

(iii) Financial success perspective:

The financial perspective considers how the organisations create value for the shareholders. It identifies core financial themes which will drive business strategy and looks at traditional measures such as revenue growth and profitability.

(iv) Process efficiency perspective:

The process perspective requires the organisation to ask itself the question 'what must we excel at to achieve our financial and customer objectives?' It must identify the business processes which are critical to the implementation of the organisation's strategy and aims to improve processes, decision making and resource utilisation.

455 In responsibility accounting, a specific manager is given the responsibility for a particular aspect of the budget, and within the budgetary control system, he or she is often made accountable for actual performance. Managers are therefore made accountable for their area of responsibility.

Responsibility accounting is based on the application of the controllability principle: a manager should be made responsible and accountable only for the costs and revenues that he or she is in a position to control.

456 The use of ROI as a performance measure might lead to dysfunctional behaviour by divisional managers. They might be tempted to avoid investing capital in their respective divisions. This would reduce the average capital employed in order to achieve a higher level of ROI.

Residual income (RI) is an alternative measure of divisional performance. It encourages divisional managers to make new investments if they add to RI. A new investment might add to RI but reduce ROI. In such a situation, measuring the performance by RI would reduce the probability of dysfunctional behaviour.

457 There is always a very strong temptation for operational managers to set as 'soft' a budget as possible, so they cannot fail to meet it and so will be assessed positively by senior managers. Soft budgets means that there is a degree of slack in there, so managers are not motivated to achieve their best possible performance, but rather one that is simply adequate.

458 Critical success factors are those areas of a business and its environment which are critical to the achievement of its goals and objectives. A company may, for example, express its main goal as being a world-class business in its chosen areas of operation. Management should identify critical success factors since failure in any one such factor may prevent or inhibit the advancement of the company and the achievement of its goals.

459 ROI is expressed as a percentage and is more easily understood by non-financial managers.

ROI can be used to compare performance between different sized divisions or companies.

It is not necessary to know the cost of capital in order to calculate ROI.

ROI may lead to dysfunctional decisions. For instance, if a division has a very high ROI of say 40% and is considering a project with an ROI of 30% which is still well above the cost of capital of say 10%, then the project should be accepted as it provides a return well in excess of the cost of capital. The division may quite possibly reject the project, however, as when added to its existing operations it will reduce the ROI from 40%.

Using residual income as a performance measure should ensure that divisions make decisions which are in the best interests of the group as a whole and should eliminate the problem outlined in the previous paragraph.

Different divisions can use different rates to reflect different risk when calculating residual income.

Residual income is not useful for comparing divisions of different sizes.

Both residual income and ROI improve as the age of the assets increase and both provide an incentive to hang onto aged possibly inefficient machines.

460 Factors that should be considered when designing divisional performance measures. These include:

Each measure should be simple to calculate and to understand so that managers can see the effect of the decisions that they make on the measurement of their division's performance.

Each measure should be fair to the manager of the division and only include items that are within their control.

461 The value for money (VFM) concept has been developed as a useful means of assessing performance in an organisation which is not seeking profit. VFM concept revolves around the 3Es, as follows:

If you follow through the diagram above, you will see that, ultimately, VFM relates money spent to objectives achieved.

- Economy (an input measure) – measures the relationship between money spent and the inputs. Are the resources used the cheapest possible for the quality required?

- Efficiency (link inputs with outputs) – is the maximum output being achieved from the resources used?

- Effectiveness (links outputs with objectives) – to what extent to which the outputs generated achieve the objectives of the organisation.

462 Internal benchmarking – comparisons between different departments or functions within an organisation.

Functional benchmarking – comparisons with organisations with similar core activities that are not a competitor.

463 Short termism vs long term performance

Linking rewards to financial performance may tempt managers to make decisions that will improve short term financial performance but may have a negative impact on long term profitability. E.g. they may decide to cut investment or to purchase cheaper but poorer quality materials.

Manipulation of results

In order to achieve the target financial performance and hence their reward, managers may be tempted to manipulate results, for example delaying a provision or accrual to achieve better financial results

Do not convey the full picture

The use of only financial performance indicators has limited benefit to the company as it does not convey the full picture regarding the factors that will drive long term profitability, e.g. customer satisfaction, quality.

Section 7

PRACTICE EXAM QUESTIONS

SECTION A

1 The following details are available for a company:

	Budgeted	Actual
Expenditure	$176,400	$250,400
Machine hours	4,000	5,000
Labour hours	3,600	5,400

The company absorbs overheads using labour hours.

What was the under or over absorption of the overheads?

A Under-absorbed by $29,900

B Under-absorbed by $14,200

C Over-absorbed by $14,200

D Over-absorbed by $64,990

2 **What type of sampling is defined as 'a sample taken in such a way that every member of the population has an equal chance of being selected'?**

A Random

B Stratified

C Quota

D Cluster

3 The following data is available for a company in period 2.

Actual overheads	$225,900
Actual machine hours	7,530
Budgeted overheads	$216,000

The budgeted overhead absorption rate was $32 per hour.

What were the number of machine hours (to the nearest hour) that were budgeted to be worked?

[6750] hours

4 In overhead absorption which of the following is the final step relating overheads to units?

  A Allocation

  B Apportionment

  C Absorption

  D Re-apportionment

5 ABC produces three main products. Which would be the most appropriate chart or diagram for showing total revenue and product analysis month by month?

  A Z chart

  B Line graph

  C Pie chart

  D Component bar chart

6 In times of decreasing prices, the valuation of inventory using the First In First Out method, as opposed to the Weighted Average Cost method, will result in which ONE of the following combinations?

	Cost of sales	Profit	Closing inventory
A	Lower	Higher	Higher
B	Lower	Higher	Lower
C	Higher	Lower	Lower
D	Higher	Higher	Lower

7 A manufacturing company uses 28,000 components at an even rate during the year. Each order placed with the supplier of the components is for 1,600 components, which is the Economic Order Quantity. The company holds a buffer inventory of 800 components. The annual cost of holding one component in inventory is $3.50.

What is the Annual cost of holding inventory of the component?

  A $2,800

  B $4,200

  C $5,600

  D $5,700

PRACTICE EXAM QUESTIONS : SECTION 7

The following data relates to Questions 8 and 9.

Normal working week	36 hours
Basic rate of pay (direct)	$6.20 per hour
Overtime pay	$7.50 per hour

Last week, the total hours worked by all these workers was 936. The overtime hours worked was 108. All employees worked at least their basic 36 hours.

8 How many workers worked last week?

  A was 23

  B was 26

  C was 29

  D cannot be determined from the above data

9 What was the total direct labour charge?

  A $810.00

  B $5,133.60

  C $5,803.20

  D $6,210.00

10 Your firm values inventory using the weighted average cost method. At 1 October 20X9, there were 50 units in inventory valued at $15 each. On 8 October, 30 units were purchased for $20 each, and a further 40 units were purchased for $17 each on 14 October. On 21 October, 60 units were sold for $1,800.

  What was the value of closing inventory at 31 October 20X9 to the nearest $?

  $ _____

11 Service costing is characterised by?

  A high levels of indirect costs as a proportion of total

  B identical output units

  C the ability to store the units

  D long shelf life of output

KAPLAN PUBLISHING 227

PAPER F2/FMA : MANAGEMENT ACCOUNTING

12 A Company has three departments – Assembly, Finishing and Maintenance. Budgeted data for each department is shown below:

	Assembly	Finishing	Maintenance
Allocated overheads	$90,000	$100,000	$10,000
Direct labour hours	5,000	6,000	Nil
Machine hours	10,000	3,000	2,000
Percentage of time spent maintaining machinery	60	40	Nil
Number of staff	60	120	10

What would be the most appropriate production overhead absorption rate to use in the Assembly department?

A $9.60 per machine hour ✓

B $9.90 per machine hour

C $17.33 per labour hour

D $18.33 per labour hour

13 Products A and B are manufactured in a joint process. The following data is available for a period:

Joint process costs		$30,000
Output:	Product A	2,000 kg
	Product B	4,000 kg
Selling price:	Product A	$12 per kg
	Product B	$18 per kg

What is Product B's share of the joint process costs if the sales value method of cost apportionment is used?

A 7,500

B 18,000

C 20,000

D 22,500

The following data relates to Questions 14 and 15.

Budgeted production details for November are as follows:

	Product X	Product Y	Product Z
Units produced	2,000	1,600	2,200
Units sold	1,800	1,500	2,000
Variable cost/unit	100	80	120
Fixed overhead absorbed/unit	30	30	50
No. of labour hours	6	4.5	5

There was no opening inventory at the beginning of November.

PRACTICE EXAM QUESTIONS : **SECTION 7**

14 What were the budgeted fixed overheads for November?

A $810,000
B $739,000
C $218,000
D $199,000

15 Which of the following statements is true?

A Absorption costing profit will be $19,000 lower than marginal costing profit
B Absorption costing profit will be $71,000 lower than marginal costing profit
C Absorption costing profit will be $19,000 higher than marginal costing profit
D Absorption costing profit will be $71,000 higher than marginal costing profit

16 The total costs incurred at various output levels in a factory have been measured as follows:

Output in units	Total cost
25	$5,500
30	$5,450
33	$5,550
44	$6,000
48	$6,500
55	$7,000

What are the variable cost per unit and the total fixed costs?

A Variable cost $50 per unit, Fixed costs $4,250
B Variable cost $53 per unit, Fixed costs $4,000
C Variable cost $56 per unit, Fixed costs $4,500
D Variable cost $59 per unit, Fixed costs £4,750

17 Which of the following statements are true and which are false when applied to fixed costs?

	True	False
Overhead costs are always fixed costs		
As production levels increase, fixed cost per unit decreases		
Fixed costs are always irrelevant in a decision making situation		
As the level of activity changes, fixed costs will also change		

18 A job is budgeted to require 3,300 productive hours but will incur 25% idle time. If the total labour cost budgeted for the job is $36,300, what is the labour cost per hour (to the nearest cent)?

$ ☐

KAPLAN PUBLISHING

PAPER F2/FMA : MANAGEMENT ACCOUNTING

19 Which of the following statements about variable costs is correct?

Variable costs are conventionally deemed to:

A   be constant per unit of output

B   vary per unit of output as production volume changes

C   vary in total when production volume is constant

D   vary, in total, from period to period when production is constant

20 In quality related costs, which of the following are conformance costs and which are non-conformance costs?

	Conformance costs	Non-conformance costs
Internal failure costs		✓
Prevention costs	✓	
Appraisal costs	✓	
External failure costs		✓

21 A business is preparing its budget for the coming year by using time series analysis. Using the following information and a 3-month moving average what is the seasonal variation for the month of October?

Month	Sales value (000s)
June	770
July	750
August	928
September	854
October	834
November	1012
December	938

A   −66

B   −38

C   +66

D   +38

230 KAPLAN PUBLISHING

PRACTICE EXAM QUESTIONS : SECTION 7

22 D Ltd operates a total absorption costing system. Budgeted fixed overheads for 2007 were $175,000 and budgeted production was 5,000 units.

During 2007, the actual fixed overheads amounted to $186,000 and actual production was 6,000 units.

What is the over or under absorption of overheads?

- A under-absorbed by $24,000
- B under-absorbed by $11,000
- C over-absorbed by $11,000
- D over-absorbed by $24,000 ✓

23 Below is the standard cost card for one unit of product K.

	$/unit
Selling price	35
Direct materials	20
Direct labour	4
Variable overhead	1
Fixed overhead	6

Production was 50,000 units and sales 60,000 units. Opening inventory was 25,000 units. The profit calculated using marginal costing was $180,000.

What is the profit using absorption costing?

- A $30,000
- B $120,000 ✓
- C $210,000
- D $240,000

24 Which of the following statements is true about direct costs?

- A they can be directly identified with a product or service ✓
- B they are directly under the control of a manager
- C they are incurred directly the factory is opened
- D they are directly charged to a department

25 What is a cost pool in ABC?

- A an activity that consumes resources and for which overhead costs are identified and allocated ✓
- B an activity that causes a cost to change
- C an item of equipment that costs are charged to
- D an area of the business that is used to store output

PAPER F2/FMA : MANAGEMENT ACCOUNTING

26 Which is the best description for a centre which is responsible for managing both costs and revenues?

- A Revenue centre
- B Investment centre
- C Profit centre
- D Cost centre

27 Using an interest rate of 15% per year the net present value (NPV) of a project has been correctly calculated as $850.

If the interest rate is increased by 5% the NPV of the project falls by $900.

What is the internal rate of return (IRR) of the project?

- A 14.7%
- B 17.4%
- C 19.7%
- D 20.3%

28 Using data from 40 counties in England and Wales, it has been calculated that the correlation between the level of trampoline ownership and the number of neck injuries is 0.75. Which TWO of the statements shown follow this?

- A High levels of trampoline ownership in a given county cause high levels of neck injuries.
- B There is a strong relationship between the level of trampoline ownership and the number of neck injuries.
- C 56% of the variation in the level of neck injuries from one county to the next can be explained by the corresponding variation in the level of trampoline ownership.
- D 75% of the variation in the level of neck injuries from one county to the next can be explained by the corresponding variation in the level of trampoline ownership.

29 The following statements refer to spreadsheets:

(1) Spreadsheets can be used for budgeting.

(2) Spreadsheets are very useful for word-processing.

(3) Spreadsheets make the manipulation of data easier and quicker.

Which of these statements are correct?

- A (1) and (2)
- B (1) and (3)
- C (2) and (3)
- D (1), (2) and (3)

PRACTICE EXAM QUESTIONS : SECTION 7

30 A company uses standard marginal costing. Last month, when all sales were at the standard selling price, the standard contribution from actual sales was $50,000 and the following variances arose:

Total variable costs variance $3,500 adverse
Total fixed costs variance $1,000 favourable
Sales volume contribution variance $2,000 favourable

What was the actual contribution for last month?

 A $46,500
 B $47,500
 C $48,500
 D $49,500

31 A production worker is paid a salary of $650 per month, plus an extra 5 cents for each unit produced during the month. **What is the best description of the type of labour cost?**

 A   A variable cost
 B   A fixed cost
 C   A step cost
 D   A semi-variable cost

32 A company achieves bulk buying discounts on quantities of raw material above a certain level. These discounts are only available for the units above the specified level and not on all the units purchased.

Which of the following graphs of total purchase cost against units best illustrates the above situation?

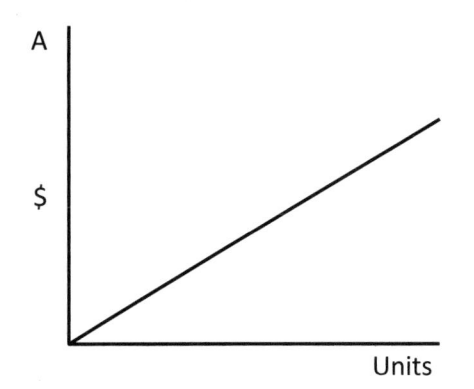

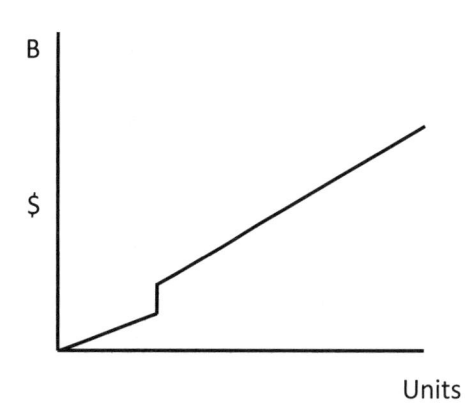

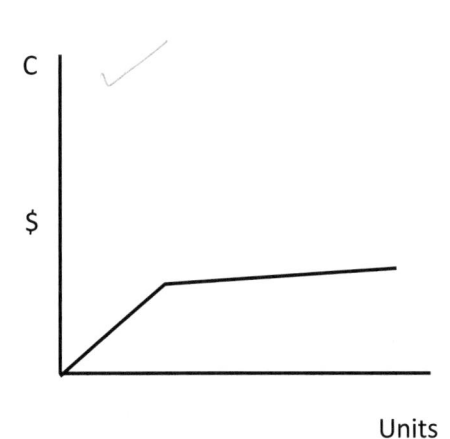

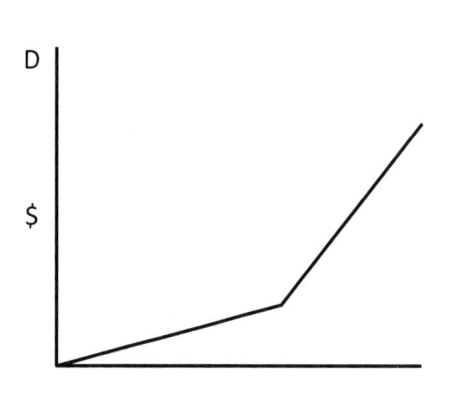

KAPLAN PUBLISHING

PAPER F2/FMA : MANAGEMENT ACCOUNTING

The following information relates to questions 33 and 34.

During the month of December, a manufacturing process incurs material costs of $8,000 and conversion costs of $4,500. 2,000 kgs of material was input. There is a normal loss of 10% and all losses have a scrap value of $1.75 per kg. During the period, 1700 kgs were output to finished goods. Opening and Closing inventories in the process were nil.

33 What was the cost per kg output?

    A $6.25

    B $6.75

    C $6.94

    D $7.35

34 What was the value of the abnormal loss written off in the statement of profit or loss?

    A $675

    B $175

    C $2,025

    D $500

35 Jojo is an assembly worker earning $12 per hour for a basic 35 hour week. Any overtime is paid at a premium of 50%.

In the last four-week period, Jojo was paid for 150 hours. During this time 15 hours were classed as idle due to a machine breaking down. Also included in the number of hours are four hours' overtime spent working for an urgent job at the request of the customer.

How much should be charged to the production overhead account for the four-week period?

    A $216

    B $240

    C $288

    D $360

SECTION B

ALL THREE QUESTIONS ARE COMPULSORY AND MUST BE ATTEMPTED

1   Mrs Glam wants to expand her clothes shop. Mrs Glam has commissioned a market research company at a cost of $3,000 to research her options for her. The company have offered two options:

    Option 1

    Remain in her the current premises and undertake an advertising campaign at a cost of $2,000 to increase the profile of the shop in the area. It is estimated that revenue will increase by 10% from its current level of $50,000 per year. The contribution earned on revenue is 30%.

    Option 2

    Move the shop to a more central location and undertake an advertising campaign to both increase the profile and the move to new premises. This more extensive campaign would cost $4,000 but revenue would be expected to increase by 18% from its current level. The level of contribution earned on revenue is not expected to change.

    There would be further costs involved in moving location which have been estimated:

    - Moving costs are estimated to be $1,500. This includes the cost of refitting the shop, and would be payable immediately
    - New shop fittings will be required costing $2,500. These will be depreciated on a straight line basis.
    - Rates of $4,000 will be payable yearly in advance. This cost is 15% higher than Mrs Glam currently pays, due to the location.

    Other information

    - Mrs Glam uses a cost of capital of 10%

    Required:

    (a) State if the following items relating to Mrs Glam's decision how to expand are relevant or irrelevant cash flows in a net present value calculation:

    (i)   The $3,000 market research fee   (1 mark)

    (ii) Depreciation of $625 per year for the new shop fittings.   (1 mark)

    (iii) The costs of $1,500 incurred in moving to the new premises.   (1 mark)

    (b) Calculate the present value of the INCREMENTAL contribution cash flow that will arise if option 2 is pursued.   (2.5 marks)

    (c) Calculate the present value of the cash flows relating to the INCREMENTAL rates that will arise if option 2 is pursued.   (2.5 marks)

PAPER F2/FMA : MANAGEMENT ACCOUNTING

(d) If Mrs Glam moved her clothes shop, she would finance the move with a small legacy of $10,000 that she has been left. She is wondering whether instead of moving the shop now, she should invest the money she has been left and use the lump sum in four years time to move to even bigger premises.

Required:

Calculate the value of the legacy in four years time, if it is invested at 10%. (2 marks)

(Total: 10 marks)

2 M Co is a small manufacturing company. The following information is available:

Budgeted
Labour rate per hour $4
Fixed overhead absorption rate per hour $2.50
Actual
Hours worked   3,000 hours
Fixed overheads $9,000
Variances
Labour rate   300 favourable
Fixed overhead expenditure   200 favourable
Fixed overhead efficiency   500 adverse

Required:

(a) Using the information available, calculate:

(i) the budgeted fixed overhead expenditure and state if the fixed overhead capacity variance would be favourable or adverse. (2 marks)

(ii) the labour efficiency variance (2 marks)

(iii) the actual labour rate per hour (2 marks)

(b) Which of the following could have caused the fixed overhead efficiency variance to arise?

A ✓ Sub contract staff being brought in to partially cover a strike by M Co's workforce

B Incorrect estimation of standard absorption rate per hour.

C A key piece of machinery breaking down and requiring repair before manufacturing could continue

D The materials supplier failing to deliver raw materials into stock as required.
(2 marks)

(c) M co is aware that next month they will have to buy their materials from a different supplier. Although this supplier charges less per unit, M Co is aware that the material will be of a lesser quality. The management of M Co wants to understand the possible effect this purchase will have on their results.

Required:

As an indirect result of this purchase, what is likely to be the effect on the materials usage and labour efficiency variances?

	Materials usage	Labour efficiency
A	Adverse	Favourable
B ✓	Adverse	Adverse
C	Favourable	Favourable
D	Favourable	Adverse

(2 marks)

(Total: 10 marks)

3 Play Co owns two indoor children's soft play centres one in Bromsgrove, one in Worcester. The following information about each centre is available:

	Bromsgrove	Worcester
Centre opened	3 years ago	6 years ago
Original cost including cost of site, building and equipment	$300,000	$150,000
Current value	$425,000	$425,000
Controllable profit	$55,000	$40,000
Depreciation policy set by head office	Reducing balance basis	Reducing balance basis

Managers are responsible for maintaining the centres to a high standard, and head office will do spot checks to ensure that no equipment is damaged.

Play Co uses an annual rate of 10% as the required return on investment and to determine residual income. Bonuses are paid if managers exceed their targets.

Required:

(a) Using the information provided, calculate for Bromsgrove:

ROI = 55,000/300,000 = 18.3%

  (i)   Return on investment using original cost   (1 mark)

  (ii) Residual income using original cost   (2 marks)

RI = 55,000 − 0.1 × 300,000 = 25,000

(b) If the current values are used for the investment, what will happen to the return on investment and residual income figures for Bromsgrove?

	Residual income	Return on investment
A	Higher	Higher
B	Lower	Higher
C	Higher	Lower
D ✓	Lower	Lower

(2 marks)

(c) The manager of the Worcester office is concerned that his controllable profit levels are so much lower than the Bromsgrove centre, despite the centres being the same size and having the same footfall. Which reason could account for the lower controllable profit:

A   Increased repair costs due to age of equipment.

B   Lower depreciation charge due to age of equipment

(1 mark)

(d) Are the following statements true or false?

Statement one: Residual income is of more use than return on investment when comparing divisions of different sizes.

Statement two: Residual income is more likely to encourage investment in new assets than return on investment is.

	Statement one	Statement two
A	True	True
B	True	False
C	False	True
D	False	False

(2 marks)

(e) Which sequence shows the level of managerial control decreasing?

A	Investment centre →	Profit centre →	Cost centre
B	Profit centre →	Investment centre →	Cost centre
C	Cost centre →	Profit centre →	Investment centre
D	Cost centre →	Investment centre →	Profit centre

(2 marks)

(Total: 10 marks)

Section 8

ANSWERS TO PRACTICE EXAM QUESTIONS

SECTION A

1   C

OAR = $176,400/3,600 = $49

	$
Amount absorbed = $49 × 5,400 =	264,600
Actual overhead	(250,400)
Over absorbed	14,200

2   A

3   6,750 hours

Budgeted hours = $\dfrac{\$216,000}{\$32}$ = 6,750 hours

4   C

5   D

A bar chart is a good way of illustrating total revenue month by month. The length of the bar each month is a measure of total revenue. The bar can be divided into three parts, to show the amount of sales achieved for each of the three products. This is called a component bar chart.

6   C

When prices are decreasing, FIFO will give a lower valuation for closing inventory, because the closing inventory will consist of the most recently-purchased items. Lower closing inventory means higher cost of sales and lower profit.

PAPER F2/FMA : MANAGEMENT ACCOUNTING

7 C

{[Buffer inventory + (EOQ ÷ 2)] × Annual holding cost per component}

= [800 units + (1,600 units ÷ 2)] × $3.50 = $5,600

8 A

Normal time = 936 – 108 = 828 hours

Number of employees = 23

9 C

Direct labour charge is **all** hours (including overtime) at normal rate:

936 × $6.20 = $5,803.20

10 $1,015

Date		Units	Unit value $	Inventory value $
1 October	Opening inventory	50	15.00	750
8 October	Purchase 30 units at $20	30	20.00	600
14 October	Purchase 40 units at $17	40	17.00	680
		120	16.92	2,030
21 October	Sold 75 units: cost	(60)	16.92	(1,015)
31 October	Closing inventory	60	16.92	1,015

11 A

12 A

	Assembly	Finishing	Maintenance
Allocated o/hs	90,000	100,000	10,000
Maintenance	6,000	4,000	(10,000)
	96,000	104,000	–

OAR for Assembly department = $96,000/10,000 machine hours = $9.60

13 D

	Output (kg)	Sales value ($)	Apportionment of joint costs ($)	
Product A	2,000	24,000	(24/96)	7,500
Product B	4,000	72,000	(72/96)	22,500
		96,000		30,000

ANSWERS TO PRACTICE EXAM QUESTIONS : SECTION 8

14   C

($30 × 2,000) + ($30 × 1,600) + ($50 × 2,200) = $218,000

15   C

All inventories are increasing, so absorption costing profits will be higher by:

($30 × 200) + ($30 × 100) + ($50 × 200) = $19,000

16   A

	Units	Total costs
High	55	$7,000
Low	25	$5,500
Difference	30	$1,500

Therefore, Variable costs = $\dfrac{\$1,500}{30 \text{ units}}$ = $50 per unit

By substitution, we find FC = $4,250.

17

	True	False
Overhead costs are always fixed costs		✓
As production levels increase, fixed cost per unit decreases	✓	
Fixed costs are always irrelevant in a decision making situation		✓
As the level of activity changes, fixed costs will also change		✓

18 $8.25

Total hours worked, and paid = 3,300/0.75 = 4,400 hours

Hourly rate = $36,300/4,400 = $8.25

19   A

20   B

	Conformance costs	Non-conformance costs
Internal failure costs		✓
Prevention costs	✓	
Appraisal costs	✓	
External failure costs		✓

KAPLAN PUBLISHING

PAPER F2/FMA : MANAGEMENT ACCOUNTING

21 A

834 − [(854 + 834 + 1,012)/3] = −66

22 D

	$
Overheads incurred	186,000
Actual absorption $\dfrac{\$175,000}{5,000} \times 6,000$	210,000
Over-absorbed	24,000

23 B

	$
Marginal costing profit	180,000
(15,000 − 25,000) × $6	(60,000)
Equals absorption costing profit	120,000

24 A

25 A

26 C

27 C

15 + [850/(850 + 50)] × (20 − 15) = 19.7%

28 B and C

29 B

30 A

Sales contribution on actual sales	$50,000
Less: Adverse total variable costs variance	($3,500)
Actual contribution	$46,500

No adjustment is required for the favourable sales volume contribution variance, as it will have already been added to the budgeted contribution to arrive at the standard contribution from actual sales ($50,000) given in the question.

31 D

ANSWERS TO PRACTICE EXAM QUESTIONS : SECTION 8

32 C

Raw materials are a variable cost so the graph will begin at the origin and increase at a gradient equal to the cost per unit. The cost per unit falls at a certain point so the gradient will become less and the graph will be flatter. Option D shows a situation where the cost per unit becomes greater above a certain volume.

33 B

Average cost = ($12,500 – $350)/(2,000 – 200) = $6.75

34 D

Income statement value = 100 × ($6.75 – $1.75) = $500

35 A

Idle time + General overtime = (15 hours × $12) + ((10 hours – 4 hours) × $6) = $216

PAPER F2/FMA : MANAGEMENT ACCOUNTING

SECTION B

1 MRS GLAM

(a) (i) Irrelevant

(ii) Irrelevant

(iii) Relevant

(b) Present value of the incremental contribution:

Option one – Contribution = $50,000 × 1.1 × 0.3 = $16,500 per annum

Present value of contribution = $16,500 × 3.170 (AF) = $52,305

Option two – Contribution = $50,000 × 1.18 × 0.3 = $17,700 per annum

Present value of contribution = £17,700 × 3.170 (AF) = $56,109

Incremental contribution = $56,109 – $52,305 = $3,804

(c) Present value of the incremental rates

Note: rates are paid in advance so payment will occur in years 0, 1, 2 and 3. The annuity factor is for years 0 to 3 = 3.487):

PV of new rates = $4,000 × 3.487 = $13,948

PV of old rates = [$4000 – ($4000/115 × 15)] × 3.487 = $12,129

Incremental rates = £13,948 – $12,129 = $1,819

(d) Value of legacy in four years time:

$10,000 × 1.1^4 = $14,641

ANSWERS TO PRACTICE EXAM QUESTIONS : SECTION 8

2 M CO

(a) Calculations:

(i) Fixed overhead expenditure = $9,000 + $200 = $9,200

Capacity variance would be adverse

Actual = 3,000 × $2.50 = $7,500

Budget = 3,680 × $2.50 = $9,200

Capacity = $7,500 – $9,200 = $1,700 Adverse

(ii) and (iii)

Ah × Ar = 3,000 × **3.90 (iii)** = $11,700

Rate = 300F

Ah × Sr = 3,000 × 4 = $12,000

Efficiency = **$800A (ii)**

Sh × Sr = 2,800* × 4 = $11,200

* to calculate the standard hours the fixed overhead efficiency variance needs to be used:

Actual = 3,000 × $2.50 = $7,500

Efficiency variance = $500 Adverse

Standard = $7,500 – $500 = $7,000

Standard hours = $7,000/$2.50 = 2,800 hours

(b) A

(c) B

3 PLAY CO

(a) Calculations

(i) ROI = $55,000/$300,000 = 18.3%

(ii) RI = $55,000 – 0.1 × $300,000 = $25,000

(b) D

(c) A

(d) C

(e) A

KAPLAN PUBLISHING

Fundamentals Level – Knowledge Module

Management Accounting

Specimen Exam applicable from June 2014

Paper F2

Time allowed: 2 hours

This paper is divided into two sections:

Section A – ALL 35 questions are compulsory and MUST be attempted

Section B – ALL THREE questions are compulsory and MUST be attempted

Formulae Sheet, Present Value and Annuity Tables are on pages 16, 17 and 18.

Do NOT open this paper until instructed by the supervisor.

This question paper must not be removed from the examination hall.

The Association of Chartered Certified Accountants

Section A – ALL 35 questions are compulsory and MUST be attempted

Please use the space provided on the inside cover of the Candidate Answer Booklet to indicate your chosen answer to each multiple choice question.
Each question is worth 2 marks.

1 A manufacturing company benchmarks the performance of its accounts receivable department with that of a leading credit card company.

What type of benchmarking is the company using?

- **A** Internal benchmarking
- **B** Competitive benchmarking
- **C** Functional benchmarking
- **D** Strategic benchmarking

2 Which of the following BEST describes target costing?

- **A** Setting a cost by subtracting a desired profit margin from a competitive market price
- **B** Setting a price by adding a desired profit margin to a production cost
- **C** Setting a cost for the use in the calculation of variances
- **D** Setting a selling price for the company to aim for in the long run

3 Information relating to two processes (F and G) was as follows:

Process	Normal loss as % of input	Input (litres)	Output (litres)
F	8	65,000	58,900
G	5	37,500	35,700

For each process, was there an abnormal loss or an abnormal gain?

	Process F	Process G
A	Abnormal gain	Abnormal gain
B	Abnormal gain	Abnormal loss
C	Abnormal loss	Abnormal gain
D	Abnormal loss	Abnormal loss

4 The following budgeted information relates to a manufacturing company for next period:

	Units		$
Production	14,000	Fixed production costs	63,000
Sales	12,000	Fixed selling costs	12,000

The normal level of activity is 14,000 units per period.

Using absorption costing the profit for next period has been calculated as $36,000.

What would be the profit for next period using marginal costing?

- **A** $25,000
- **B** $27,000
- **C** $45,000
- **D** $47,000

5 The Eastland Postal Service is government owned. The government requires it to provide a parcel delivery service to every home and business in Eastland at a low price which is set by the government. Express Couriers Co is a privately owned parcel delivery company that also operates in Eastland. It is not subject to government regulation and most of its deliveries are to large businesses located in Eastland's capital city. You have been asked to assess the relative efficiency of the management of the two organisations.

Which of the following factors should NOT be allowed for when comparing the ROCE of the two organisations to assess the efficiency of their management?

- A Differences in prices charged
- B Differences in objectives pursued
- C Differences in workforce motivation
- D Differences in geographic areas served

6 **Under which sampling method does every member of the target population has an equal chance of being in the sample?**

- A Stratified sampling
- B Random sampling
- C Systematic sampling
- D Cluster sampling

7 A Company manufactures and sells one product which requires 8 kg of raw material in its manufacture. The budgeted data relating to the next period are as follows:

	Units
Sales	19,000
Opening inventory of finished goods	4,000
Closing inventory of finished goods	3,000
	Kg
Opening inventory of raw materials	50,000
Closing inventory of raw materials	53,000

What is the budgeted raw material purchases for next period (in kg)?

- A 141,000
- B 147,000
- C 157,000
- D 163,000

8 Up to a given level of activity in each period the purchase price per unit of a raw material is constant. After that point a lower price per unit applies both to further units purchased and also retrospectively to all units already purchased.

Which of the following graphs depicts the total cost of the raw materials for a period?

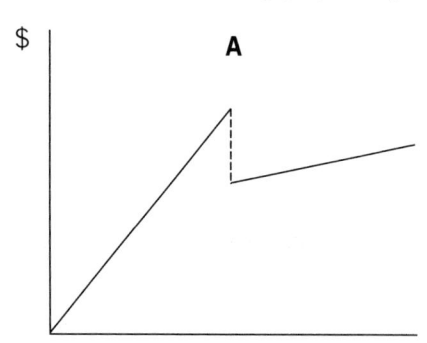

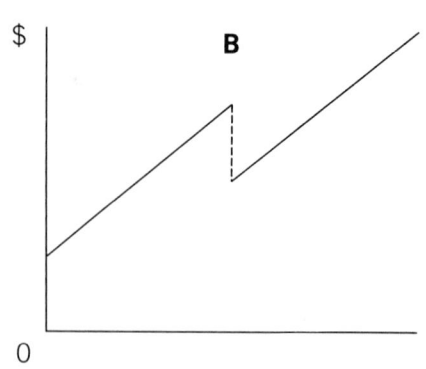

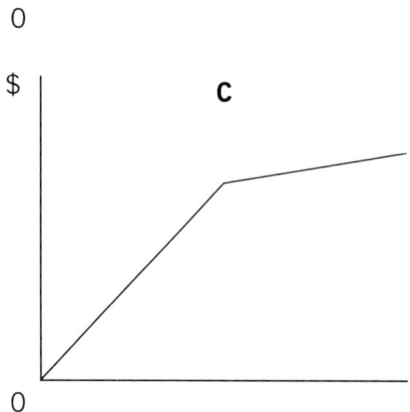

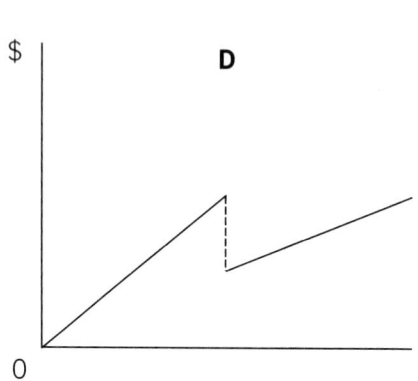

A Graph A
B Graph B
C Graph C
D Graph D

9 **Which of the following are benefits of budgeting?**

1 It helps coordinate the activities of different departments
2 It fulfils legal reporting obligations
3 It establishes a system of control
4 It is a starting point for strategic planning

A 1 and 4 only
B 1 and 3 only
C 2 and 3 only
D 2 and 4 only

10 The following statements relate to the participation of junior management in setting budgets:

1. It speeds up the setting of budgets
2. It increases the motivation of junior managers
3. It reduces the level of budget padding

Which statements are true?

A 1 only
B 2 only
C 2 and 3 only
D 1, 2 and 3

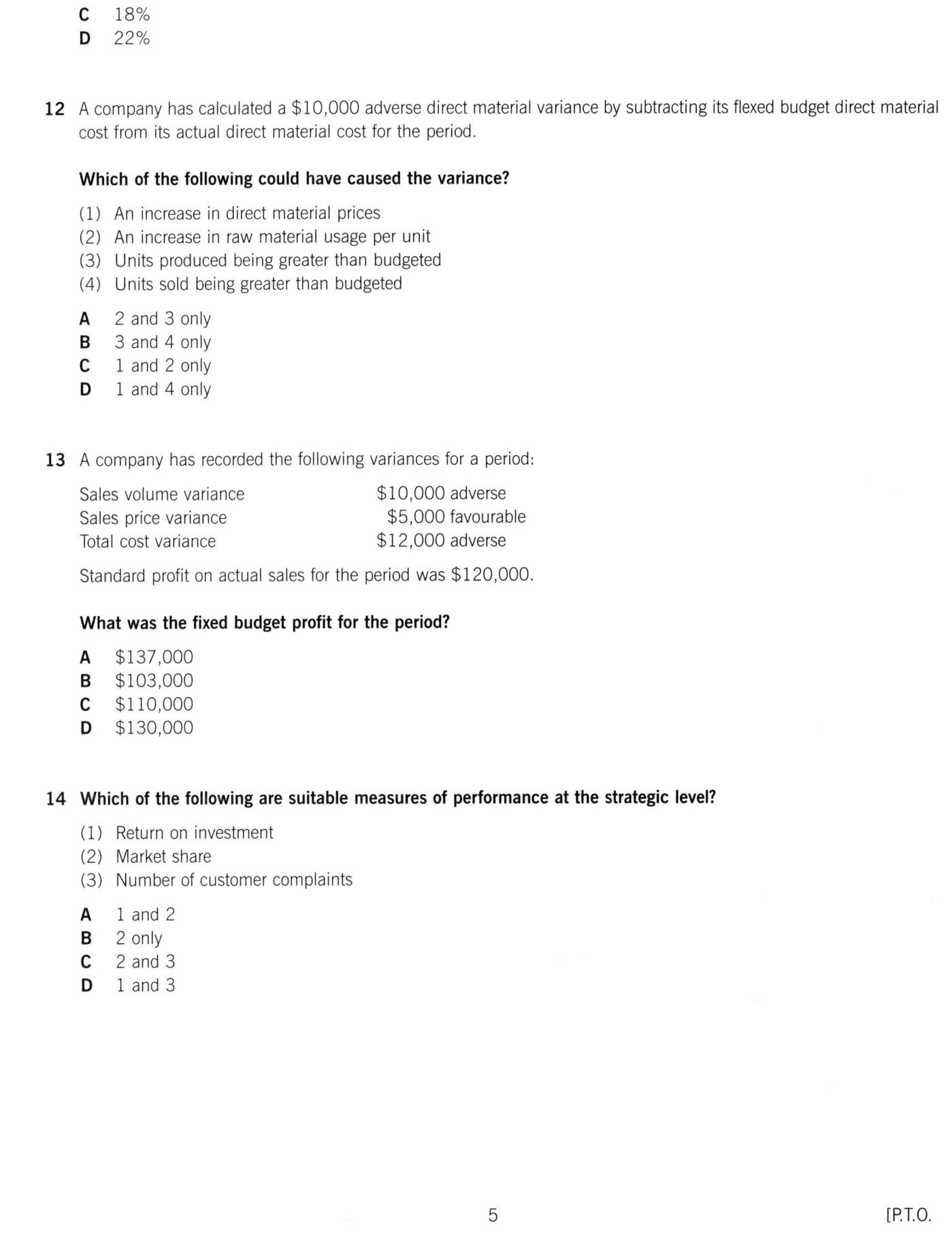

11 A company has a capital employed of $200,000. It has a cost of capital of 12% per year. Its residual income is $36,000.

What is the company's return on investment?

A 30%
B 12%
C 18%
D 22%

12 A company has calculated a $10,000 adverse direct material variance by subtracting its flexed budget direct material cost from its actual direct material cost for the period.

Which of the following could have caused the variance?

(1) An increase in direct material prices
(2) An increase in raw material usage per unit
(3) Units produced being greater than budgeted
(4) Units sold being greater than budgeted

A 2 and 3 only
B 3 and 4 only
C 1 and 2 only
D 1 and 4 only

13 A company has recorded the following variances for a period:

Sales volume variance $10,000 adverse
Sales price variance $5,000 favourable
Total cost variance $12,000 adverse

Standard profit on actual sales for the period was $120,000.

What was the fixed budget profit for the period?

A $137,000
B $103,000
C $110,000
D $130,000

14 Which of the following are suitable measures of performance at the strategic level?

(1) Return on investment
(2) Market share
(3) Number of customer complaints

A 1 and 2
B 2 only
C 2 and 3
D 1 and 3

15 Which of the following are feasible values for the correlation coefficient?

1 +1·40
2 +1·04
3 0
4 −0·94

A 1 and 2 only
B 3 and 4 only
C 1, 2 and 4 only
D 1, 2, 3 and 4

16 A company's operating costs are 60% variable and 40% fixed.

Which of the following variances' values would change if the company switched from standard marginal costing to standard absorption costing?

A Direct material efficiency variance
B Variable overhead efficiency variance
C Sales volume variance
D Fixed overhead expenditure variance

17 ABC Co has a manufacturing capacity of 10,000 units. The flexed production cost budget of the company is as follows:

Capacity	60%	100%
Total production costs	$11,280	$15,120

What is the budgeted total production cost if it operates at 85% capacity?

A $13,680
B $12,852
C $14,025
D $12,340

18 Using an interest rate of 10% per year the net present value (NPV) of a project has been correctly calculated as $50. If the interest rate is increased by 1% the NPV of the project falls by $20.

What is the internal rate of return (IRR) of the project?

A 7·5%
B 11·7%
C 12·5%
D 20·0%

19 D — $128,500

20 D — Lower EOQ, Lower annual holding cost

21 A — $19,910

22 A — $5,000 Adverse

23 The following statements have been made about value analysis.

(1) It seeks the lowest cost method of achieving a desired function
(2) It always results in inferior products
(3) It ignores esteem value

Which is/are true ?

A 1 only
B 2 only
C 3 only
D 1 and 3 only

24 Under which of the following labour remuneration methods will direct labour cost always be a variable cost?

A Day rate
B Piece rate
C Differential piece rate
D Group bonus scheme

25 A company manufactures and sells a single product. In two consecutive months the following levels of production and sales (in units) occurred:

	Month 1	Month 2
Sales	3,800	4,400
Production	3,900	4,200

The opening inventory for Month 1 was 400 units. Profits or losses have been calculated for each month using both absorption and marginal costing principles.

Which of the following combination of profits and losses for the two months is consistent with the above data?

	Absorption costing profit/(loss)		Marginal costing profit/(loss)	
	Month 1	Month 2	Month 1	Month 2
	$	$	$	$
A	200	4,400	(400)	3,200
B	(400)	4,400	200	3,200
C	200	3,200	(400)	4,400
D	(400)	3,200	200	4,400

26 The following statements relate to the advantages that linear regression analysis has over the high low method in the analysis of cost behaviour:

1. the reliability of the analysis can be statistically tested
2. it takes into account all of the data
3. it assumes linear cost behaviour

Which statements are true?

A 1 only
B 1 and 2 only
C 2 and 3 only
D 1, 2 and 3

27 A company operates a process in which no losses are incurred. The process account for last month, when there was no opening work-in-progress, was as follows:

Process Account

	$		$
Costs arising	624,000	Finished output (10,000 units)	480,000
		Closing work-in-progress (4,000 units)	144,000
	624,000		624,000

The closing work in progress was complete to the same degree for all elements of cost.

What was the percentage degree of completion of the closing work-in-progress?

A 12%
B 30%
C 40%
D 75%

28 Which of the following would not be expected to appear in an organisation's mission statement?

A The organisation's values and beliefs
B The products or services offered by the organisation
C Quantified short term targets the organisation seeks to achieve
D The organisation's major stakeholders

29 An organisation operates a piecework system of remuneration, but also guarantees its employees 80% of a time-based rate of pay which is based on $20 per hour for an eight hour working day. Three minutes is the standard time allowed per unit of output. Piecework is paid at the rate of $18 per standard hour.

If an employee produces 200 units in eight hours on a particular day, what is the employee's gross pay for that day?

A $128
B $144
C $160
D $180

30 A company uses an overhead absorption rate of $3·50 per machine hour, based on 32,000 budgeted machine hours for the period. During the same period the actual total overhead expenditure amounted to $108,875 and 30,000 machine hours were recorded on actual production.

By how much was the total overhead under or over absorbed for the period?

A Under absorbed by $3,875
B Under absorbed by $7,000
C Over absorbed by $3,875
D Over absorbed by $7,000

31 Which of the following statements relating to management information are true?

1. It is produced for parties external to the organisation
2. There is usually a legal requirement for the information to be produced
3. No strict rules govern the way in which the information is presented
4. It may be presented in monetary or non monetary terms

A 1 and 2
B 3 and 4
C 1 and 3
D 2 and 4

32 A company's sales in the last year in its three different markets were as follows

	$
Market 1	100,000
Market 2	150,000
Market 3	50,000
Total	300,000

In a pie chart representing the proportion of sales made by each region what would be the angle of the section representing Market 3 (to the nearest whole degree)?

A 17 degrees
B 50 degrees
C 61 degrees
D 120 degrees

33 Which of the following BEST describes a flexible budget?

A A budget which shows variable production costs only
B A monthly budget which is changed to reflect the number of days in the month
C A budget which shows sales revenue and costs at different levels of activity
D A budget that is updated halfway through the year to incorporate the actual results for the first half of the year

34 The purchase price of an item of inventory is $25 per unit. In each three month period the usage of the item is 20,000 units. The annual holding costs associated with one unit equate to 6% of its purchase price. The cost of placing an order for the item is $20.

What is the Economic Order Quantity (EOQ) for the inventory item to the nearest whole unit?

A 730
B 894
C 1,461
D 1,633.

35 Two products G and H are created from a joint process. G can be sold immediately after split-off. H requires further processing into product HH before it is in a saleable condition. There are no opening inventories and no work in progress of products G, H or HH. The following data are available for last period:

	$
Total joint production costs	350,000
Further processing costs of product H	66,000

Product	Production units	Closing inventory
G	420,000	20,000
HH	330,000	30,000

Using the physical unit method for apportioning joint production costs, what was the cost value of the closing inventory of product HH for last period?

A $16,640
B $18,625
C $20,000
D $21,600

(70 marks)

Section B – ALL THREE questions are compulsory and MUST be attempted

1   Cab Co owns and runs 350 taxis and had sales of $10 million in the last year. Cab Co is considering introducing a new computerised taxi tracking system.

The expected costs and benefits of the new computerised tracking system are as follows:

(i) The system would cost $2,100,000 to implement.

(ii) Depreciation would be provided at $420,000 per annum.

(iii) $75,000 has already been spent on staff training in order to evaluate the potential of the new system. Further training costs of $425,000 would be required in the first year if the new system is implemented.

(iv) Sales are expected to rise to $11 million in Year 1 if the new system is implemented, thereafter increasing by 5% per annum. If the new system is not implemented, sales would be expected to increase by $200,000 per annum.

(v) Despite increased sales, savings in vehicle running costs are expected as a result of the new system. These are estimated at 1% of total sales.

(vi) Six new members of staff would be recruited to manage the new system at a total cost of $120,000 per annum.

(vii) Cab Co would have to take out a maintenance contract for the new system at a cost of $75,000 per annum for five years.

(viii) Interest on money borrowed to finance the project would cost $150,000 per annum.

(ix) Cab Co's cost of capital is 10% per annum.

Required:

(a) State whether each of the following items are relevant or irrelevant cashflows for a net present value (NPV) evaluation of whether to introduce the computerised tracking system.

   (i) Computerised tracking system investment of $2,100,000;
   (ii) Depreciation of $420,000 in each of the five years;
   (iii) Staff training costs of $425,000;
   (iv) New staff total salary of $120,000 per annum;
   (v) Staff training costs of $75,000;
   (vi) Interest cost of $150,000 per annum.

Note: The following mark allocation is provided as guidance for this requirement:

   (i) 0·5 marks
   (ii) 1 mark
   (iii) 0·5 marks
   (iv) 1 mark
   (v) 1 mark
   (vi) 1 mark

(5 marks)

(b) Calculate the following values if the computerised tracking system is implemented.

   (i) Incremental sales in Year 1;
   (ii) Savings in vehicle running costs in Year 1;
   (iii) Present value of the maintenance costs over the life of the contract.

Note: The following mark allocation is provided as guidance for this requirement:

   (i) 1 mark
   (ii) 0·5 marks
   (iii) 1·5 marks

(3 marks)

(c) Cab Co wishes to maximise the wealth of its shareholders. It has correctly calculated the following measures for the proposed computerised tracking system project:

- The internal rate of return (IRR) is 14%,
- The return on average capital employed (ROCE) is 20% and
- The payback period is four years.

Required:

Which of the following is true?

- **A** The project is worthwhile because the IRR is a positive value
- **B** The project is worthwhile because the IRR is greater than the cost of capital
- **C** The project is not worthwhile because the IRR is less than the ROCE
- **D** The project is not worthwhile because the payback is less than five years

(2 marks)

(10 marks)

2 Castilda Co manufactures toy robots. The company operates a standard marginal costing system and values inventory at standard cost.

The following is an extract of a partly completed spreadsheet for calculating variances in month 1.

	A	B	C	D
1	Standard Cost Card - Toy Robot		$ per robot	
2	Selling price		120	
3	Direct material	1 material per unit	20	
4	Direct labour	6 hours @ $8 per hour	48	
5	Production overhead		24	
6	Standard contribution		28	
7	Actual and budgeted activity levels in units	Budget	Actual	
8	Sales	25,000	25,600	
9	Production	25,000	26,000	
10	Actual sales revenue and variable costs	$		
11	Sales	3,066,880		
12	Direct material (purchased and used)	532,800		
13	Direct labour (150,000 hours)	1,221,000		
14	Variable production overhead	614,000		
15	Variances	$		
16	Total direct materials variances	12,800	Adverse	
17	Direct labour rate variances	21,000	Adverse	
18	Direct labour efficiency variances	48,000	Favourable	
19	Total variable production overhead variances	10,000	Favourable	

Required:

(a) Which formula will correctly calculate the direct labour efficiency variance in cell B18?

  A   = (C9*C4) - B13
  B   = B13 - (C9*C4)
  C   = (C9*C4) - (150,000*8)
  D   = (150,000 - (C9*6))*8

(2 marks)

(b) Calculate the following for month 1:

  (i) Sales volume variance and state whether it is favourable or adverse;
  (ii) Sales price variance and state whether it is favourable or adverse.

  Note: The total marks will be split equally between each part. (5 marks)

(c) Castilda's management accountant thinks that the direct labour rate and efficiency variances for Month 1 could be interrelated.

Required:

Briefly explain how the two direct labour variances could be interrelated. (3 marks)

(10 marks)

3 Nicholson Co sells mobile telephones. It supplies its customers with telephones and wireless telephone connections. Customers pay an annual fee plus a monthly charge based on calls made.

The company has recently employed a consultant to install a balanced scorecard system of performance measurement and to benchmark the results against those of Nicholson Co's competitors. Unfortunately the consultant was called away before the work was finished. You have been asked to complete the work. The following data is available.

Nicholson Co
Operating data for the year ended 30 November 2013

Sales revenue	$480 million
Sales attributable to new products	$8 million
Average capital employed	$192 million
Profit before interest and tax	$48 million
Average numbers of customers	1,960,000
Average number of telephones returned for repair each day	10,000
Number of bill queries	12,000
Number of customer complaints	21,600
Number of customers lost	117,600
Average number of telephones unrepaired at the end of each day	804

Required:

(a) Calculate the following ratios and other statistics for Nicholson Co for the year ended 30 November 2013.

(i) Return on capital employed;
(ii) Return on sales (net profit percentage);
(iii) Asset turnover;
(iv) Average wait for telephone repair (in days);
(v) Percentage of customers lost per annum;
(vi) Percentage of sales attributable to new products.

Note: The following mark allocation is provided as guidance for this requirement:

(i) 1·5 marks
(ii) 1·5 marks
(iii) 1·5 marks
(iv) 1·5 marks
(v) 1 mark
(vi) 1 mark

(8 marks)

(c) A balanced scorecard measures performance from four perspectives: customer satisfaction, growth, financial success and process efficiency.

Required:

Briefly explain any ONE of the four perspectives above. (2 mark)

(10 marks)

15 [P.T.O.

Formulae Sheet

Regression analysis

$$y = a + bx$$

$$a = \frac{\sum y}{n} - \frac{b \sum x}{n}$$

$$b = \frac{n \sum xy - \sum x \sum y}{n \sum x^2 - (\sum x)^2}$$

$$r = \frac{n \sum xy - \sum x \sum y}{\sqrt{(n \sum x^2 - (\sum x)^2)(n \sum y^2 - (\sum y)^2)}}$$

Economic order quantity

$$= \sqrt{\frac{2 C_0 D}{C_h}}$$

Economic batch quantity

$$= \sqrt{\frac{2 C_0 D}{C_h (1 - \frac{D}{R})}}$$

Present Value Table

Present value of 1 i.e. $(1 + r)^{-n}$

Where r = discount rate
       n = number of periods until payment

Discount rate (r)

Periods (n)	1%	2%	3%	4%	5%	6%	7%	8%	9%	10%	
1	0·990	0·980	0·971	0·962	0·952	0·943	0·935	0·926	0·917	0·909	1
2	0·980	0·961	0·943	0·925	0·907	0·890	0·873	0·857	0·842	0·826	2
3	0·971	0·942	0·915	0·889	0·864	0·840	0·816	0·794	0·772	0·751	3
4	0·961	0·924	0·888	0·855	0·823	0·792	0·763	0·735	0·708	0·683	4
5	0·951	0·906	0·863	0·822	0·784	0·747	0·713	0·681	0·650	0·621	5
6	0·942	0·888	0·837	0·790	0·746	0·705	0·666	0·630	0·596	0·564	6
7	0·933	0·871	0·813	0·760	0·711	0·665	0·623	0·583	0·547	0·513	7
8	0·923	0·853	0·789	0·731	0·677	0·627	0·582	0·540	0·502	0·467	8
9	0·941	0·837	0·766	0·703	0·645	0·592	0·544	0·500	0·460	0·424	9
10	0·905	0·820	0·744	0·676	0·614	0·558	0·508	0·463	0·422	0·386	10
11	0·896	0·804	0·722	0·650	0·585	0·527	0·475	0·429	0·388	0·305	11
12	0·887	0·788	0·701	0·625	0·557	0·497	0·444	0·397	0·356	0·319	12
13	0·879	0·773	0·681	0·601	0·530	0·469	0·415	0·368	0·326	0·290	13
14	0·870	0·758	0·661	0·577	0·505	0·442	0·388	0·340	0·299	0·263	14
15	0·861	0·743	0·642	0·555	0·481	0·417	0·362	0·315	0·275	0·239	15

(n)	11%	12%	13%	14%	15%	16%	17%	18%	19%	20%	
1	0·901	0·893	0·885	0·877	0·870	0·862	0·855	0·847	0·840	0·833	1
2	0·812	0·797	0·783	0·769	0·756	0·743	0·731	0·718	0·706	0·694	2
3	0·731	0·712	0·693	0·675	0·658	0·641	0·624	0·609	0·593	0·579	3
4	0·659	0·636	0·613	0·592	0·572	0·552	0·534	0·516	0·499	0·482	4
5	0·593	0·567	0·543	0·519	0·497	0·476	0·456	0·437	0·419	0·402	5
6	0·535	0·507	0·480	0·456	0·432	0·410	0·390	0·370	0·352	0·335	6
7	0·482	0·452	0·425	0·400	0·376	0·354	0·333	0·314	0·296	0·279	7
8	0·434	0·404	0·376	0·351	0·327	0·305	0·285	0·266	0·249	0·233	8
9	0·391	0·361	0·333	0·308	0·284	0·263	0·243	0·225	0·209	0·194	9
10	0·352	0·322	0·295	0·270	0·247	0·227	0·208	0·191	0·176	0·162	10
11	0·317	0·287	0·261	0·237	0·215	0·195	0·178	0·162	0·148	0·135	11
12	0·286	0·257	0·231	0·208	0·187	0·168	0·152	0·137	0·124	0·112	12
13	0·258	0·229	0·204	0·182	0·163	0·145	0·130	0·116	0·104	0·093	13
14	0·232	0·205	0·181	0·160	0·141	0·125	0·111	0·099	0·088	0·078	14
15	0·209	0·183	0·160	0·140	0·123	0·108	0·095	0·084	0·074	0·065	15

Annuity Table

Present value of an annuity of 1 i.e. $\dfrac{1-(1+r)^{-n}}{r}$

Where r = discount rate
       n = number of periods

Discount rate (r)

Periods (n)	1%	2%	3%	4%	5%	6%	7%	8%	9%	10%	
1	0·990	0·980	0·971	0·962	0·952	0·943	0·935	0·926	0·917	0·909	1
2	1·970	1·942	1·913	1·886	1·859	1·833	1·808	1·783	1·759	1·736	2
3	2·941	2·884	2·829	2·775	2·723	2·673	2·624	2·577	2·531	2·487	3
4	3·902	3·808	3·717	3·630	3·546	3·465	3·387	3·312	3·240	3·170	4
5	4·853	4·713	4·580	4·452	4·329	4·212	4·100	3·993	3·890	3·791	5
6	5·795	5·601	5·417	5·242	5·076	4·917	4·767	4·623	4·486	4·355	6
7	6·728	6·472	6·230	6·002	5·786	5·582	5·389	5·206	5·033	4·868	7
8	7·652	7·325	7·020	6·733	6·463	6·210	5·971	5·747	5·535	5·335	8
9	8·566	8·162	7·786	7·435	7·108	6·802	6·515	6·247	5·995	5·759	9
10	9·471	8·983	8·530	8·111	7·722	7·360	7·024	6·710	6·418	6·145	10
11	10·37	9·787	9·253	8·760	8·306	7·887	7·499	7·139	6·805	6·495	11
12	11·26	10·58	9·954	9·385	8·863	8·384	7·943	7·536	7·161	6·814	12
13	12·13	11·35	10·63	9·986	9·394	8·853	8·358	7·904	7·487	7·103	13
14	13·00	12·11	11·30	10·56	9·899	9·295	8·745	8·244	7·786	7·367	14
15	13·87	12·85	11·94	11·12	10·38	9·712	9·108	8·559	8·061	7·606	15

(n)	11%	12%	13%	14%	15%	16%	17%	18%	19%	20%	
1	0·901	0·893	0·885	0·877	0·870	0·862	0·855	0·847	0·840	0·833	1
2	1·713	1·690	1·668	1·647	1·626	1·605	1·585	1·566	1·547	1·528	2
3	2·444	2·402	2·361	2·322	2·283	2·246	2·210	2·174	2·140	2·106	3
4	3·102	3·037	2·974	2·914	2·855	2·798	2·743	2·690	2·639	2·589	4
5	3·696	3·605	3·517	3·433	3·352	3·274	3·199	3·127	3·058	2·991	5
6	4·231	4·111	3·998	3·889	3·784	3·685	3·589	3·498	3·410	3·326	6
7	4·712	4·564	4·423	4·288	4·160	4·039	3·922	3·812	3·706	3·605	7
8	5·146	4·968	4·799	4·639	4·487	4·344	4·207	4·078	3·954	3·837	8
9	5·537	5·328	5·132	4·946	4·772	4·607	4·451	4·303	4·163	4·031	9
10	5·889	5·650	5·426	5·216	5·019	4·833	4·659	4·494	4·339	4·192	10
11	6·207	5·938	5·687	5·453	5·234	5·029	4·836	4·656	4·486	4·327	11
12	6·492	6·194	5·918	5·660	5·421	5·197	4·988	4·793	4·611	4·439	12
13	6·750	6·424	6·122	5·842	5·583	5·342	5·118	4·910	4·715	4·533	13
14	6·982	6·628	6·302	6·002	5·724	5·468	5·229	5·008	4·802	4·611	14
15	7·191	6·811	6·462	6·142	5·847	5·575	5·324	5·092	4·876	4·675	15

End of Question Paper

Answers

Fundamentals Level – Knowledge Module, Paper F2
Management Accounting

Specimen Exam Answers

Section A

1 C

2 A

3 C

	(litres)	Normal loss	Actual loss	Abnormal loss	Abnormal gain
Process F		5,200	6,100	900	–
Process G		1,875	1,800	–	75

4 B
Marginal costing profit:
(36,000 – (2,000*(63,000/14,000))
$27,000

5 C

6 B

7 B
Budgeted production (19,000 + 3,000 – 4,000) = 18,000 units
RM required for production (18,000*8) = 144,000 kg
RM purchases (144,000 + 53,000 – 50,000) = 147,000 kg

8 D

9 B

10 B

11 A
(36,000 + (200,000 x 12%))/200,000 = 30%

12 C

13 D
Sales volume variance:
(budgeted sales units – actual sales units) * standard profit per unit = 10,000 adverse
Standard profit on actual sales: (actual sales units * std profit per unit) = $120,000
Fixed budget profit: (120,000 +10,000) = $130,000

14 A

15 B

16 C

17 A
Variable production cost per unit = (15,120 − 11,280)/(10,000 − 6,000) = 3,840/4,000 = $0·96
Fixed cost = 11,280 − (6,000 x 0·96) = $5,520
85% capacity = 8,500 units.
Flexible budget allowance for 8,500 units = $5,520 + (8,500 x 0·96) = $13,680

18 C
At 13% NPV should be −10
Using interpolation: 10% + (50/60)(10% − 13%) = 12·5%

19 D
Direct cost	$95,000
Proportion of cost centre X (46,000 + (0·10*30,000))*0·50	$24,500
Proportion of cost centre Y (30,000*0·3)	$9,000
Total overhead cost for P	$128,500

20 D

21 A
1,700 units*10	$17,000
300 units*0·4*10	$1,200
Opening work in progress value	$1,710
Total value	$19,910

22 A
(Actual hours − Budgeted hours) * standard rate
(24,000 − 25,000)*5 = $5,000 adverse

23 A

24 B

25 C
Month 1: production >sales   Absorption costing > marginal costing
Month 2: sales> production   marginal costing profit> absorption costing profit
A and C satisfy month 1, C and D satisfy month 2; therefore C satisfies both

26 B

27 D
Cost per equivalent unit (480,000/10,000) = $48
Degree of completion= ((144,000/48)/4,000) = 75%

28 C

29 D
200 units*(3/60)*18 = $180

30 A
Actual cost	$108,875
Absorbed cost	$105,000
Under absorbed	$3,875

31 B

32 C
Total number of degrees = 360
Proportion of market 3 sales: (50,000/300,000) = 0·1666 = 0·17
0·17*360 = 61

33 C

34 C
$\{(2*20*(4*20,000))/(0·06*25)\}^{0·5}$
1,461 units

35 C
Joint costs apportioned to H: ((330,000/(420,000 + 330,000))*350,000 = $154,000
Closing inventory valuation(HH): (30,000/330,000)*(154,000 + 66,000) = $20,000

Section B

1 **(a)** **(i)** relevant

(ii) irrelevant

(iii) relevant

(iv) relevant

(v) irrelevant

(vi) irrelevant

(b) **(i)** Increase in sales = ($11m – $10m) = $1m

Increase due to the project = ($1m – $0·2m) = $800,000

(ii) Total sales in year 1 = $11m

Savings ($11m*0·01) = $110,000

(iii) Annuity factor for five years at 10% = 3·791

Present value ($75,000*3·791) = $284,325

(c) B

2 **(a)** C

(b) **(i)** Sales volume variance:

Budgeted to sale 25,000 units but sold 25,600 units
(25,600 – 25,000)*$28
$16,800 favourable

(ii) Sales price variance:

Budgeted to sale at $120 per unit (25,600*$120) = $3,072,000
Actual sales were $3,066,880
Variance ($3,066,880 – $3,072,000) = $5,120 adverse

(c) The direct labour variance is adverse while the efficiency variance is favourable for month 1. This indicates some interdependences between the two variances. Possible reason could be that Castilda employed a more skilled or experienced work force who demanded a higher rate of pay, resulting in an adverse labour rate variance. However, the more experienced labour resulted in high productivity, hence a favourable efficiency variance.

3 **(a)** **(i)** Profit before interest and tax/Capital employed:
$48m ÷ $192m = 25%

- **(ii)** Profit before interest and tax/Sales revenue:
  $48m ÷ $480m = 10%

- **(iii)** Sales revenue/capital employed = $480m ÷ 192m = 2·5

- **(iv)** Average number of telephones unrepaired at the end of each day/Number of telephones returned for repair:
  (804 ÷ 10,000)*365 days = 29·3 days

(b) **(i)** Percentage of customers lost per annum = number of customers lost ÷ total number of customers x 100% = 117,600 ÷ 1,960,000 = 6%

- **(ii)** Percentage of sales attributable to new products = Sales attributable to new products/total sales x 100% = $8m ÷ $480m = 1·67%

(c) **(i)** **Customer satisfaction perspective:**

The customer perspective considers how the organisation appears to existing and new customers. It aims to improve quality of service to customers and looks at cost, quality, delivery, inspection, handling, etc.

- **(ii)** **Growth perspective:**

The learning and growth perspective requires the organisation to ask itself whether it can continue to improve and create value. If an organisation is to continue having loyal, satisfied customers and make good use of its resources, it must keep learning and developing.

- **(iii)** **Financial success perspective:**

The financial perspective considers how the organisations create value for the shareholders. It identifies core financial themes which will drive business strategy and looks at traditional measures such as revenue growth and profitability.

- **(iv)** **Process efficiency perspective:**

The process perspective requires the organisation to ask itself the question 'what must we excel at to achieve our financial and customer objectives?' It must identify the business processes which are critical to the implementation of the organisation's strategy and aims to improve processes, decision making and resource utilisation.

(Note: Only one was required)